A STATISTICAL PROFILE OF CANADIAN SOCIETY

McGRAW-HILL RYERSON SERIES IN CANADIAN SOCIOLOGY

GENERAL EDITOR -- LORNE TEPPERMAN

Department of Sociology and Anthropology

University of Toronto

DEMOGRAPHIC BASES OF CANADIAN SOCIETY

Warren Kalbach and Wayne McVey

A STATISTICAL PROFILE OF CANADIAN SOCIETY

Daniel Kubat and David Thornton

Forthcoming

IDEOLOGICAL PERSPECTIVES ON CANADA

M. Patricia Marchak

SOCIAL STRATIFICATION IN CANADA

Dennis Forcese

SOCIAL MOBILITY IN CANADA

Lorne Tepperman

ETHNIC GROUP RELATIONS IN CANADA

Wsevolod Isajiw

SOCIAL CHANGE IN CANADA

Lorna Marsden

A STATISTICAL PROFILE OF CANADIAN SOCIETY

Daniel Kubat
University of Waterloo

David Thornton
Mount Saint Vincent University

McGRAW-HILL RYERSON LIMITED

Toronto   Montreal   New York   London   Sydney
Johannesburg   Mexico   Panama   Düsseldorf
Singapore   São Paulo   Kuala Lumpur   New Delhi

A STATISTICAL PROFILE OF CANADIAN SOCIETY

ISBN 0-07-077799-3

  2345678910 AP-74 32109876

Printed and bound in Canada

Contents

Preface

Each decade seems to have its own emphasis on topics of
social import and it may well be that the present one is
a decade of a tangible concern with population issues.
Not that population issues have not been discussed in the
past. They have been, but mostly in terms of and as
concern for the developing countries unfortunate enough
to be experiencing a very rapid population growth. Rapid
growth, however, has never been foreign to Canada. It is
only now, with the energy crises and the ecological
reverberations of our economic exuberance and technological
comfort, that population and an understanding of it has
gained its well deserved recognition at home.

What we are presenting to the reader is essentially a
pocketbook of numerical documentation of Canadian society.
We hope that this numerical documentation will translate
into a numerical awareness of the same kind which the
reader holds of his bank account and of the government
spending. Dollar valuation translating social exchanges
into an understandable scheme of things is pretty well
established but consideration of societies in terms of
their demographic make-up has been left to actuarial
statisticians and demographers. What we have done is to
provide numerical data series on Canadian population in
terms of events like births, deaths, and migrations, and
in terms of basic social institutions like families,
schools, and work. To present complex human behaviour in
a tabular form seems an outrage to many, but the patterns
and orderliness of human events and of social institutions
become clearer for it.

The sophistication with which people handle money can
easily be transformed into sophistication with which
people handle other numerical data which is arranged simply.
Exercising one's imagination on time series of data on
population growth and composition will make it possible
for everyone to understand Canadian society better,
perhaps, than they would if they read volumes of interpretive
literature where facts and personal biases are not
easily disentangled. This does not mean that the sparse
comments prefacing each section are free of bias and of
particular point of view. On the contrary, the position
on certain population issues taken is unambiguous and,
at least for one of us, quite adamant. However, the
reader will be able to come to conclusions quite
independently of the text and it is the numerical content
of this little volume, we submit, which should contribute
to an understanding of the Canadian society.

Our thanks go to our respective institutions which enabled
us to work on this project over the years. The University
of Waterloo awarded a summer stipend to Daniel Kubat in
1970 so that a conceptual framework and organisation of
source materials be undertaken. Our colleagues in our
departments of sociology have been supportive and helpful.
Professor J. L. Elliott of Dalhousie University proved to
be a stern critic. Our ladies Nelda Kubat and Gail Thornton
attempted to mute our metaphors. Over the years, an
enormous amount of typing and retyping has been done and
to all those who helped, our appreciation. The manuscript
passed the scrutiny of our copy editor, Anne Sinclair.
We would also like to acknowledge the editorial presence
of Gordon Van Tighem, of McGraw-Hill Ryerson, who saw the
manuscript to a swift publication, after some delays not
of his making. The offices of Statistics Canada harbour
the most helpful and kind public servants, and we should
like to thank those with whom we have come in contact:
F.C. Boardman, M.E. Fleming, A. Kempster, J.Lindsay,
J.F. Macmillan, G. Priest, D. Viveash and, in particular,
R. Bradley.

Should there be merits in our work, we share them equally.
Should there be deficiencies, the blame should be allotted
to the names in order of appearance.

                                        D. K.
                                        D. T.

List of Tables

List of Charts

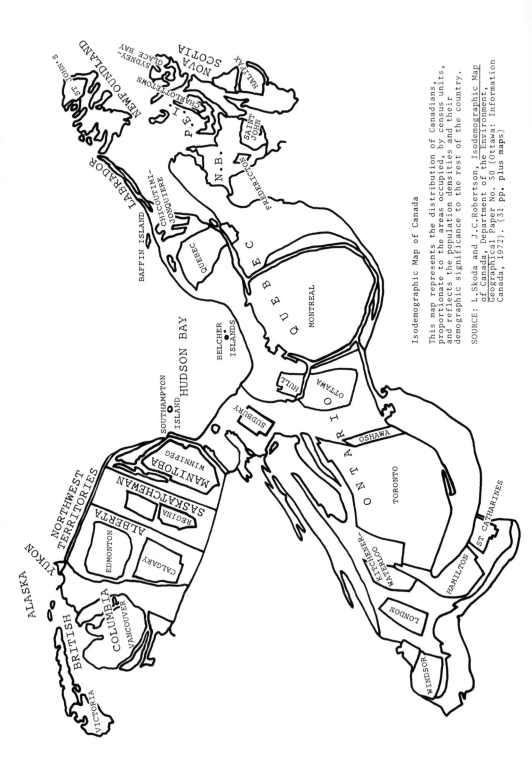

Isodemographic Map of Canada

This map represents the distribution of Canadians, proportionate to the areas occupied, by census units, and reflects the population densities and their demographic significance to the rest of the country.

SOURCE: L. Skoda and J.C. Robertson, Isodemographic Map of Canada, Department of the Environment, Geographical Paper No. 50 (Ottawa: Information Canada, 1972). (31 pp. plus maps)

Introduction and Overview

The domain of a statistical representation of
society has remained unclaimed except by few.
It is not because statistics on the social reality
of the country are unavailable or cumbersome to
use; nor is it that their categories are of an
unclear purpose. It is because even those who use
demographic data to illustrate social themes have
displayed a mode of thinking which fails to relate
the political with the demographic fact.

In the realm of statistical data on Canadian
society two concerns are foremost: (1) the selection
principle of the substantive areas and the manner
in which the materials are presented, including
the logic of tabular organization; and (2) the accuracy
of the figures and the caveats concerning the
exactitude of final digits.

The selection of substantive areas has been
guided partly by the general availability of
statistics but primarily by their particular emphasis
on population processes and on three social institutions
-- the family, education and work -- considered tied
to the population base. The population base itself
is, of course, the result of combined processes: growth
through births and immigration, curtailed through
deaths and emigration, and redistributed across the
country through internal migration. The births take
place, in most cases, in the family, the maintenance
of which reflects the occupational standing of its
adult members, whose educational attainment has been
translated into economic terms. Thus, there is a
close interface between the family and socialization
into adulthood through schools, and the level of
maintenance of self and family as determined by
performance in the world of work, with the family as
the interstitial link to the basic demographic
processes.

There are, of course, other social institutions
derivative of the three aforementioned -- the polity,
for instance. It is the polity, the institution
of government, which appears to subsume all demographic
behaviour, all varieties of socialization, and all
types of employment under the various forms of
government. Yet if all forms of demographic processes
take place under all forms of government, does this
not indicate that forms of population and forms of
government are related?

There is no need to remonstrate against the
accepted practices of sociological analysis nor
against those of other social sciences. There is,
however, a need to emphasize that alternate explanations
of society may be arrived at through demographic
analysis. The parsimony of thought and demonstration
using demographic variables and demographic indices
of social institutions should be sufficiently
convincing as to justify this approach to Canadian
society.

1

For the main part of the book (chapters 1,2 and 3) the organization of data follow roughly the same scheme: to offer time series on events and on population counts from the year of availability; the simpler the event or count, the earlier the record. However, vital statistics were not collected in any highly organized fashion prior to 1921, and today's releases are more revealing than those of decades past, in any case. Only recent censuses, for example, have cross-tabulated schooling and family patterns by rural and urban residence.

The last three decades have seen a formidable increase in the complexity of Canadian social structure, a complexity witnessed by considerable changes in household and family formation, schooling patterns and employment patterns; it is these last few decades which are documented most fully.

The main sources of data are for decennial intervals (quinquennial for the "mini-censuses" since 1956); vital registration data are patterned decennially as well to coincide with the census information. Where there are variations in the vital statistics that exceed the normal, they have been recorded in the appropriate tables.

Not all the data published by governmental and other agencies are in a form suitable for a sociological cross-classification, nor are they offered in a manner which would facilitate comparisons. Considerable effort has been devoted to rearranging and occasionally recomputing the data to provide tables pleasing to a sociological eye. One thing immediately apparent in the organization of the tables is that the most recent year is featured first (usually on the left side of the tables) and the data are presented in descending order. That the same variable is presented sometimes in rows and sometimes in columns is a matter of expediency.

One must, of course, be cautioned regarding the accuracy of the data. The types of errors affecting census data are not only those of collection and processing but also those of discontinuity of classifications.(1) As a rule of thumb, however, error

(1) Sampling and nonsampling errors are the two main sources of inaccuracies in census data. The nonsampling errors are those of data coding and general data processing, interviewer biases, and the time lag between the collection and publication of the data. A major nonsampling error is the error in coverage: particular groups in a population are more likely to be "missed" by enumerators than others. The coverage error rate for the 1961 census, for instance, is estimated at about 2.5 to 3.0 per cent of the total population. Males fifteen to twenty-five years of age, however, may be "missed" at much higher rates, given the high degree of mobility within this category. Besides age and sex, coverage also varies by socioeconomic area. Those occupying a lower-class status in an

in excess of 3 per cent in any one category is rare, and the overall error is much less, even though the farther one reaches into the past the more one has to expect that the last two or three digits of any number may not be an exact rendering of facts. Registration of vital events is subject to minor inaccuracies as well, births being more likely underreported than deaths and migration being merely an estimate of actual movement of the population. Data based on surveys carry their own error estimates, always reported in their respective sources.

The sources for the data and other technical literature follow every chapter so that additional data and methodological hints can be pursued further. A general bibliography is in appendix A.

The intent of this collection of statistical information on Canadian society is not only to provide a profile of the country and its population but also to provide a handbook so that rates and ratios and other useful indices of the social structure may be computed for the country or for specific provinces and various regions of Canada.

The material in the tables has been organized into four chapters, three dealing with Canada only and the fourth offering comparative data on similar countries,but mostly on the United States. Chapters 2 and 3 are subdivided into three parts each, and each subdivision or unsubdivided chapter is prefaced by substantive comments on that segment of Canadian society depicted in the tables. Each section contains a graph or a chart summarizing a societal feature in a self-explanatory fashion.

Chapter 1 deals with an overall view of Canadian population history (thirteen tables), outlining the population growth and distribution in the provinces, the distribution of the farm population, the various facets of urban population, the racial and ethnic mix, distribution by religion, and including population projections until 1984.

Chapter 2 is divided into three sections dealing with the three demographic processes: (1) fertility (seven tables), which traces the changes in the legitimate and illegitimate birthrates by the age of women, and the distribution of child-woman ratios for the provinces, and also profiles by religion the childbearing behaviour of cohorts of older women;

---

urban area tend to be underenumerated by substantially more than the national average. A coverage error, however, is crucial only when dealing with small area statistics. The introduction of self-enumeration for the 1971 census effectively reduced the coverage error, and the sampling errors may be easily estimated statistically. With the exception of a few basic questions directed to the total population in 1971, most other questions were addressed to a 33.3 per cent sample of the population. A greater accuracy of the data appears to result from self-enumeration than from counts by enumerators.

(2) mortality (nine tables), which covers death rates by age, deaths by causes, life expectancies at different ages, and for the Province of Ontario, causes of death cross-classified by marital status and sex; and (3) migration (eight tables), which deals with the history of immigration into Canada and emigration of Canadians to the United States, with immigration after World War II and with the migration patterns of families.

Chapter 3 is divided into three parts covering three major social institutions: (1) family (nine tables), which records the distribution of households and families across provinces and over time, family formation practices (i.e., age at marriage), and includes economic profiles of Canadian families and their current spending patterns; (2) education (eleven tables), which deals with the population enrolled in schools at all levels and the education attainment and profiling of university students by type of study and by their social backgrounds; (3) employment (seven tables), which details the distribution of the labour force in various occupations and the resulting income differences and regional variations.

Chapter 4 offers comparisons (eleven tables), between Canada and other similar countries, mostly with the United States, on basically two sets of indices: those of individual behaviour errors (e.g., teen childbearing, suicide deaths, mental illness and crime) and those of institutional inequities (occupational distribution, educational attainment, income and poverty).

Out of a sea of statistical data, tables have been selected which fit the intellectual imagery of order and purpose in society. No doubt some may argue that real life is far more manifold than it appears in this selection, and far more irregular. Those who do not fail to see the numbers for the digits will profit by this collection of statistics the most.

4

BIBLIOGRAPHY

Selected titles follow each section of tables.
The selection principle was that 1) the literature
refers to the topic or topics covered by the tables,
and 2) the basis for the literature is data similar
in nature to those in the tables.

GOVERNMENT PUBLICATIONS

The Government of Canada issues a wealth of statistical
data through its agencies and crown corporations. The
data best pertaining to Canadian population and the
social institutions anchored in the population structure
are found in the publications of Statistics Canada
(formerly Dominion Bureau of Statistics) and best
located through the Catalogue (e.g. Catalogue 1971
Publications, Data Files and Unpublished Information.
Ottawa: Information Canada. Updated with supplements
and occasionally reissued; available free upon request
to Information Canada, Ottawa, Canada). The data
based on analysis of economic trends as relating to
Canadian social structure are found in the publications
of the Economic Council of Canada. A host of ad hoc
Royal Commissions, Task Forces, and various governmental
Bureaus address themselves to current social problems.
Most libraries have a section on government publications
and occasional browsing there will yield exciting
finds to those who remain reasonably persistent.

Dominion Bureau of Statistics, General Review:
  Administrative Report of the 1961 Census, Bulletin
  No. 7.2-12 Ottawa: Queen's Printer, 1970. (371 pp.)

  Population Sample: Introductory Report to Volume IV,
  1961 Census, Bulletin No. 4.1-11. Ottawa: Queen's
  Printer, 1970. (67 pp.)

  "Sampling in the 1971 Census. Background Material
  for the Committee on the 1971 Census (1969). (37 pp.)

Winkworth, A.V. "Evaluation of Canadian Census".
  Statistical Observer, Vol. 5 no. 2 (1970): 3-5

1 Population of Canada

Sketching out the broad parameters of population
allows us to document the sequence of political
events and succession of governmental deeds which
underlie the history of Canada. To a sociologist
and to a historian alike there are three features
of our population which ought to be reckoned with:
the growth in numbers, the urbanization, and the
cultural mix.

The growth of the population in Canada has
been close to sixfold in the last one hundred years.
To contemplate as sizeable a growth in the next
one hundred years would indeed be considered an act
of folly, the talk about the open spaces and
greenbelts in the North notwithstanding. Using
population density per square mile of occupied
agricultural land for comparison (see table P-1)
one finds that the provinces of Ontario and Quebec
have a population density similar to that of Europe
as a whole, and Canada has a proportionately higher
density than the United States.

The decline of the farm population throughout
this century has been slower in Canada than in
comparable countries but the last two decades have
seen a sharp decline in the number of farms in
Canada as well. The 40 per cent decrease in the
number of farms(1)and the halving of the farming
population was not at all matched by a decrease of the
farm acreage, which declined only by about 3 per cent
during the same period (see table P-2). The trend
toward the depopulation of rural areas was more
pronounced in the Maritime Provinces than in the rest
of the country. Traditionally, the farms in the
east are smaller; the average farm in Newfoundland
was 60 acres in 1971 as compared with about 460
acres in Saskatchewan and 170 acres in Ontario.
A small farming operation is unlikely to remain
self-sustaining for long in today's Canada.

It is true that the growth of the Canadian
population has been checked to the extent that the
next doubling may be at least half a century away.
The growth in the past has been primarily through
births and the slow growth of the future will have
to be primarily through reproductive restraint. The
immigrants did, in the past, contribute their share
to the population growth. For instance, in the
five years preceding the 1971 census, the number of
immigrants was equal to about one-fourth of all
births for that period; the same was true for the
decade 1951 to 1961. The first decade of this
century saw the number of immigrants equal to more
than one-third of the births, but at the other

---

(1) A census "farm" is defined as an agricultural
    holding of at least one acre and with sales of
    agricultural products of at least fifty dollars
    during the preceding twelve months.

Chart 1. Elements of Population Growth:Canada 1966–1972

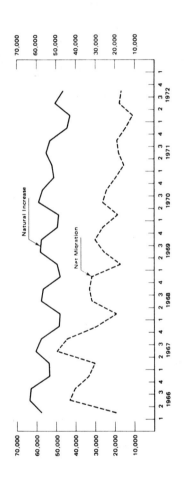

Source: Statistics Canada Daily, January 3, 1973, page 2.

times - during the Great Depression or the economic
uncertainties of the last century, for instance -
there was a net exodus from the country (see table P-3).

In a natural population there are as many men
as women, slightly more men during the early years of
life and more women during the late years of life.
The population of Canada is not natural in this sense,
as it has always registered more men than women.
This is largely owing to the immigration factor:
the majority of immigrants are male (when including
estimates of illegal immigration). Even a casual
scrutiny of the age and sex structure of the Canadian
population over time (see table P-4) will tell the
history of all immigration, and to imaginative minds
it will suggest accounts of competitive courtships.
Future censuses, however, are likely to record natural
sex and age distributions, where women will have an
assured, even though slight, numerical advantage.

The urban character of the Canadian population
may be demonstrated in two ways. For one, in the census
definitions those places are urban which are either
incorporated or have at least 1,000 inhabitants, or
which constitute parts of the metropolitan fringe
with an "urban" density of population.(2)

In this definition, about 80 per cent of the
population has been enumerated as urban in 1971, as
compared to about 20 per cent which would have been
defined as urban one hundred years ago (see table P-5).
Secondly, if life styles and standard of living are
seen as social indicators of urbanization, there is
no doubt that about the same proportion of the
population could be defined as urban as by using the
technical definition. The life styles depend primarily
on the communication remove from any urbanized area.

It is the metropolitan areas(3)which account for
just about three-fourths of all urban population;
their share since the beginning of this century has
close to tripled (see table P-6). It is fair to
estimate that a good portion of growth of the
metropolitan centres has been at the expense of
smaller fringe cities. Changes in metropolitan
area boundaries, annexations and redefinitions of
older settlements as census metropolitan areas can boost
the urban population overnight, even though, for
instance, the villagers around Montreal may go about
their daily tasks without taking notice.

(2) The 1961 census followed the following criteria for
    urban: "(1) incorporated cities, towns and villages
    of at least 1,000 population; (2) unincorporated
    agglomerations (generally considered as towns or
    villages) of at least 1,000 population; and (3)
    built-up fringes of incorporated cities, towns and
    villages (of at least 5,000 population) with a
    population density of at least 1,000 persons per
    square mile" (Stone, Urban Development, p5).

(3) Cities with at least 50,000 population and
    contiguous settled areas dependent economically
    on the central city.

Where the growth has not been taking place is in the small towns of a few thousand population. These now account for less than 10 per cent. No doubt their children are those who swell the metropolitan population. In all, the metropolitanization of Canada is as pronounced and as cumbersome as anywhere else in the world, even though its impact is mitigated by a reasonable level of affluence within and apart from the larger urbanized areas.

The growth rates of the principal regions of metropolitan development in Canada (see table P-6) exceed by far the overall population growth. For instance, London increased by close to 60 per cent during the last decade and Calgary by 85 per cent during the decade before that. During the first decade of the century, however, the population of Edmonton increased about sixfold, a growth rate which could not even be considered for a modern city. In terms of numbers, however, the recent growth of Toronto, Montreal or Vancouver substantially exceeds the numbers added in the past. The future actually may see a decrease in metropolitan populations like that registered for Sudbury by this last census, especially if the massive infusion of immigrants into the main metropolitan areas should subside.

The cultural mix of the Canadian population is expressed in the growth and urbanization of Canada. Not only did the newcomers add directly to the population but also they tended to concentrate in large urban centres, Toronto being their main port of entry for the last twenty-five years. In contrast, the native peoples have not been given much consideration as a part of the cultural mix. Due in part to the regional isolation in which the approximately 16,000 Eskimos live and due in part to residence on reserves where some 200,000 Indians live, the native peoples have stayed very much outside the Canadian society. Their combined numbers have tripled in the last one hundred years (see table P-7) and yet it could be another generation before a major residential and social integration of the native people occurs and they take their rightful place in the Canadian society.

At present, Indians are widely scattered over all provinces; about one-fifth of them live in Ontario and another one-fifth live in British Columbia; most of the rest live in the Prairie Provinces (see table P-8). Like the Eskimos, the Indians have very high rates of natural increase despite the medical-care disadvantages; at present, these two groups are the fastest growing segment of Canadian society except for, perhaps, Hutterites or similar religious communities.

The ethnic diversity of the Canadian population stems from the open immigration policy and active recruitment of immigrants, a practice lasting well into this century. Even though the immigration policies of the last two decades or so were based primarily on the recruitment of skilled and professional persons, a variety of humanitarian measures invited

9

populations from all parts of the globe. The great
bulk of the two million or more immigrants entering
Canada between 1946 and 1966 came from Europe
(see table P-9); nonetheless, the very recent years
saw an increasing proportion of immigrants from
countries with distinctly non-European populations.
Numerically, the recent immigration is of a small
impact on the population structure of Canada. The
cultural diversity, on the other hand, has been kept
alive by newcomers, especially if their ethnic groups
are numerous enough to maintain a separate identity.

Data on ethnic and racial origins as traced by
the male ancestor first coming to this continent
have been collected conscientiously since 1871. At
that time, about 60 per cent of the population was of
British origin, slightly over 30 per cent of French
origin and close to 6 per cent of German origin. The
other European groups were of little numerical and
proportionate import. One hundred years later the
situation has not changed much for the French, but
those of British origin are now about 40 per cent,
those of German origin still about 6 per cent, and
the remainder is widely distributed among the European
nations (see table P-10). The difference now is that
the 2.5 per cent of the population in 1971 may
represent, for example, over half a million Canadians
with strong Italian identification, probably
concentrated in a few metropolitan centres.

Another measure of ethnicity may be gained from
mother-tongue statistics (see table P-11). Ranking
the 1971 population by mother tongue, we notice that
the first three languages, English, French and German
have not changed their relative rank since 1941, being
60, 27 and 3 per cent of the population respectively.
On the other hand, some of the Mediterranean groups,
the Greeks and Portuguese in particular, have gained
considerably since 1941. Of course, the mother-tongue
enumeration does not guarantee that the language is
commonly spoken in the family but it does identify
cultural influences which may translate themselves
ultimately into political choices. Likewise, some of
the ethnic identification of the Canadian population
may be only of sentimental interest and of culinary
consequence.

Religious affiliation has been followed by the
Canadian census as carefully as the ethnic origin
(see table P-12). In 1871, about 42 per cent of all
Canadians were Catholics and after minor fluctuation,
the figure is about 45 per cent in 1971. This small
change may well be attributed to the immigration of
ethnic groups with Catholic background as much as to
the higher fertility of Catholic women. Two major
Protestant denominations account for another 30 per
cent of the population, the rest being fragmented
among a host of churches and sects. One of the
characteristics of well-established churches like
the Anglican and the United Church may be that
they attract population of British ancestry. The
effect of "majority" churches on the behaviour of the
parishioners may be easily overstated, but "minority"
religions like Mennonites and a variety of

fundamentalist Protestant denominations may well
exact some behavioural conformity from their parishioners.
To what extent Canadians will align themselves along
abstract religious lines remain open questions. There
is some evidence that an alignment along religious lines
may be encouraged in the metropolitan melting pot.

As much as growth and cultural diversity were
the major features of the Canadian population, one may
very well ask how long a country can sustain such
growth, sustain substantial immigration, and sustain
the drain of governmental resources to coordinate her
cultural mosaic. The very recent experience of
immigration and fertility in 1972 would point to an
expected population of about 25 million by 1984. The
bulk of this population, namely 65 per cent, would be
in the age span between fifteen and sixty-four years,
from which the labour force is customarily recruited,
thus presaging an economically advantageous population
structure. Whether this prediction series (see table
P-13) or any revised series occasionally issued by
Statistics Canada will prove reliable is hard to say.
The issue of population projections is a very
unrewarding one since in the past,very few forecasts
have been borne out. Throughout the course of history,
an atmosphere of gloom has been accompanied by
slow population growth, and an atmosphere of
unrestrained optimism, by rapid population growth;
however, the country may not be well served by
either combination in the future.

TABLE P-1 POPULATION OF CANADA BY PROVINCE, BY PER CENT OF POPULATION IN PROVINCE, BY PER CENT OF POPULATION IN URBAN PLACES, AND BY POPULATION DENSITY (PER SQUARE MILE OF OCCUPIED AGRICULTURAL LAND AS ENUMERATED IN 1966), AT CENSUS YEARS SINCE 1851

	Census Years						
	1971	1966	1961	1956	1951	1941	1931
Canada							
Population	21,568,311	20,014,880	18,238,247	16,080,791	14,009,429	11,506,655	10,376,786
Per cent urban	76.1	73.6	69.7	66.3	62.4	55.7	52.5
Density (per square mile)	79.3	73.6	67.0	59.1	51.5	42.3	38.1
Newfoundland							
Population	522,104	493,396	457,853	415,074	361,416	--	--
Per cent urban	57.2	54.1	50.7	45.0	43.3	--	--
Per cent of total population	2.4	2.5	2.5	2.6	2.6	--	--
Density	6,780.6	6,407.7	5,946.1	5,390.6	4,693.7	--	--
Prince Edward Island							
Population	111,641	108,535	104,629	99,285	98,429	95,047	88,038
Per cent urban	38.3	36.6	32.4	30.7	25.1	22.1	19.5
Per cent of total population	0.5	0.6	0.6	0.6	0.7	0.8	0.8
Density	77.1	75.0	72.3	68.6	67.9	65.6	60.8
Nova Scotia							
Population	788,960	756,039	737,007	694,717	642,584	577,962	512,846
Per cent urban	56.7	58.1	54.3	57.0	54.5	52.0	46.6
Per cent of total population	3.7	3.8	4.0	4.3	4.6	5.0	4.9
Density	272.7	261.3	254.7	240.1	222.1	199.7	177.3
New Brunswick							
Population	634,557	616,788	597,936	554,616	515,697	457,401	408,219
Per cent urban	56.9	50.6	46.5	45.8	42.8	38.7	35.4
Per cent of total population	2.9	3.0	3.3	3.4	3.7	4.0	3.9
Density	224.1	217.9	211.2	195.9	182.2	161.6	144.2

TABLE P-1 continued

Census Years

	1971	1966	1961	1956	1951	1941	1931
Quebec							
Population	6,027,764	5,780,845	5,259,211	4,628,378	4,055,681	3,331,882	2,874,662
Per cent urban	80.6	78.3	74.3	70.0	66.8	61.2	59.5
Per cent of total population	27.9	28.9	28.8	28.8	28.9	28.9	27.7
Density	299.4	287.1	261.2	229.9	201.4	165.5	142.7
Ontario							
Population	7,703,106	6,960,870	6,236,092	5,404,933	4,597,542	3,787,655	3,431,683
Per cent urban	82.4	80.4	77.3	75.3	72.5	67.5	63.1
Per cent of total population	35.7	34.8	34.2	33.6	32.8	32.9	33.1
Density	283.9	256.5	229.8	199.2	169.4	139.6	126.5
Manitoba							
Population	988,247	963,066	921,686	850,040	776,541	729,744	700,139
Per cent urban	69.5	67.1	63.9	59.6	56.0	45.7	45.2
Per cent of total population	4.6	4.8	5.1	5.3	5.5	6.3	6.7
Density	33.1	32.3	30.9	28.5	26.0	24.5	23.5
Saskatchewan							
Population	926,242	955,344	925,181	880,665	831,728	895,992	921,785
Per cent urban	53.0	49.0	43.0	36.6	30.4	21.3	20.3
Per cent of total population	4.3	4.8	5.1	5.5	5.9	7.8	8.9
Density	9.1	9.3	9.0	8.6	8.1	8.7	9.0
Alberta							
Population	1,627,874	1,463,203	1,331,944	1,123,116	939,501	796,169	731,605
Per cent urban	73.5	68.8	63.3	56.4	47.6	31.9	31.8
Per cent of total population	7.5	7.3	7.3	7.0	6.7	6.9	7.1
Density	21.3	19.1	17.4	14.7	12.3	10.4	9.5

TABLE P-1 continued

Census Years

	1971	1966	1961	1956	1951	1941	1931
British Columbia							
Population	2,184,621	1,873,674	1,629,082	1,398,464	1,165,210	817,861	694,263
Per cent urban	75.7	75.3	72.6	71.9	68.6	64.0	62.3
Per cent of total population	10.1	9.4	8.9	8.7	8.3	7.1	6.7
Density	264.2	226.6	197.0	169.1	140.9	98.9	83.9
Yukon and Northwest Territories							
Population	53,195	43,120	37,626	31,503	25,090	16,942	13,546
Per cent urban	52.7	-	-	-	-	-	-
Per cent of total population	0.2	0.2	0.2	0.2	0.2	0.1	0.1
Density	5,910.6	4,791.1	4,180.6	3,500.3	2,787.7	1,182.4	1,505.1

Census Years

	1921	1911	1909	1891	1881	1871	1861	1851
Canada								
Population	8,787,949	7,206,643	5,371,315	4,833,239	4,324,810	3,689,257	3,229,633	2,436,297
Per cent urban	47.4	41.8	34.9	29.8	23.3	18.3	15.8	13.1
Density (per square mile)	32.3	26.4	19.7	17.2	15.9	13.6	11.9	8.9
Newfoundland								
Population	-	-	-	-	-	-	-	-
Per cent urban	-	-	-	-	-	-	-	-
Per cent of total population	-	-	-	-	-	-	-	-
Density	-	-	-	-	-	-	-	-
Prince Edward Island								
Population	88,615	93,728	103,259	109,078	108,891	94,021	80,857	62,678
Per cent urban	18.8	16.0	14.5	13.1	10.5	9.4	9.3	-
Per cent of total population	1.0	1.3	2.0	2.2	2.5	2.5	2.5	2.5
Density	61.2	64.7	71.3	75.3	75.2	64.9	55.0	47.3

14

TABLE P-1 continued

	Census Years							
	1921	1911	1901	1891	1881	1871	1861	1851
Nova Scotia								
Population	523,837	492,338	459,574	450,396	440,572	387,800	330,857	276,854
Per cent urban	44.8	36.7	27.7	19.4	14.7	8.3	7.6	7.5
Per cent of total population	6.0	6.8	8.6	9.3	10.2	10.5	10.3	11.0
Density	181.1	170.2	158.8	155.7	152.3	134.0	114.4	95.7
New Brunswick								
Population	387,876	351,889	331,120	321,263	321,233	285,594	252,043	193,800
Per cent urban	35.2	26.7	23.1	19.9	17.6	17.6	13.1	14.0
Per cent of total population	4.4	4.9	6.2	6.7	7.4	7.8	7.8	8.0
Density	137.0	124.3	116.9	113.5	113.5	100.1	89.0	68.4
Quebec								
Population	2,360,510	2,005,776	1,648,898	1,488,535	1,359,027	1,191,516	1,111,566	890,261
Per cent urban	51.8	44.5	36.1	28.6	23.8	19.9	16.6	14.9
Per cent of total population	26.9	27.8	30.7	30.8	31.4	32.3	34.4	37.0
Density	177.2	99.6	81.9	73.9	67.5	59.2	55.2	44.2
Ontario								
Population	2,933,662	2,527,292	2,182,947	2,114,321	1,926,922	1,620,851	1,396,091	952,004
Per cent urban	58.8	49.5	40.3	35.0	27.1	20.6	18.5	14.0
Per cent of total population	33.4	35.1	40.6	43.8	44.6	43.9	43.2	39.0
Density	108.1	93.1	80.4	77.9	71.0	59.7	51.4	35.1
Manitoba								
Population	610,118	461,396	255,211	152,506	62,260	25,228	(b)	(b)
Per cent urban	41.5	39.3	24.9	23.3	14.9	-	-	-
Per cent of total population	6.9	6.4	4.8	3.2	1.4	0.7	-	-
Density	20.5	15.5	8.5	5.1	2.8	0.8	-	-

TABLE P-1 continued

| | Census Years | | | | | | | |
	1921	1911	1901	1891	1881	1871	1861	1851
Saskatchewan								
Population	757,510	492,432	91,279	(b)	(b)	(b)	(b)	(b)
Per cent urban	16.8	16.1	6.1	-	-	-	-	-
Per cent of total population	8.6	6.8	1.7	-	-	-	-	-
Density	7.4	4.8	.9	-	-	-	-	-
Alberta								
population	588,454	374,295	73,022	(b)	(b)	(b)	(b)	(b)
Per cent urban	30.7	29.4	16.2	-	-	-	-	-
Per cent of total population	6.7	5.2	1.4	-	-	-	-	-
Density	7.7	4.9	1.0	-	-	-	-	-
British Columbia								
Population	524,582	392,480	178,657	98,173	49,459	36,247	51,524	55,000
Per cent urban	50.9	50.9	46.4	42.6	18.3	9.0	-	-
Per cent of total population	6.0	5.4	3.3	2.0	1.2	0.9	1.6	2.3
Density	63.4	47.5	21.6	11.9	5.9	4.4	6.2	6.6
Yukon and Northwest Territories								
Population	12,300(c)	28,641(c)	47,348	98,967	56,446	48,000	6,691	5,700
Per cent urban	-	-	-	-	-	-	-	-
Per cent of total population	0.1	0.4	0.9	2.1	1.3	1.3	0.2	0.2
Density	1,366.6	3,182.3	5,260.9	10,996.3	6,271.8	5,333.3	743.4	633.3

Note: Occupied agricultural land: improved (crops and summer fallows; pasture; other);unimproved (forest; other). Generally, productive forest land is excluded.

(a) Included in the Canadian census since 1951.
(b) Included with Northwest Territories.
(c) Underenumerated.

Sources: Statistics Canada Weekly (29 December 1972), p.7; 1971 Census of Canada, Population by Federal Electoral Districts, Advance Bulletin 1AP-1 (May 1972); Canada Year Book, 1969, tables 5, 47; Urquhart and Buckley, Historical Statistics, Series A2-14.

TABLE P-2 FARMS AND FARM POPULATION, CANADA AND PROVINCES, BY SELECTED CENSUS YEARS SINCE 1921

		Canada	Nfld.	P.E.I.	N.S.	N.B.	Que.	Ont.	Man.	Sask.	Alta.	B.C.
Farm Population (a)	1971	1,489,565	5,156	21,338	26,977	27,453	334,579	391,713	131,202	233,792	237,924	79,353
	1951	2,911,996	19,975	46,855	115,414	149,916	792,756	702,778	219,233	399,473	345,222	120,292
	1921	4,426,037	-	69,522	296,799	263,432	1,068,630	1,227,060	348,502	538,552	365,550	177,020
No. of farms occupied	1971	366,128	1,042	4,543	6,008	5,485	61,257	94,722	34,981	76,970	62,702	18,400
	1951	623,091	3,626	10,137	23,515	26,431	134,336	149,920	52,383	172,018	84,315	26,406
	1921	711,000	-	13,701	47,432	36,655	137,619	198,053	53,252	119,451	82,954	21,973
Per cent owned (b)	1971	68.6	89.6	76.4	79.9	81.5	86.3	73.8	61.8	53.9	59.3	78.2
	1951	77.3	93.8	97.5	97.7	97.1	96.9	89.2	77.8	65.5	65.9	74.0
	1921	86.5	-	95.6	96.1	96.1	94.9	85.2	82.0	77.6	80.3	86.3
Mean age of operators	1971	49	51	50	52	52	48	49	49	49	48	49
	1951	-	-	-	-	-	-	-	-	-	-	-
	1921	43	-	48	50	47	44	46	41	38	39	45
No. of acres (in 000s)	1971	169,669	63	775	1,329	1,339	10,801	15,963	19,008	65,057	49,506	5,823
	1951	174,047	85	1,095	3,174	3,470	16,786	20,880	17,730	61,663	44,460	4,702
	1921	140,888	-	1,216	4,724	4,270	17,257	22,629	14,616	44,023	29,293	2,861

Note: Census farm is at least 1 acre, and at least $50 of sales for the preceding twelve months.

(a) For 1971 and 1951, defined as rural farm. For 1921, defined as rural population, not all living on farms.
(b) For 1951, operated by owner and fully owned.

Sources: 1971 Census of Canada, Agriculture, Advance Bulletin AA-61 (October 1972); 1951 Census of Canada, vol. VI, tables 1,2,15; 1921 Census of Canada, vol. V, tables II, 61.

17

TABLE P-3 COMPONENTS OF GROWTH OF THE CANADIAN POPULATION FOR INTERCENSAL INTERVALS
SINCE 1871 (IN THOUSANDS)

Census Interval	Population at Beginning of the Interval	Births	Deaths	Natural Increase	Immigration	Emigration	Net Migration
1966-1971	20,015	1,845	771	1,074	838	359	479
1961-1966	18,238	2,249	731	1,518	539	280	259
1951-1961	14,009	4,468	1,320	3,148	1,543	462	1,081
1941-1951	11,507	3,184	1,214	1,970	548	379	169
1931-1941	10,377	2,294	1,072	1,222	150	242	-92
1921-1931	8,788	2,415	1,055	1,360	1,203	974	229
1911-1921	7,207	2,338	988	1,350	1,612	1,381	231
1901-1911	5,371	1,931	811	1,120	1,759	1,043	716
1891-1901	4,833	1,546	828	718	326	506	-180
1881-1891	4,325	1,538	824	714	903	1,109	-206
1871-1881	3,689	1,477	754	723	353	440	-87

Note: Emigration figures are estimates only and include residual and error values.

Sources: Statistics Canada, 1971 Immigration (Ottawa, 1972), tables 1,2; Urquhart and
Buckley, Historical Statistics, Series A244, 253; Dominion Bureau of Statistics
Migration Projections for Canada 1969-1984 (Ottawa, 1970), tables 1,2; Canada Year Book,
1969, p. 156; Statistics Daily, passim; Vital Statistics Trends 1921-1954 (Ottawa,
1963), tables 1,2; 1961 Census of Canada, Bull. 7.1-1, Introduction table 3.

TABLE P-4 CANADIAN POPULATION BY AGE AND SEX RATIO, BY CENSUS YEARS SINCE 1851

CENSUS YEAR		ALL AGES	0-4	5-9	10-14	15-19	20-24	25-29	30-34	35-39	40-44	45-49	50-54	55-59	60-64	65-69	70+
1971	N(a)	21,568	1,816	2,254	2,311	2,114	1,889	1,584	1,305	1,264	1,263	1,239	1,053	955	777	620	1,124
	SR(b)	100.2	104.9	104.6	104.6	103.3	99.4	102.2	102.5	104.2	103.1	98.1	97.2	98.0	96.6	91.4	76.1
1961	N	18,238	2,256	2,080	1,856	1,433	1,184	1,209	1,272	1,271	1,119	1,015	863	706	584	487	903
	SR	101.2	104.6	104.7	104.4	103.6	98.3	103.2	102.7	98.6	100.2	103.2	105.5	105.2	100.7	97.2	92.3
1951	N	14,009	1,722	1,398	1,131	1,058	1,089	1,130	1,043	999	869	745	663	571	506	433	652
	SR	102.4	104.1	104.4	103.4	101.1	97.6	95.1	96.8	101.6	105.4	108.7	105.6	105.4	109.1	111.2	97.9
1941	N	11,507	1,052	1,046	1,101	1,120	1,032	967	844	760	677	635	592	507	407	307	460
	SR	105.3	103.1	103.3	103.0	101.8	100.8	101.9	104.9	109.1	106.4	109.9	114.5	118.5	115.9	112.4	98.3
1931	N	10,377	1,075	1,135	1,074	1,040	912	787	709	689	646	586	489	367	295	230	345
	SR	107.5	102.3	103.1	102.3	102.3	100.2	101.0	107.9	109.1	116.8	122.0	121.3	118.5	113.8	110.0	101.8
1921	N	8,788	1,059	1,050	914	805	713	688	655	634	529	436	363	281	240	173	248
	SR	106.4	101.7	101.5	102.0	101.3	97.5	102.6	110.9	117.9	119.1	119.6	117.4	112.0	112.4	111.0	100.0
1911	N	7,207	890	785	702	686	712	663	559	470	392	333	287	214	179	132	203
	SR	112.9	102.3	101.7	102.2	107.3	121.1	129.4	127.2	123.2	121.5	117.6	115.8	114.0	113.1	106.3	101.0
1901	N	5,371	646	618	583	557	515	430	369	336	294	242	206	162	142	106	165
	SR	105.0	101.9	102.3	104.2	102.9	102.0	105.3	108.5	110.0	111.5	110.4	108.1	105.1	107.2	105.8	103.7
1891	N	4,833	611	592	554	521	482	395	326	275	235	198	173	130	121	85	135
	SR	103.7	102.3	102.7	103.7	101.2	100.8	101.6	105.7	107.6	106.1	106.3	106.3	106.3	108.6	112.5	107.7
1881	N	4,325	599	562	513	483	436	337	265	232	196	171	143	112	98	69	109
	SR	102.5	103.1	102.3	104.4	98.8	97.3	99.4	101.5	101.7	103.1	106.0	104.4	107.4	115.2	115.6	109.6
1871	N	3,689	541	519	476	408	351	281	223	188	157	139	112	90	69	56	79
	SR	102.7	104.2	103.5	104.4	98.1	96.1	95.8	99.1	100.0	103.1	107.5	113.2	114.3	122.6	124.0	119.4
1861	N	3,230	543	429	399	374	305	254	201	161	136	111	89	71	58	42	57
	SR	105.7	104.1	103.3	103.6	100.0	102.7	103.2	106.2	109.1	112.5	115.7	117.1	115.2	123.1	133.3	115.4
1851	N	2,436	451	346	308	277	223	183	145	118	101	81	64	49	35	23	42
	SR	105.4	106.9	100.0	104.1	96.5	100.9	102.2	107.1	110.7	114.9	113.2	120.7	122.7	118.6	130.0	110.0

(a) Both sexes.
(b) Sex ratio.

Sources: Statistics Canada, Census Division, Demographic and Social Characteristics Section, 1972 (informal release of 1971 data); Canada Year Book, 1969, p. 17; Urquhart and Buckley, Historical Statistics, Series A44-59; Keyfitz, "The Growth of the Canadian Population", p. 50.

TABLE P-5 DISTRIBUTION OF POPULATION IN URBAN AREAS OF 1,000 PERSONS AND OVER, BY SIZE OF URBAN CENTRES, BY CENSUS YEARS SINCE 1871

Census Year		1,000-4,999	5,000-29,999	30,000-99,999	100,000 and over(a)	Total Urban
				SIZE		
1971	N	1,640,745	2,593,280	1,930,590	10,246,170	16,410,785
	%	10.0	15.8	11.8	62.4	100.0
1961	N	1,595,070	1,641,406	1,646,703	8,400,859	13,971,937
	%	11.5	12.7	11.8	64.0	100.0
1951	N	1,166,584	1,198,365	1,230,731	5,221,957	8,817,637
	%	13.2	13.6	14.0	59.2	100.0
1941	N	909,728	1,370,375	928,367	2,645,133	5,853,603
	%	15.5	23.4	15.9	45.2	100.0
1931	N	430,742	1,305,304	696,680	2,328,175	5,160,901
	%	16.1	25.3	13.5	45.1	100.0
1921	N	764,836	1,057,965	495,566	1,658,697	3,977,064
	%	19.1	26.6	12.5	41.8	100.0
1911	N	655,097	782,771	488,748	1,080,960	3,007,576
	%	21.8	26.0	16.3	35.9	100.0
1901	N	545,037	503,187	343,266	475,770	1,867,260
	%	29.2	26.9	18.4	25.5	100.0
1891(b)	N	427,310	390,670	224,760	397,865	1,440,605
	%	29.7	27.1	15.6	27.6	100.0
1881(b)	N	(c)	298,371	220,922	140,747	(c)
	%	-	-	-	-	-
1871(b)	N	(c)	228,354	115,791	107,225	(c)
	%	-	-	-	-	-

(a) Includes Census Metropolitan Areas since 1951; the incorporated places included in the CMA total do not show in the preceding three columns for 1951 and 1961.
(b) Yukon and the Northwest Territories excluded.
(c) Centres of 1,000-4,999 estimated: 1881, 316,000; 1871, 196,000.

Sources: 1971 Census of Canada, vol. I part 1 Bull. 1.1-9, inside front cover; 1961 Census of Canada, Bull. 7.1-2, table V; Urquhart and Buckley, Historical Statistics, Series A20-24.

TABLE P-6 POPULATION AND PER CENT CHANGE IN POPULATION SINCE LAST CENSUS FOR PRINCIPAL
REGIONS OF METROPOLITAN DEVELOPMENT IN CANADA, BY CENSUS YEARS SINCE 1901.

CENSUS YEARS

Principal Regions of Metropolitan Development	1971 N (000s)	1971 Per Cent Change	1961 N (000s)	1961 Per Cent Change	1951 N (000s)	1951 Per Cent Change	1941 N (000s)	1941 Per Cent Change	1931 N (000s)	1931 Per Cent Change	1921 N (000s)	1921 Per Cent Change	1911 N (000s)	1911 Per Cent Change	1901 N (000s)
Halifax	223	21.2	184	37.3	134	38.8	99	25.5	79	4.1	75	30.6	58	13.4	51
Saint John	132	37.5	96	22.0	78	10.5	71	13.1	63	2.5	61	14.2	54	4.7	51
Montreal	2,743	27.2	2,156	43.3	1,504	23.6	1,216	12.1	1,086	36.3	796	29.2	616	48.6	415
Quebec	481	25.6	383	29.2	297	23.0	241	16.7	207	30.7	158	18.5	133	13.9	117
Hamilton	499	39.0	359	34.9	266	28.7	207	8.8	190	23.7	154	37.5	112	40.6	79
Kitchener-Waterloo	227	28.3	177	40.1	126	27.8	99	9.9	90	19.4	75	20.2	63	19.0	53
London	286	58.0	181	40.6	129	32.7	97	11.6	87	18.0	74	20.9	61	18.5	52
Ottawa	603	38.3	436	47.2	296	25.3	236	19.9	197	17.6	168	26.4	133	28.4	103
Sudbury	155	-6.6	166	51.4	110	35.6	81	38.7	58	35.4	43	44.5	30	84.9	16
Toronto	2,628	35.3	1,942	53.6	1,264	26.2	1,002	11.2	901	31.3	686	43.6	478	57.7	303
Windsor	259	34.9	192	17.6	163	26.1	129	10.6	117	77.2	66	103.4	32	44.7	22
Winnipeg	540	13.5	476	33.4	357	18.1	302	2.4	295	28.7	229	46.0	157	223.7	48
Calgary	403	39.0	290	85.8	156	39.7	112	8.1	103	33.0	78	39.5	56	570.2	8
Edmonton	496	32.6	374	77.1	211	55.1	136	17.9	116	32.4	87	83.0	48	215.5	15
Vancouver	1,082	37.0	790	40.6	562	42.7	394	16.5	338	51.3	224	-	-	-	-
Victoria	196	21.0	162	33.5	122	41.5	86	23.3	70	9.1	64	-	-	-	-

Sources: Statistics Canada, Division of the Census, Population by Census Metropolitan Areas (for 1971 limits),
January 1973 (advance release); Stone, Urban Development, p. 278.

TABLE P-7 NATIVE PEOPLES OF CANADA BY SELECTED YEARS SINCE 1871

Year	Indians		Eskimos	Estimated Total
	Male	Female		
1971	297,000(a)		18,000(a)	315,000(a)
1969	244,113		16,000	260,113
1966	224,164			
1961	191,709			
1956			11,000	
1954	77,626	73,932		
1951				165,607
1941				125,521
1931				128,890
1921				113,724
1911				105,611
1901				127,941
1881				108,547
1871(b)				23,037

(a) 1971 census.
(b) Includes the four original provinces only.

Sources: Private communication by R. Bradley, Chief, Demographic and
Social Characteristics Section, Census Division, Statistics
Canada, June 1973; Department of Indian Affairs and Northern
Development, Annual Report, 1969-1970 (Ottawa: Queen's Printer,
1970, p.117; Canada Year Book, 1969, population table 36;
Canada Year Book, 1957-58, population table 31; Urquhart and
Buckley, Historical Statistics, Series A75-113.

TABLE P-8 INDIAN POPULATION BY PROVINCE, BY SELECTED YEARS
SINCE 1949

Province	Years			
	1969	1965	1961	1949
P.E.I.	435	393	348	273
N.S.	4,512	4,099	3,746	2,641
N.B.	4,274	3,824	3,397	2,139
Que.	27,050	24,446	21,793	15,970
Ont.	54,052	49,556	44,942	34,571
Man.	34,392	29,996	25,681	17,549
Sask.	35,062	30,086	25,334	16,308
Alta.	28,443	24,587	20,931	13,805
B.C.	47,138	43,250	38,616	27,936
Y.T.	2,484	2,292	2,006	1,443
N.W.T.	6,271	5,569	4,915	3,772
Canada	244,113	218,098	191,709	136,407

Sources: Canada Year Book, 1970-71, p.245; Department of Indian
Affairs and Northern Development, Annual Report, 1969-70
(Ottawa: Queen's Printer, 1970), p.117

23

TABLE P-9 NUMBER AND PROPORTION OF IMMIGRANTS TO CANADA
BY SOURCE AREA, SINCE 1946

Source Area		1971	1970	1969	1968	1967	1946-66
Europe	Number	52,031	75,609	88,363	120,702	159,979	2,248,515
	%	42.68	51.19	54.70	65.61	71.78	83.32
Africa	Number	2,841	2,863	3,297	5,204	4,608	25,362
	%	2.33	1.94	2.04	2.82	2.06	0.94
Asia	Number	22,171	21,170	23,319	21,686	20,740	92,802
	%	18.19	14.33	14.44	11.78	9.30	3.44
Austral-asia	Number	2,906	4,388	4,414	4,818	6,179	33,362
	%	2.38	2.97	2.73	2.62	2.77	1.24
North and Central America	Number	36,019	37,795	36,693	28,551	28,043	257,345
	%	29.55	25.59	22.72	15.52	12.58	9.54
South America	Number	5,058	4,943	4,767	2,693	3,090	29,085
	%	4.5	3.35	2.95	1.46	1.38	1.07
Oceania and other	Number	874	945	678	320	237	12,292
	%	0.72	0.63	0.42	0.17	0.10	0.45
Totals	Number	121,900	147,713	161,531	183,974	222,876	2,698,763
	%	100.00	100.00	100.00	100.00	100.00	100.00

Source: Department of Manpower and Immigration, Quarterly Immigration
Bulletin (Ottawa, 1971), pp. 4,8,9.

TABLE P-10 ETHNIC AND RACIAL ORIGINS OF THE CANADIAN POPULATION BY SELECTED CENSUS YEARS
SINCE 1871

CENSUS YEARS

ETHNIC and RACIAL GROUP	1971 (in 000s)		1961		1951		1941		1931	
	N	%	N	%	N	%	N	%	N	%
British	9,624	44.6	7,996,669	43.8	6,709,685	47.9	5,715,904	49.7	5,381,071	51.9
English	6,246	29.0	4,195,175	23.0	3,630,344	25.9	2,968,402	25.8	2,741,419	26.4
Irish	1,581	7.3	1,753,351	9.6	1,439,635	10.3	1,267,702	11.0	1,230,808	11.9
Scottish	1,720	8.0	1,902,302	10.4	1,547,470	11.0	1,403,974	12.2	1,346,350	13.0
Other	86	0.4	145,841	0.8	92,236	0.7	75,826	0.7	62,494	0.6
Other European	11,139	51.6	9,657,195	53.0	6,872,889	49.1	5,526,964	48.0	4,753,242	45.8
French	6,180	28.7	5,540,346	30.4	4,319,167	30.8	3,483,038	30.3	2,927,990	28.2
Austrian(a)	42	0.2	106,535	0.6	32,031	0.2	37,715	0.3	48,639	0.5
Belgian	51	0.2	61,382	0.3	35,148	0.2	29,711	0.3	27,585	0.3
Czech and Slovak	82	0.4	73,061	0.4	63,959	0.5	42,912	0.4	30,401	0.3
Danish	76	0.3	85,473	0.5	42,671	0.3	37,439	0.3	34,118	0.3
Finnish(b)	59	0.3	59,436	0.3	43,745	0.3	41,683	0.4	43,885	0.4
German	1,317	6.1	1,049,599	5.8	619,995	4.4	464,682	4.0	473,544	4.6
Greek	124	0.6	56,475	0.3	13,966	0.1	11,692	0.1	9,444	*
Hungarian(c)	132	0.6	126,220	0.7	60,460	0.4	54,598	0.5	40,582	0.4
Icelandic	28	0.1	30,623	0.2	23,307	0.2	21,050	0.2	19,382	0.2
Italian	731	3.4	450,351	2.5	152,245	1.1	112,625	1.0	98,173	0.9
Jewish	297	1.4	173,344	0.9	181,670	1.3	170,241	1.5	156,726	1.5
Lithuanian	25	0.1	27,629	0.2	16,224	0.1	7,789	*	5,876	*
Netherlander	426	2.0	429,679	2.4	264,267	1.9	212,863	1.8	148,962	1.4
Norwegian	179	0.8	148,681	0.8	119,266	0.8	100,718	0.9	93,243	0.9
Polish	316	1.5	323,517	1.8	219,845	1.6	167,485	1.5	145,503	1.4
Romanian(d)	27	0.1	43,805	0.2	23,601	0.2	24,689	0.2	29,056	0.3
Russian(e)	64	0.3	119,168	0.7	91,279	0.6	83,708	0.7	88,148	0.8
Scandinavian(f)										
Swedish	102	0.5	121,757	0.6	97,780	0.7	85,396	0.7	81,306	0.8
Ukrainian	580	2.7	473,337	2.6	395,043	2.8	305,929	2.7	225,113	2.2
Yugoslavic	105	0.5	68,587	0.4	21,404	0.1	21,214	0.2	16,174	0.2
Other	195	0.9	88,190	0.5	35,616	0.2	9,787	*	9,392	*

25

TABLE P-10 continued

ETHNIC AND RACIAL GROUP	1921 N	1921 %	1911 N	1911 %	1901 N	1901 %	1881 N	1881 %	1871 N	1871 %
					CENSUS YEARS					
British	4,868,738	55.4	3,999,081	55.5	3,063,195	57.0	2,548,514	58.9	2,110,502	60.5
English	2,545,358	29.0	1,871,268	26.0	1,260,899	23.5	881,301	20.4	706,369	20.3
Irish	1,107,803	12.6	1,074,738	14.9	988,721	18.4	957,403	22.1	846,414	24.3
Scottish	1,173,625	13.3	1,027,015	14.2	800,154	14.9	699,863	16.2	549,946	15.8
Other	41,952	0.5	26,060	0.4	13,421	0.2	9,947	0.2	7,773	0.2
Other European	3,699,846	42.1	3,006,502	41.7	2,107,327	39.2	1,598,386	37.0	1,322,813	37.9
French	2,452,743	27.9	2,061,719	28.6	1,649,371	30.7	1,298,929	30.0	1,082,940	31.1
Austrian	107,671	1.2	44,036	0.6	10,947	0.2	-	-	-	-
Belgian	20,234	0.2	9,664	0.1	2,994	*	-	-	-	-
Czech and Slovak	8,840	0.1	-	-	-	-	-	-	-	-
Danish	21,124	0.2	-	-	-	-	-	-	-	-
Finnish	21,494	0.2	15,500	0.2	2,502	*	-	-	-	-
German	294,635	3.3	403,417	5.6	310,501	5.8	254,319	5.9	202,991	5.8
Greek	5,740	*	3,614	*	291	*	-	-	39	*
Hungarian	13,181	0.1	11,648	0.2	1,549	*	-	-	-	-
Icelandic	15,876	0.2	-	-	-	-	-	-	-	-
Italian	66,769	0.8	45,963	0.6	10,834	0.2	1,849	*	1,035	*
Jewish	126,196	1.4	76,199	1.1	16,131	0.3	667	*	125	-
Lithuanian	1,970	-	-	-	-	-	-	-	-	-
Netherlander	117,505	1.3	55,961	0.8	33,845	0.6	30,412	0.7	29,662	0.8
Norwegian	68,856	0.8	-	-	-	-	-	-	-	-
Polish	53,403	0.6	33,652	0.5	6,265	0.1	-	-	-	-
Romanian	13,470	0.1	5,883	*	354	*	-	-	-	-
Russian	100,064	1.1	44,376	0.6	19,825	0.4	1,227	*	607	*
Scandinavian	-	-	112,682	1.6	31,042	0.6	5,223	0.1	1,623	*
Swedish	61,503	0.7	75,432	1.0	5,682	0.1	-	-	-	-
Ukrainian	106,721	1.2	-	-	-	-	-	-	-	-
Yugoslavic	3,906	*	-	-	-	-	-	-	-	-
Other	17,945	0.2	6,756	*	5,174	0.1	5,760	0.1	3,791	0.1

TABLE P-10 continued

ETHNIC and RACIAL GROUP	1971 N	1971 %	1961 N	1961 %	CENSUS YEARS 1951 N	1951 %	1941 N	1941 %	1931 N	1931 %
Asiatic	286	1.3	121,753	0.7	72,827	0.5	74,064	0.6	84,548	0.8
Chinese	119	0.6	58,197	0.3	32,528	0.2	34,627	0.3	46,519	0.4
Japanese	37	0.2	29,157	0.2	21,663	0.1	23,149	0.2	23,342	0.2
Other	129	0.6	34,399	0.2	18,636	0.1	16,288	0.1	14,687	0.1
Other Origins	520	2.4	462,650	2.5	354,028	2.5	189,723	1.6	157,925	1.5
Native Indian and Eskimo(h)	314	1.5	220,121	1.2	165,607	1.2	125,521	1.1	128,890	1.2
Negro	34	0.2	32,127	0.2	18,020	0.1	22,174	0.2	19,456	0.2
Other and not stated(i)	172	0.8	210,382	1.2	170,401	1.2	42,028	0.4	9,579	0.1
Total	21,568	100.0	18,238,247	100.0	14,009,429	100.0	11,506,655	100.0	10,376,786	100.0

ETHNIC and RACIAL GROUP	1921 N	1921 %	1911 N	1911 %	CENSUS YEARS 1901 N	1901 %	1881 N	1881 %	1871 N	1871 %
Asiatic	65,914	0.7	43,213	0.6	23,731	0.4	4,383	0.1	4	*
Chinese	39,587	0.4	27,831	0.4	17,312	0.3	4,383	0.1	-	-
Japanese	15,868	0.2	9,967	0.1	4,738	*	-	-	-	-
Other	10,459	0.1	6,315	*	1,681	*	-	-	4	*
Other Origins	153,451	1.7	157,847	2.2	177,062	3.3	173,527	4.0	52,442	1.5
Native Indian and Eskimo	113,724	1.3	105,611	1.5	127,941	2.4	108,547	2.5	23,037	0.7
Negro	18,291	0.2	16,994	0.2	17,437	0.3	21,394	0.5	21,496	0.6
Other and not stated	21,436	0.2	35,242	0.5	31,684	0.6	43,586	1.0	7,909	0.2
Total	8,787,949	100.0	7,206,643	100.0	5,371,315	100.0	4,324,810	100.0	3,485,761	100.0

(a) Not otherwise specified; for 1901, includes Bohemian, Bukovinian and Slavic.
(b) Includes Estonian prior to 1951; see note e.
(c) Includes Lithuanian and Moravian for 1901 and 1911.
(d) Includes Bulgarian for 1901 and 1911.
(e) Includes Finnish and Polish for 1881 and 1871.
(f) Since 1921 listed under Danish, Finnish, Icelandic and Swedish.
(g) For 1921 includes Bukovinian, Galician and Ruthenian.
(h) For 1941, excludes Métis; see note i.
(i) For 1941, includes 35,416 Métis.
* Less than one-tenth of 1 per cent.

Source: Private communication by R. Bradley, Chief, Demographic and Social Characteristics Section. Census Division, Statistics Canada, June 1973; Urquhart and Buckley, Historical Statistics, Series A75-113; 1961 Census of Canada, Bull.1.2-5, table 34.

TABLE P-11 POPULATION OF CANADA BY MOTHER TONGUE AND BY RANK OF PROPORTIONATE REPRESENTATION BY CENSUS YEARS SINCE 1941

Mother Tongue	1971 No.	1971 Rank	1961 No.	1961 Rank	1951 No.	1951 Rank	1941 No.	1941 Rank
English	12,973,810	1	10,660,534	1	8,280,809	1	6,488,190	1
French	5,793,650	2	5,123,151	2	4,068,850	2	3,354,753	2
German	561,085	3	563,713	3	329,302	4	322,228	3
Italian	538,365	4	339,626	5	92,244	8	80,260	7
Ukrainian	309,860	5	361,496	4	352,323	3	313,273	4
Native Indian and Eskimo	179,820	6	166,531	7	144,787	5	-	-
Netherlands	144,925	7	170,177	6	87,935	9	53,215	9
Polish	134,780	8	161,720	8	129,238	6	128,711	6
Greek	104,450	9	40,455	15	8,036	26	8,747	22
Chinese	94,860	10	49,099	11	28,289	16	33,500	15
Portuguese	86,925	11	-	-	-	-	-	-
Magyar	86,830	12	85,939	9	42,402	12	41,287	12
Croatian, etc.	74,190	13	-	-	-	-	-	-
Serbian, etc.	49,890	14	28,866	19	11,031	23	14,863	20
Yiddish	45,145	15	82,448	10	103,593	7	129,806	5
Czech and Slovak	36,730	16	42,546	14	45,516	10	37,604	13
Finnish	32,555	17	44,785	12	31,771	15	37,331	14
Indo-Pakistani	31,740	18	-	-	-	-	-	-
Russian	28,550	19	42,903	13	39,223	13	52,431	10
Arabic,Syrian	27,405	20	12,999	25	5,475	28	8,111	23
Norwegian	27,390	21	40,054	16	43,831	11	60,084	8
Danish	24,360	22	35,035	17	15,714	18	-	-
Gaelic and Welsh	23,815	23	10,573	26	13,974	19	32,708	16
Spanish	21,680	24	-	-	-	-	-	-
Swedish	16,985	25	32,632	18	36,096	14	49,547	11
Japanese	14,725	26	17,856	20	17,589	17	22,359	17
Lithuanian	14,520	27	14,997	21	12,307	21	6,910	24
Estonian	14,240	28	13,830	24	8,784	25	-	-
Flemish	14,135	29	14,304	22	12,623	20	14,557	21
Lettish	11,300	30	14,062	23	7,019	27	-	-
Romanian	7,860	31	10,165	27	10,105	24	16,402	18
Icelandic	-	-	8,993	28	11,207	22	15,510	19

Sources; From private files of F.C.Boardman, chief (retired), Demographic and Social Characteristics Section, Census Division, Statistics Canada, 1971; 1961 Census of Canada, Bull.7.1-9, table 8; 1951 Census of Canada, vol.X, table 46.

TABLE P-12 NUMBER AND PER CENT OF CANADIAN POPULATION BY PRINCIPAL RELIGIOUS DENOMINATIONS, BY CENSUS YEARS SINCE 1871

RELIGIOUS DENOMINATION	1971 N	%	1961 N	%	1951 N	%	1941 N	%	1931 N	%
Anglican	2,543,180	11.8	2,409,068	13.2	2,060,720	14.7	1,754,368	15.2	1,639,075	15.8
Baptist	667,245	3.1	593,553	3.3	519,585	3.7	484,465	4.2	443,944	4.3
Greek Orthodox	316,605	1.3	239,766	1.3	172,271	1.2	139,845	1.2	102,529	1.0
Jewish	276,025	1.3	254,368	1.4	240,836	1.5	168,585	1.5	155,766	1.5
Lutheran	715,740	3.3	662,744	3.6	444,923	3.2	401,836	3.5	394,920	3.8
Mennonite	168,150	0.8	152,452	*	125,938	*	111,554	1.0	88,837	*
Methodist	-	-	-(e)	-	-(e)	-	-(e)	-	-(e)	-
Pentecostal	220,390	1.0	143,877	*	95,131	*	57,742	*	26,349	*
Presbyterian	872,335	4.0	818,558(c)	4.5	781,747(c)	5.6	830,597(c)	7.2	872,428(c)	8.4
Roman Catholic	9,974,895	46.2	8,342,826	45.7	6,069,496	43.3	4,806,431	41.8	4,102,960	39.5
Salvation Army	119,665	0.6	92,054	*	70,275	*	33,609	*	30,773	*
Ukrainian Catholic	227,730	1.1	189,653	1.0	190,831	1.4	185,948	1.6	186,879	1.8
United	3,768,800	17.5	3,664,008	20.2	2,867,271	20.5	2,208,658	19.2	2,021,065	19.5
Other	1,697,555	7.8	675,320	3.7	405,805	2.9	323,017	2.8	311,261	3.0
Total	21,568,310	100.0	18,238,247		14,009,429		11,506,655		10,376,786	

29

TABLE P-12 continued

RELIGIOUS DENOMINATION	1921 N	1921 %	1911 N	1911 %	CENSUS YEARS 1901 N	1901 %	1891 N	1891 %	1881 N	1881 %	1871 N	1871 %
Anglican	1,407,780	16.0	1,043,017	14.5	681,494	12.7	646,059	13.4	574,818	13.3	501,269	13.6
Baptist	421,730	4.8	382,720	5.3	318,005	5.9	303,839	6.3	296,525	6.9	243,714	6.5
Greek Orthodox	169,832	1.9	88,507	1.2	15,630	*	-	-	-	-	18	*
Jewish	125,197	1.4	74,564	1.0	16,401	*	6,414	*	2,393	*	1,115	*
Lutheran	286,458	3.3	229,864	3.2	92,524	1.7	63,982	1.3	46,354	1.1	37,935	1.0
Mennonite	58,797	*	44,625	*	31,797	*	-	-	-	-	-	-
Methodist	1,159,246	13.2	1,079,993	15.0	916,886	17.1	847,765	17.5	742,981	17.2	578,161	15.7
Pentecostal	7,003	*	513	*	-	-	-	-	-	-	-	-
Presbyterian	1,409,406	16.0	1,116,071	15.5	842,531	15.7	755,326	15.6	676,165	15.6	574,577	15.6
Roman Catholic	3,389,626	38.6	2,833,041	39.3	2,229,600	41.5	1,992,017	41.2	1,791,982	41.4	1,532,471	41.5
Salvation Army	24,733	*	18,834	*	10,308	*	13,949	*	-	-	-	-
Ukrainian Catholic	-	-	-	-	-	-	-	-	-	-	-	-
United	8,728	*	-	-	-	-	-	-	-	-	-	-
Other	319,413	3.6	294,894	4.1	216,139	4.0	203,888	4.2	193,596	4.4	219,997	6.0
Total	8,787,949		7,206,643		5,371,315		4,833,239		4,324,810		3,689,257	

Note: * negligible percentage.

(a) Churches observing the Greek Orthodox rite, e.g., Russian Orthodox, Ukrainian Orthodox, and Syrian Orthodox.
(b) Includes Hutterite.
(c) Not included in United Church.
(d) Includes Evangelical United Brethren.
(e) Included in United Church.
(f) Includes 29,575 of no religion.

Sources: 1971 Census of Canada, Bull. 1.3-3, Table 9; 1961 Census of Canada, Bull. 1.2-6, Table 41; Bull. 7.1-11, Table 1.

TABLE P-13 PROJECTED AGE COMPOSITION OF CANADIAN POPULATION,
         BOTH SEXES, FOR 1974 and 1984.

Year/Age (as of June 1)	SeriesA	Series B	Series C	Series D
		In thousands		
1969				
0-14	6,518.6	6,518.6	6,518.6	6,518.6
15-64	12,903.3	12,903.3	12,903.3	12,903.3
65+	1,639.1	1,639.1	1,639.1	1,639.1
All ages	21,061.0	21,061.0	21,061.0	21,061.0
1974				
0-14	6,502.6	6,341.8	6,285.4	6,173.9
15-64	14,760.0	14,609.0	14,458.1	14,307.4
65+	1,830.3	1,824.9	1,819.3	1,813.9
All ages	23,093.1	22,775.6	22,563.0	22,295.1
1984				
0-14	8,165.1	7,178.5	6,964.8	6,419.0
15-64	17,939.0	17,457.4	16,976.3	16,494.6
65+	2,368.7	2,347.3	2,325.8	2,304.4
All ages	28,472.8	26,983.3	26,266.8	25,222.2
		In percentages		
1969				
0-14	30.95	30.95	30.95	30.95
15-64	61.27	61.27	61.27	61.27
65+	7.78	7.78	7.78	7.78
All ages	100.00	100.00	100.00	100.00
1974				
0-14	28.16	27.84	27.86	27.69
15-64	63.92	64.14	64.08	64.17
65+	7.93	8.01	8.06	8.14
All ages	100.00	100.00	100.00.	100.00

In percentages			
1984			
0-14	28.68	26.60	26.52	25.47
15-64	63.00	64.70	64.63	65.40
65+	8.32	8.70	8.85	9.14
All ages	100.00	100.00	100.00	100.00

Notes:Series A: High fertility, net migration of 140,000 per year.
        B: Medium fertility, net migration of 100,000 per year.
        C: Medium fertility, net migration of 60,000 per year.
        D: Low fertility, net migration of 20,000 per year.

Source: Dominion Bureau of Statistics, The Population Projections
        for Canada 1969-1984, Analytical and Technical Memorandum
        No. 4 (Ottawa: April 1970), table 11.

BIBLIOGRAPHY

Bladen,V.W., Canadian Population and Northern Colonisation.
Toronto: Toronto University Press, 1962. (158 pp.)

Dominion Bureau of Statistics, Dominion Bureau of Statistics:
History, Function, Organisation. Ottawa: Queen's Printer
1958. (56 pp.)

_____, Canada, One Hundred Years: 1867-1967. Ottawa:
Queen's Printer, 1967. (504 pp.)

Hurd, W.B., Racial Origins and Nativity of the Canadian People.
1931 Census Monograph. Ottawa: King's Printer, 1937. (292 pp.)

_____, Ethnic Origin and Nativity of the Canadian People.
1941 Census Monograph. Ottawa: Queen's Printer, n.d. (251 pp.)

Joy, R., Languages in Conflict. Toronto: McClelland and Stewart,
1972. (149 pp.)

Kalbach, W., and McVey,W., The Demographic Bases of Canadian
Society. Toronto: McGraw-Hill, 1971. (354 pp.)

Keyfitz, N., "The Growth of the Canadian Population".
Population Studies 4 (1950): 47-63.

Lieberson,S., Language and Ethnic Relations in Canada.
New York: Wiley, 1970. (264 pp.)

Porter, J., Canadian Social Structure: A Statistical Profile.
Toronto: McClelland and Stewart, 1967. (159 pp.)

Royal Commission on Bilingualism and Biculturalism, The Cultural
Contribution of the Other Ethnic Groups. Book IV. Ottawa:
Queen's Printer, 1970. (352 pp.)

Richmond, A.H., Ethnic Residential Segregation in Metropolitan
Toronto. Toronto: York University Survey Research Centre,
1972. (90 pp.)

Ryder, N.B., "Components of Canadian Population Growth",
Population Index 20 (1964): 71-81.

_____, "The Interpretation of Origin Statistics",
Canadian Journal of Economics and Political Science 21
(1955): 466-479.

Simmons, J., and Simmons, R., Urban Canada. Toronto: Copp
Clark, 1964. (167 pp.)

Statistics Canada, Canada Year Book, 1972. Ottawa:
Information Canada, 1972. (1,404 pp.; annual)

_____, Canada 1972. Ottawa: Information Canada, 1972.
(336 pp.; annual)

Stone, L.O., Urban Development in Canada. 1961 Census
Monograph. Ottawa: Queen's Printer, 1967. (293 pp.)

Urquhart, M.C., and Buckley, K.A.H., eds., Historical
Statistics of Canada. Toronto: Macmillan, 1965. (672 pp.)

2 Three Demographic Processes

FERTILITY

There are two ways in which changes in the childbearing
patterns of Canadian women are usually recorded. One is
through the registration of births (which is the responsibility
of the provinces) and one is through the decennial censuses
(which are the responsibility of the federal government).
The first has the advantage that current changes in the
number of children being born are easily followed from year
to year. Such measures as the Crude Birthrate, for instance,
are often quoted and referred to in the public media. The
second has the advantage that a variety of social and
economic characteristics of women and their families can be
linked to childbearing behaviour, on an aggregate level, of
course. Furthermore, total histories of childbearing can be
traced as long as there are enough female respondents of
any age, thus offering the student of population an overview
of what has happened in the past.

The disadvantages of both types of data are equally
apparent. The registration data provide only minimal
information and are usually not cross-classified to any
extent. The enumeration data, on the other hand, are quite
rich in information but their publication schedules are
cumbersome and they are late in appearing.

Chart 2. Birth Rates in Canada, since 1969

Notes: For explanation of terms, see Appendix B

Source: Vital Statistics November 1972. Ottawa: Statistics Canada,
Vital Statistics Section of the Health and Welfare Division,
January 1973.

At the present time, Canada is experiencing its lowest
birthrate ever. Based on the number of children born per
1,000 women of childbearing age in any given year (see table
F-1), 1969 was the first time that the number of children
born to all women aged fifteen to forty-nine years fell under
the level of 100. The decline in fertility has become
most pronounced in the cities and in the most populous
and fastest growing provinces. Urbanization and fertility
have again become incompatible, as they were held to be
some thirty years ago.

Since the birthrate started its downward trend about ten years ago, it has been commented upon quite extensively. The world population growth is a likely topic for almost any conversation, and an awareness of the relationship between population growth and economic growth and the quality of life in Canada has come to the foreground. Growth and prosperity are no longer thought synonymous.

The demographic analysts, in contrast to laymen, have been very cautious in commenting on the decline of births. One of the cautious explanations of the present fertility decline is that which assumes that Canadian women are only delaying their births for the time being. Sooner or later, they will complete their family, which will have the familiar three or four children, thus confirming the traditionally pronatalist culture of the land. On the other hand, there is the real possibility that the hold of the pronatalist ideology has been shattered and that the cohorts of young women now entering their childbearing prime will either have small families or will choose to remain childless. At the risk of appearing overly optimistic, one can say that the decline in births has been demonstrated for all provinces and for all age groups, discounting certain self-contained religious and cultural communities of no numerical impact.

The traditionally high fertility of married women aged fifteen to nineteen has shown a decrease exceeding that of the Great Depression (see tableF-2). Even though this group represents but a fraction of all women in their late teens, it betrays an interesting and new trend in childbearing behaviour. Some ten years ago, women in their late teens who were married wed possibly because they were already pregnant; that is why close to half the married women under twenty years of age bore children. Considering that there must have been some fetal loss through still-births and abortions and considering the relative subfecundity characteristic of that population, the fertility achieved by this group would have been matched only by early settlers, present-day Hutterites, or similar child-happy populations. What the decline in births in this group portends is perhaps one of the most significant changes in the institutional arrangement of modern societies: the dissociation of marriage and parenthood, and that exactly for those women who until recently were unable and unwilling to separate the two.

If the decline of fertility among the pre-twenty-year-old women is seen as one of the correlates of the divorce between marriage and parenthood, the increase of illegitimacy in births is, perhaps, another correlate of the same phenomenon. Canada shares in this trend with all developed nations (the illegitimacy in other countries can be traced to different social arrangements for marriage), although it is by no means a leader in this respect. In 1970, illegitimate births accounted for almost one-tenth of all live births by Canadian women. Curiously enough, those provinces which have an overall higher fertility also have a higher percentage of illegitimate births (table F-3). What is reflected in the numerical growth of illegitimate births is a greater tolerance of such births, making a recourse to abortion, or contraception, or sexual abstention less imperative.

Looking back, provinces which at present have the
highest proportion of illegitimate births had lower-than-
average illegitimacy rates in the past, with the singular
exception of Nova Scotia. This may be accounted for by
two cultural forces:(1) camouflaging an early pregnancy
by marriage used to be quite widespread; and (2) the shotgun
argument is not so convincing to many as it once was. In
the provinces where the decline in births by teenage women
was very pronounced, as in Quebec and Ontario, the rise
in illegitimate births was slower than in those provinces
where the decline in teenage childbearing was relatively
slow. Such an emerging pattern of childbearing represents
a form of institutional transformation where the acceptance
of alternate behavioural models for women encourages
underplaying childbearing and may even negate it as an
obligation. This transformation may seem rather slow, but
appearing as it does after timeless pressure for the
survival of the species, it is truly revolutionary.

There is no question that the childbearing patterns
of Canadian women have undergone a considerable change.
The main feature is the reduction in the time span needed
to complete the family size. Most women bear most of their
children in a span of less than ten years, whereas twenty
years ago the span was twenty years. At present, about two-
thirds of all births are occurring when the women are in
their early and middle twenties (see table F-4).

The impact of this compact childbearing on the social
structure is bound to be profound, if for no other reason
than it frees a great number of women from staying at home
and makes them socially "visible", be it in the marketplace
of jobs or in the marketplace of daily encounters. After
the age of thirty-five or forty, most women become
functionally "childless"; that is, their children are grown up
enough to free them from daily childrearing preoccupations.
As happens to any human behaviour, once this becomes visible
it becomes institutionalized, which in turn allows for
natural childlessness to become accepted. Perhaps one
may argue that inasmuch as the older-age "childlessness"
has preceded the late-teen-married decline in childbearing,
alternate models of behaviour for women were visible a
while before they became actively emulated by the youth.
This again contributes to the dissociation between marriage
and parenthood and is bound to bring zero population
growth to Canada smoothly and without much of a future
shock.

Traditionally, the first-born children are understood
to be in the advantageous position over their subsequent
siblings. This is not only because the parents are young
and under no pressure to divide their attention to all the
other children, but also because their resources are not
strained to accommodate the new arrival. It should be no
great surprise that the lowering of the birthrate brings
the proportion of the first-born up (see table F-5).
More than one-third of all births are now first births, with
all the eugenic and other positive consequences. However,
close to one-fifth of current births are of the fourth
or a higher parity and most of them are disproportionately
concentrated among income groups with the least resources.
Forty years ago, such large families were not uncommon
and by necessity were more equally distributed in the social
and economic strata of the Canadian society. Should the

trend toward small families (two children) continue, every other Canadian would be first-born. Furthermore, the proportion of Canadians enjoying economic advantages has been steadily on the increase. The combination of small families and privileged social circumstances should have an impact on the quality of life, which is being threatened by adverse environmental strains.

Historically, religion has been a fairly good indicator of family size (see table F-6). As with most indicators, however, this one seems to apply only for the period of transition from a high to a low fertility. When fertility was high (six or more children), most women had large families; now, when fertility is low (about two children), religious conviction seems to make little difference in the number of children women have. During the transition period, Catholic women and women identifiable as fundamentalist Protestants (for example, Hutterites or Mennonites) lagged behind Jews and secular Protestants in adopting small-family values. But the retarding force of religion is better tied to broad, cultural value patterns than to ecclesiastical interpretations of the Holy Writ. Since it could be shown rather easily that some cultural groups in the Canadian mosaic traditionally have had a higher fertility than the majority of urban Canadians, religion may be only symptomatic of other forces which bond people together and impose conformity from within. For example, were Catholicism alone responsible for high fertility it would not explain the sharp drop in the birthrate in Quebec. On the other hand, the religious factor is contributory inasmuch as it is meshed with other cultural values which population subgroups may share.

Education, on the other hand, continues to act as a fertility depressant for Canadian women. The overall evidence from other countries and the available Canadian evidence point to the unambiguous influence that the education of women has on their fertility. Education as a fertility depressant assures us of small families, which in turn prove to be little burden to Canadian women, thus allowing them full participation in the modern world. Today's educational policies put every Canadian through some ten to twelve years of schooling at the minimum, which should translate into a decreasing birthrate.

One approximate measure of fertility is the child-women ratio (see table F-7), indicating the number of children up to four years of age in relation to the number of women of childbearing age. This ratio has dropped from 555 in 1951 to 390 in 1971 for Canada and from 582 to 350 for Quebec during the same period, even though in the smaller provinces either in the Maritimes or in the Prairies, the decline has been less dramatic.

No doubt, there will be additional evidence on Canadian fertility patterns, but the trend toward small families both in Canada and the rest of the civilized world may prove difficult to disconfirm.

TABLE F-1 NUMBER OF CHILDREN BORN PER 1,000 MARRIED WOMEN AGED 15 TO 49, FOR CANADA AND PROVINCES, FOR SELECTED CENSUS YEARS SINCE 1831

Year	Canada	Nfld.	P.E.I.	NS.	NB.	Que.	Ont.	Man.	Sask.	Alta.	B.C.	Y.and NWT.
1969(a)	98(b)	9	130	108	119	96	95	104	110	106	90	(c)
1966	112(b)	198(d)	146	124	138	119	107	110	121	115	95	186(e)
1961	153(b)	237(f)	194	162	185	167	142	147	157	162	131	238(e)
1956	163(b)	-	186	167	197	188	146	148	163	172	141	230(e)
1951	159(b)	220(g)	186	162	200	193	138	147	152	160	130	224(e)
1941	149	-	167	165	194	201	118	133	141	139	116	-
1931	161	-	176	169	201	225	130	138	158	152	98	-
1921	204	-	210(h)	187	218(i)	283	165	194	193	167(j)	126	-
1911	256	-	-	247	-	299	209	275	331	-	228	-
1891	285	-	-	291	-	312	245	406	-	-	310	-
1871	378	-	-	366	-	355	358	-	-	-	-	-
1861	-	-	-	378	-	370	376	-	-	-	-	-
1851	-	-	-	-	-	357	362	-	-	-	-	-
1842	-	-	-	-	-	-	482	-	-	-	-	-
1831	-	-	-	-	-	419	-	-	-	-	-	-

(a) Reporting of legitimate fertility discontinued as of 1970.
(b) Includes Newfoundland.
(c) Not available for intercensal years.
(d) Arithmetically adjusted from 231 for women 15 to 44.
(e) Yukon and Northwest Territories combined; N.W.T.usually higher in fertility.
(f) Arithmetically adjusted from 276 for women 15 to 44.
(g) For 1952.
(h) Arithmetically adjusted from 245 for women 15 to 44.
(i) Arithmetically adjusted from 254 for women 15 to 44.
(j) Arithmetically adjusted from 195 for women 15 to 44.

Sources: Henripin, Tendences et Facteurs de la Fécondité au Canada, table 2.5; Dominion Bureau of Statistics, Vital Statistics, 1969, table B.7; Vital Statistics, 1968, table B.7; Canada Year Book, 1927-28, p.164.

TABLE F-2 AGE-SPECIFIC FERTILITY RATES PER 1000 MARRIED WOMEN AGED 15 TO 49 FOR CANADA, FOR CENSUS YEARS SINCE 1921.

Year	Age Group							Gross Reproduction Rate (All Women)
	15-19	20-24	25-29	30-34	35-39	40-44	45-49	
1969(a)	350.4	249.5	172.5	91.1	47.7	13.3	1.2	1.122(b)
1966	465.8	280.2	187.3	112.5	62.5	21.0	2.0	1.369
1961	541.2	374.4	255.6	161.4	89.9	32.1	2.8	1.868
1956	551.5	381.7	265.5	169.8	101.0	35.6	3.4	1.874
1951	498.5	350.4	218.1	168.7	100.8	36.6	3.7	1.701
1941	453.1	340.2	237.8	158.3	99.1	38.9	4.5	1.377
1931	485.0	357.6	257.7	180.9	123.1	52.5	6.5	1.555
1921	472.9	396.7	300.7	225.6	152.8	70.6	9.5	1.733(c)

Note: Excludes Newfoundland for all years and the Yukon and Northwest Territories through 1941.
(a) Reporting of legitimate fertility discontinued as of 1970.
(b) For 1970.
(c) Arithmetically transformed total fertility rate of 3,536.

Sources: Henripin, Tendences et Facteurs, p.376; Canada Year Book, 1969, p.235; Vital Statistics, 1969, table B.7; Vital Statistics, 1968, table B.7; Vital Statistics 1961, table B.7; Vital Statistics, 1956, table II. 13; Vital Statistics, 1944, table 6.

TABLE F-3 ILLEGITIMATE LIVE BIRTHS AND PER CENT OF ALL LIVE BIRTHS FOR CANADA AND PROVINCES, FOR CENSUS YEARS SINCE 1921

Provinces	1971 No.	%	1966 No.	%	1961 No.	%	1956 No.	%	1951 No.	%	1941 No.	%	1931 No.	%	1921 No.	%
CANADA(a)	32693	9.0	29391	7.6	21490	4.5	17510	3.9	14537	3.8	10430	4.0	8543	3.5	3347	2.0
Newfoundland	1229	9.6	832	5.9	666	4.3	529	3.6	417	3.6	329	4.0	178	2.7	-	-
Prince Edward Island	171	8.1	145	6.6	135	4.8	154	5.8	138	5.2	96	4.7	71	3.8	49	2.3
Nova Scotia	1664	11.7	1551	10.2	1334	6.9	1194	6.2	1147	6.7	977	7.0	630	5.4	396	3.0
New Brunswick	1177	9.7	882	6.9	735	4.4	688	4.2	643	4.0	452	3.5	367	3.4	205	1.8
Quebec	7087	7.9	6366	5.8	4931	3.6	4454	3.2	3650	3.0	2646	3.0	2450	2.9	-	-
Ontario	8492	6.5	8476	6.4	5456	3.5	4415	3.1	3807	3.3	3384	4.7	2773	4.0	1592	2.1
Manitoba	2338	13.0	1844	10.2	1469	6.3	1002	4.6	771	3.9	517	3.5	513	3.6	420	2.3
Saskatchewan	2257	14.1	1923	10.1	1419	5.9	1058	4.4	971	4.5	641	3.5	638	3.0	258	1.1
Alberta	3638	11.9	3198	10.5	2430	6.2	1674	4.8	1272	4.7	720	4.2	635	3.7	299	1.8
British Columbia	4236	12.2	3926	12.1	2680	6.9	2207	6.1	1633	5.8	688	4.6	288	2.8	128	1.2
Yukon	125	24.7	72	19.5	94	16.8	60	12.5	41	12.0	-	-	-	-	-	-
Northwest Territories	279	21.7	176	15.2	141	12.6	75	9.6	47	7.2	-	-	-	-	-	-

(a) Excludes Newfoundland prior to 1951. Excludes Quebec for 1921.

Sources: Vital Statistics 1971 Preliminary Report, table 9; Vital Statistics, 1970, table B.7; Vital Statistics, 1961, table B.7; Canada Year Book, 1969, p.232; Canada Year Book, 1922-23, p. 190.

TABLE F-4 PERCENTAGE DISTRIBUTION OF BIRTHS BY AGE OF MOTHER,
FOR CANADA, BY CENSUS YEARS SINCE 1931

Age of Mother	Year						
	1970	1966	1961	1956	1951	1941	1931
Under 20	8.5	8.9	7.3	6.1	5.6	5.8	5.4
20-24	35.5	32.2	29.3	27.7	27.1	27.4	25.1
25-29	31.8	27.8	28.4	29.7	31.0	30.4	27.8
30-34	15.0	17.4	18.9	21.2	20.8	20.2	21.0
35-39	7.0	10.1	11.4	11.5	11.6	11.6	14.4
40-44	2.1	3.3	3.5	3.5	3.5	4.1	5.6
45-49	.2	.3	.3	.3	.3	.4	.6
Average age for all birth	29.1(a)	27.5	28.1	-	28.4	28.5	29.2

Note: Deals with legitimate live births. Excludes Newfoundland; prior
to 1961 excludes Yukon and Northwest Territories.

(a) Estimate based on 1968 illegitimacy by age figures.

Sources: Vital Statistics, 1970 (Preliminary Report), table 6;
Vital Statistics, 1968, table C; Vital Statistics, 1956, table D.

TABLE F-5 LIVE BIRTHS BY LIVE BIRTH ORDER AS PER CENT OF ALL BIRTHS FOR
CANADA, FOR SELECTED CENSUS YEARS SINCE 1931

Birth Order	Year						
	1971	1966	1961	1956	1951	1941	1931
First	40.7	29.9	24.1	25.2	26.7	32.7	23.0
Second	29.3	25.5	23.6	24.3	25.8	21.8	19.3
Third	14.9	16.9	18.5	18.3	17.6	13.5	14.0
Fourth or higher	15.1	27.6	33.8	32.2	29.9	32.0	43.8

Note: Deals with legitimate live births only. Excludes Newfoundland
prior to 1950. Excludes Yukon and Northwest Territories.

Sources: Vital Statistics 1971 Preliminary report, table 8;
Vital Statistics, 1970, table B.10; Vital Statistics, 1968,
table D.

41

TABLE F-6 PER CENT DISTRIBUTION OF EVER-MARRIED WOMEN, AGED 15 TO 44 AND 45 AND OVER IN 1961, BY MAJOR RELIGIOUS GROUPINGS AND NUMBER OF CHILDREN EVER BORN, FOR CANADA

Age and Religious Group	Children Born per 1,000 Women	Per Cent of Women Bearing Children, by Number of Children Born					Women Ever Married
		0	1-2	3-4	5-6	7 or more	
15 to 44 years							
Catholics (Roman, Ukrainian, Greek Orthodox)	2,844	13.1	40.0	27.9	11.2	7.7	1,144,211
Protestants	2,355	13.8	45.9	30.4	7.2	2.6	1,176,691
Mennonites, Hutterites, Mormons	2,997	11.1	34.3	34.2	13.8	7.9	24,613
Jewish	1,961	12.0	58.6	27.7	1.7(a)	-	35,616
Other	2,454	14.6	42.6	30.9	8.6	3.3	82,027
45 years and over							
Catholics	4,613	12.9	23.1	22.1	15.2	26.7	740,304
Protestants	2,791	14.9	39.6	27.1	10.5	7.8	1,052,320
Mennonites, Hutterites, Mormons	4,898	7.8	17.7	25.4	21.3	25.8	19,399
Jewish	1,854	10.5	50.3	30.0	9.2(a)	-	37,565
Other	3,301	13.5	32.1	28.1	14.3	11.9	70,366

(a) Five children or more.

Sources: Recalculated, 1961 Census of Canada, Bull. 7.2-2, table 5.

TABLE F-7 CHILD-WOMAN RATIOS, FOR CANADA AND PROVINCES,
BY CENSUS YEARS SINCE 1951

	1971	1966	1961	1956	1951
Canada	390	530	606	583	555
Newfoundland	581	725	797	803	824
Prince Edward Island	538	642	720	667	687
Nova Scotia	435	582	637	610	606
New Brunswick	446	609	692	674	695
Quebec	350	499	596	650	582
Ontario	382	515	579	546	504
Manitoba	423	539	591	564	518
Saskatchewan	444	594	648	616	562
Alberta	432	581	665	631	565
British Columbia	385	508	584	548	496
Yukon and Northwest Territories	660	870	843	506	376

Note: Ratio calculated from number of children aged 0 to 4 per 1,000
women aged 15 to 45.

Sources: Statistics Canada, Census Division, Demographic and Social
Characteristics Section, 1972 (informal release on age and
sex, 1971 census); 1966 Census of Canada, vol. 1 (1-10),
table 19; 1961 Census of Canada, Bull. 1.2-2, table 20.

BIBLIOGRAPHY

Allingham, J.D., Balakrishman, T.R., and Kantner, J.F.,
"Use of Oral Contraception and the Differential Diffusion of
Oral Anovulants", Population Studies 23 (1969): 43-51.

Balakrishnan, T.R., Ross, S., Allingham, J.D., and Kantner, J.F.,
"Attitudes Toward Abortion of Married Women in Metropolitan
Toronto", Social Biology 19 (1972): 35-42.

Barratt, T.R., "An Analysis of Fertility Trends in Ontario",
Ontario Economic Review 9 (May-June 1971): 2-15.

Bourvier, L.F., "The Spacing of Births Among French Canadian
Families", The Canadian Review of Sociology and Anthropology
5 (1968): 17-26.

Charles,E., The Changing Size of the Family in Canada. 1941 Census
Monograph. Ottawa: King's Printer, 1948. (311 pp.)

Dominion Bureau of Statistics/Statistics Canada, Vital Statistics.
Ottawa: Queen's Printer (Information Canada), annual.

Henripin, J., Tendences et Facteurs de la Fécondité au Canada.
1961 Census Monograph. Ottawa: Queen's Printer, 1968. (428 pp.)

Henripin, J., and Legare, J.,"Recent Trends in Canadian Fertility",
The Canadian Review of Sociology and Anthropology 8 (1971):
106-118.

Hurd, B.W., "The Decline in the Canadian Birth Rate", Canadian
Journal of Economics and Political Science 3 (1937): 40-57.

Krotki, K.J., and LaPierre, E., "La Fécondité au Canada selon la
Religion, l'Origine Éthnique et l'État Matrimonial",
Population 23 (1968): 815-834.

Miraben, J.N. and Legare, J., "Nouvelles Données sur la Natalité et
la Fécondité au Canada", Population 22 (1967): 255-286.

Murphy, E.M., and Nagnur, D.M., "A Gompertz Fit that Fits:
Application to Canadian Fertility Patterns", Demography 9 (1972)
35-50.

Romaniuk, A., and Piche, V., "Natality Estimates for the Canadian
Indians by Stable Population Models, 1900-1969", The Canadian
Review of Sociology and Anthropology 9 (1972): 1-20.

Tracey, W.R., Fertility of the Population of Canada. 1931
Census Monograph. Ottawa: King's Printer, 1941. (207 pp.)

Veevers, J.E., "Childlessness and Age at First Marriage",
Social Biology 18 (1971): 285-291.

_____, "Rural-urban Variation in the Incidence of Childlessness",
Rural Sociology 36 (1971): 547-553.

MORTALITY

Unlike births, deaths do not weigh heavily on the national mind, for at least three reasons. First, Canada has one of the lowest death rates in the world; as a matter of fact, its mortality for the last ten years has been lower than that of any other country with predominantly European population. Secondly, the thought of death should not concern the adult population, as the probability of dying is now very low until an advanced age. And thirdly, institutional arrangements to deal with death remove its reality even further from our daily routines.

The legal implications of death, on the other hand, primarily with regard to estate settlements and property transfers, brought forth a good registration system. Even though systematic death registration for Canada and provinces is not available until as of 1921 (for Quebec as of 1926, and for Territories as of 1950), there are historical records locally in parishes and other administrative areas which allow an estimate of death rates for about 200 years back. For example, during the decade 1851-1860, the crude death rate for Quebec was about 19, twice as much as the 100 years prior to that.

Crude death rate leaves much to be desired as a measure of mortality, as it only reflects the number of deaths in a population. As an indicator of trends, however, and as a comparative index between provinces, it remains fairly useful. Standardized- that is, adjusted for the differences in age distribution- death rates by sex indicate a continuous downward trend in mortality across all provinces (see table D-1). During the last decade or so death rates have stabilized at a level somewhere between 7 and 9 for males and between 5 and 6 for females. For the Territories, the decline in mortality has been retarded, in part because of the difficulties of providing effective health services to isolated populations, and in part because of the reluctance of those populations to accept modern health practices.

One of the chief features of mortality statistics is their remarkable stability from year to year. It is as if the proverbial certainty of death has become translated into a statistical series. Implications of this are quite considerable. Whereas analysis of fertility data, for instance, has to be fairly cautious as regards short-term fluctuations, minor changes in mortality data represent true changes over time.

The substantial reduction in Canadian mortality during the last fifty years did not occur uniformly across the various age groups nor for both sexes. Advances in medical technology reduced the mortality rate of both sexes through to their middle years of life, although the patterns by sex differ (see table D-2). For males, the greatest decline has occurred at the child and adolescent levels, while for females the reduction has been significant for all years up to about forty. Beyond that age, however, two shifts in this pattern appear: (1) for both sexes the reduction has not been as dramatic as for those below age forty; and (2) reductions for women after the middle years are substantially higher than the reductions for men.

Chart 3. Crude and Standardized Death Rates[1] for Diseases of the Heart, by Sex,
Canada, 1950-1968.

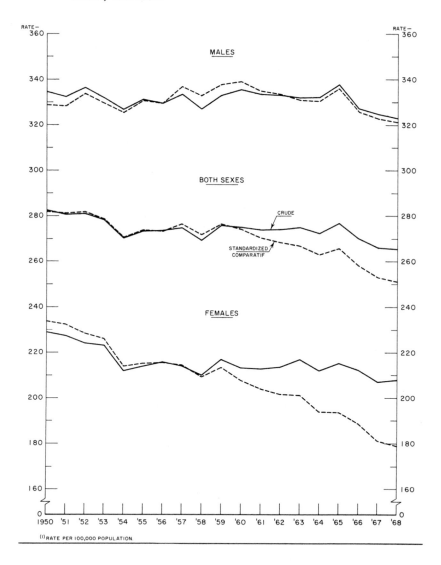

Note: For definition of terms, consult Appendix B

Source: Statistics Canada. Cardiovascular-renal Mortality 1950-1968. Ottawa:
Information Canada, 1973, Chart 2, page 33.

Whereas the decline in mortality of children and adolescents can be explained largely by the success of combatting infectious diseases, the decline in mortality of women in their young adulthood is explained by the decline in deaths through pregnancy and childbirth complications. Up to about 1930, women in their twenties had a slightly higher mortality than men in that age group. Today, however, their mortality in that age is negligible.

One sensitive measure of the efficacy of public health provisions is infant mortality. The last fifty years saw a very pronounced decline in infant deaths, from some 90 for each 1,000 live births to about 19 in 1971. For some of the provinces, the decline was even more pronounced, for instance, in New Brunswick or Nova Scotia, or Quebec (see table D-3). What is most striking in the infant mortality figures is the discrepancy in death rates for the two sexes. The higher the infant mortality, the higher the discrepancy disfavouring boys. Also, as a closer look at the infant mortality rates would show, the higher the infant mortality the greater the proportion of deaths attributable to environmental conditions and lack of proper health care.

The rise of the average age at death by about twenty years between 1921 and 1971 is partially accounted for by the sharp decline of infant deaths and by the reduction of death at young ages. Noticeable increases in the age at death occurred around the time when a variety of public-health measures and a variety of social-care measures were being introduced and became effective. Median age at death which is a more expressive measure than average age at death now stands at about sixty-eight years for men and seventy-four for women (see table D-4). There is some variation between the provinces, men in Saskatchewan living considerably longer than men in Quebec. As for women, the median age at death in present-day Prince Edward Island is seventy-nine but only about seventy-two in Quebec.

This variation is not easily explained. The arguments of urban and rural differences in death rates can be only partially supported by evidence. Likewise, it is only partly convincing to argue that the surviving population represents cohorts which were exposed to severe attrition through infant mortality and childhood diseases and thus longevity is favoured by "natural selection" in rural areas unaided by urban health-care facilities. On the other hand, one may argue that the different age composition of the two provinces (Quebec being considerably younger) accounts for the difference in median age at death. Death affects all ages, the very young somewhat, middle-aged minimally, and the aged considerably. If the proportion of the very young is fairly high, their deaths, few as they may be, depress the median age at death by contributing to the quota of the first half of all deaths. On the other hand, when the population is demographically old, the median age at death is elevated, as it takes older persons to fill the quota for the first half of all deaths in any given year.

Economic and social consequences of aging are, of course, enormous, especially since the distribution of population by age groups is unfavourable usually to those provinces which are the least vigorous economically. Were one to think of the future holding to the median age at death of seventy-five years, this would mean that birth cohorts which some fifteen years ago

47

were about 450,000 annually, would fifty-five years from now be diminished only by one-half. As the recent birth cohorts have decreased by over 20 per cent, the old-age dependency ratio about forty years from now will become quite pronounced and, above all, unprecedented, thus requiring new government spending priorities.

Mankind is still far from having a perfect health record and even countries like Canada, which enjoys a high standard of living and a very good system of health care, have to grapple with a host of diseases which shorten man's life. The success in combatting disease, however, is remarkable. As compared with 1931, four major communicable diseases and tuberculosis have all but disappeared as causes of death (see table D-5). Other diseases, such as influenza, have been substantially reduced. On the other hand, diseases which occur later in life have assumed a prominent role as causes of death. Cancer, for instance, has registered a 50 per cent increase as compared to 1931. The changes in the relative status of diseases as leading causes of death have to be interpreted with caution. On the whole, degenerative and chronic diseases are bound to increase when the population at risk increases. Furthermore, part of the increase may reflect improved diagnostic procedures.

It can be shown that the age-specific death rates due to malignancy (e.g., cancer) have remained fairly stable over the years, even though the actual number of cases does show considerable increase (see table D-6). Strangely enough, as in the case of cancer, the age-specific rates for males have increased since 1931 but those for women for the several age categories over forty-five have decreased, or at least remained stable. Explanation for this sex discrepancy is difficult to suggest in view of the fact that the causes of cancer are as yet not entirely known. Were one to think back, however, to the life styles of those who are currently in old age, the difference in smoking, for instance, among men and women may have been considerable.

For the population up to the age of forty, accidents now appear to be the chief cause of death, substantially more for men than for women. This not only reflects some cultural arrangements and a differential exposure to hazardous working conditions but also the male tendency to take physical risks, as the difference between boys and girls in accidental deaths cannot be explained in occupational terms, for instance.

Cultural and social restraints may be powerful determinants of human behaviour resulting in death. Taking Ontario as an example (see table D-7), one can see that being married improves one's chances of avoiding death, be it death by a natural cause or by an accident, poisoning or violence. On the other hand, being widowed or divorced (or separated) is detrimental, particularly to males in their middle years between twenty-five through sixty-four, when being married is the norm in this society. Even though there are some genetic differences operative in establishing differential death rates for men and women, these differences seem to be accentuated by social arrangements favouring women.

All the differences in susceptibility to disease and resulting death, the differences in genetic endowment to survive, the social arrangements encouraging risk-taking behaviour, all of these are summarized in a statistical probability of

48

living a certain number of years into the future. At birth
Canadians now may expect to live some sixty-nine years if they
are men and some seventy-five years if they are women, slightly
less for both sexes in Quebec and slightly more for both sexes
in the Prairie Provinces (see table D-8). Those in their
midyears (at forty) still have some thirty-three years to live
if men and some thirty-eight years if women, again slightly
less in Quebec and slightly more in the Prairies.

Since 1931, the life expectancy at birth has increased
close to nine years for men and thirteen years for women for
Canada as a whole, but by close to twelve years for men and
sixteen years for women in Quebec (see table D-9). Were one
to argue for social change from mortality data, such a dramatic
increase in life expectancy at birth in Quebec must be
attributed to a considerable decrease in births with the
concomitant decrease in large families and the concomitant
decrease in infant mortality and maternal mortality, a change
which could be demonstrated by fertility data as well. The
interrelatedness of demographic variables is thus more
pronounced than the two seemingly disparate events of death
and birth may betray.

TABLE D-1 STANDARDIZED (AGE-ADJUSTED) DEATH RATES BY SEX, FOR CANADA AND PROVINCES, FOR SELECTED YEARS SINCE 1921 (Standardized on 1956 population)

Year	Canada	Nfld.	PEI.	N.S.	N.B.	Que.	Ont.	Man.	Sask.	Alta.	B.C.	Yuk.	NWT.
Male													
1971	8.4	8.2	8.1	8.8	8.6	9.1	8.4	7.9	7.3	7.7	8.1	10.6	13.5
1966	8.8	8.4	8.6	8.8	8.5	9.3	9.0	8.3	7.5	7.9	8.5	7.7	10.4
1961	9.0	8.2	8.2	8.7	8.7	9.7	9.2	8.3	7.8	8.2	8.5	10.0	17.0
1956	9.4	9.0	8.7	8.6	9.0	10.3	9.6	8.8	7.9	8.5	9.1	10.7	19.7
1951	10.0	9.3	8.3	9.3	10.0	11.2	9.9	9.2	8.4	9.2	9.7	11.3	18.4
1946	10.7	9.9(a)	8.6	10.3	11.1	11.8	10.3	10.0	9.4	10.2	10.5	14.4	23.7(
1945	10.9	-	8.3	9.7	11.6	12.2	10.4	10.3	9.4	9.9	10.8	-	-
1944	11.3	-	9.1	10.8	12.4	12.8	10.6	10.7	9.6	9.9	10.8	-	-
1943	11.8	-	9.6	11.6	11.9	13.3	11.2	11.4	10.1	11.0	11.7	-	-
1942	11.6	-	9.5	11.7	12.5	13.2	10.9	10.6	9.4	10.3	11.2	-	-
1941	12.0	-	11.0	12.8	12.9	13.6	11.4	11.2	9.6	10.9	11.3	-	-
1931	12.7	-	9.7	11.9	12.7	15.1	12.4	10.8	10.0	10.9	11.2	-	-
1921	13.3	-	12.9	13.2	15.5	17.1c)	14.1	12.4	10.5	12.5	11.8	-	-
Female													
1971	5.2	5.6	4.7	5.3	5.1	5.7	5.0	5.0	4.5	4.9	5.0	5.1	9.6
1966	5.7	6.0	5.8	5.8	5.7	6.3	5.6	5.4	5.1	5.3	5.4	6.1	9.7
1961	6.3	7.2	6.0	6.1	6.5	7.1	6.2	5.7	5.3	5.5	5.6	6.2	11.4
1956	7.0	7.7	6.0	6.4	7.3	8.0	6.8	6.4	6.1	6.1	6.5	3.8	16.1
1951	8.0	8.5	6.5	7.3	8.5	9.3	7.6	7.4	7.1	7.3	6.9	6.1	18.2
1946	9.0	8.4(a)	7.2	8.7	9.9	10.4	8.3	8.8	8.1	8.4	8.3	7.5b)	21.9(
1945	9.2	-	8.2	8.0	10.0	10.5	8.6	8.9	8.6	8.6	8.3	-	-
1944	9.7	-	8.8	9.3	10.9	11.4	8.8	9.3	8.8	8.6	8.6	-	-
1943	10.1	-	8.1	9.6	10.5	11.6	9.4	10.1	9.0	9.2	9.3	-	-
1942	9.8	-	9.4	9.8	11.3	11.4	9.0	9.3	8.5	8.8	8.3	-	-
1941	10.3	-	10.5	10.9	11.3	12.1	9.3	9.3	8.7	9.2	8.7	-	-
1931	11.7	-	9.0	11.3	12.1	14.1	11.0	10.0	10.0	10.1	9.5	-	-
1921	12.4	-	12.5	11.9	14.7	16.7c)	13.2	11.6	10.3	11.8	9.8	-	-

(a) For 1949
(b) For 1950
(c) For 1926

Sources: Vital Statistics, 1971, vol. 3: Deaths, table 16 (Ottawa: Information Canada, 1974). Vital Statistics, 1968, table D6.

TABLE D-2 AGE-SPECIFIC DEATH RATES (PER 1,000 POPULATION) BY SEX AND AGE, FOR CANADA CENSUS YEARS SINCE 1921

Age Group	M 1971	F	M 1966	F	M 1961	F	M 1956	F	M 1951	F	M 1941	F	M 1931	F	M 1921(a)	F
Under 1 yr.(b)	19.9	15.1	25.8	20.2	30.5	23.7	35.0	28.7	42.7	34.0	67.0	51.9	94.4	74.4	98.2	77.4
1-4	0.9	0.8	1.1	0.9	1.3	1.0	1.6	1.4	2.1	1.8	4.7	4.0	6.8	6.1	7.9	6.8
5-9	0.6	0.4	0.6	0.4	0.6	0.4	0.8	0.5	1.0	0.7	1.7	1.3	2.2	1.7	3.1	2.7
10-14	0.5	0.3	0.6	0.3	0.6	0.3	0.6	0.4	0.8	0.5	1.4	1.0	1.5	1.5	2.1	1.9
15-19	1.4	0.6	1.3	0.5	1.2	0.5	1.2	0.5	1.4	0.9	2.0	1.5	2.5	2.2	3.1	2.7
20-24	1.8	0.6	1.8	0.5	1.7	0.6	1.7	0.6	1.9	1.0	2.6	2.0	3.2	3.2	3.7	3.7
25-29	1.5	0.6	1.6	0.6	1.5	0.5	1.6	1.0	1.8	1.1	2.7	2.8	3.4	3.4	4.0	4.1
30-34	1.6	0.9	1.7	0.9	1.6	0.9	1.8	1.1	2.1	1.5	2.8	2.8	3.5	4.2	3.8	4.5
35-39	2.2	1.3	2.2	1.3	2.3	1.4	2.3	1.5	2.5	2.0	3.8	3.4	4.2	4.8	4.7	5.5
40-44	3.6	2.1	3.4	2.0	3.4	2.0	3.4	2.4	3.9	3.0	5.0	4.5	5.4	5.0	5.6	5.9
45-49	5.7	3.0	5.7	3.3	5.8	3.2	5.8	3.7	6.4	4.5	7.3	6.0	7.2	6.6	7.3	7.1
50-54	9.3	4.6	9.7	5.0	9.6	5.3	9.6	5.7	10.4	6.5	10.6	8.1	10.7	9.0	9.8	10.2
55-59	14.6	7.2	15.4	7.7	15.2	8.0	15.5	8.8	16.2	10.2	16.0	12.3	15.4	13.4	15.2	13.5
60-64	22.9	11.0	24.0	12.2	24.0	12.8	24.0	13.8	24.5	16.1	24.2	18.5	22.9	20.7	21.9	19.7
65-69	34.7	17.3	36.2	19.5	35.7	21.4	35.7	22.3	35.1	24.9	37.3	30.4	35.2	30.3	33.4	33.2
70-74	51.9	28.3	53.1	30.9	54.0	34.2	53.4	37.0	54.5	46.6	58.5	47.0	55.0	49.1	56.9	52.8
75-79	79.0	48.1	79.9	53.3	81.8	59.2	82.8	66.8	87.6	73.3	95.7	79.2	87.4	82.9	89.4	80.9
80-84	118.8	82.4	124.0	93.6	125.1	101.2	132.6	110.5	135.5	120.7	147.6	131.2	134.1	127.1	133.8	122.4
85 and over	198.8	163.3	213.4	183.4	208.9	192.2	221.9	198.3	235.1	212.0	241.9	229.3	228.1	212.6	228.2	224.9
Total all Ages	8.5	6.1	8.7	6.2	9.0	6.5	9.4	7.0	10.1	7.8	10.8	9.1	10.5	9.6	10.9	10.2
Average age at death	63.0	68.2	62.0	65.9	59.7	63.1	58.0	60.6	56.3	58.7	51.5	53.4	43.1	44.8	41.7	43.5
Median age at death	68.5	74.7	68.4	73.5	67.9	72.2	67.0	70.6	65.5	68.8	61.2	63.6	50.8	52.1	-	-

Note: Data not available for Newfoundland prior to 1949, Yukon and Northwest Territories prior to 1950.

(a) Excludes Quebec.
(b) Per 1000 live births.

Sources: Vital Statistics, 1971, Vol.3: Deaths, tables 13A, 13B and 14; Vital Statistics, 1968, table D5; Vital Statistics, 1961, table D6; Canada Year Book, 1969, p. 242.

TABLE D-3 INFANT DEATH RATES, BY SEX, FOR CANADA AND PROVINCES, BY CENSUS YEARS SINCE 1921. RATE PER 1,000 LIVE BIRTHS (MALES,FEMALES).

Province	1971 M	1971 F	1966 M	1966 F	1961 M	1961 F	1956 M	1956 F	1951 M	1951 F	1941(a) M	1941(a) F	1931(a) M	1931(a) F	1921(b) M	1921(b) F
Canada	20	15	26	20	30	24	35	29	43	34	67	52	94	74	98	77
Newfoundland	26	19	33	23	42	33	45	41	60	48	-	-	-	-	-	-
Prince Edward Island	26	17	30	22	37	28	46	33	44	23	95	63	78	57	89	78
Nova Scotia	22	15	28	22	31	24	33	25	39	30	77	53	86	71	110	91
New Brunswick	21	13	25	23	29	23	42	37	58	46	83	69	102	72	125	101
Quebec	21	16	28	23	35	28	45	37	54	42	85	66	126	99	-	-
Ontario	17	13	23	17	26	20	28	22	34	28	51	40	77	62	102	79
Manitoba	20	15	25	17	29	22	33	29	36	30	59	47	74	55	92	74
Saskatchewan	23	17	28	20	30	21	32	25	32	30	56	46	78	59	90	70
Alberta	21	15	24	18	31	23	28	21	39	27	57	44	76	63	95	72
British Columbia	21	16	26	21	27	22	28	24	34	26	41	32	55	44	62	51
Yukon (c)	29	22	49	60	46	36	42	55	58	53	-	-	-	-	-	-
Northwest Territories(c)	59	38	74	82	128	93	166	131	136	81	-	-	-	-	-	-

(a) Excludes the Yukon and Northwest Territories.
(b) Excludes Quebec and the Yukon and Northwest Territories (data rounded to nearest whole number).
(c) Rate fluctuates.

Sources: Vital Statistics, 1971, Vol. 3: Deaths, table 25;Canada Year Book, 1957-1958, p. 215.

TABLE D-4 MEDIAN AGE AT DEATH, BY SEX, FOR CANADA AND PROVINCES, BY CENSUS YEARS SINCE 1921

Province	1970 M	1970 F	1966 M	1966 F	1961 M	1961 F	1956 M	1956 F	1951 M	1951 F	1941(a) M	1941(a) F	1931-35(b) M	1931-35(b) F	1921-25(b) M	1921-25(b) F
Canada	68.4	74.1	68.4	73.5	67.9	72.2	67.0	70.6	65.5	68.8	61.2	63.6	46.4	48.1	41.7	43.5
Newfoundland	66.6	72.3	64.5	70.4	63.7	69.9	62.9	66.2	58.2	63.8	-	-	-	-	-	-
Prince Edward Island	71.2	79.0	72.9	77.4	71.8	77.1	71.2	75.4	71.8	74.1	68.2	69.5	54.4	55.7	50.6	52.5
Nova Scotia	69.9	75.5	69.3	75.0	69.0	73.5	68.8	73.0	68.0	72.0	62.1	65.6	50.7	53.5	46.2	49.2
New Brunswick	70.1	75.1	69.3	73.9	69.0	73.0	67.0	71.1	65.5	68.8	60.0	60.5	46.2	48.4	40.4	42.4
Quebec	65.8	71.6	64.8	70.5	64.0	69.0	62.5	66.4	60.4	64.2	52.8	55.3	38.4	41.0	-	-
Ontario	68.4	75.5	68.6	74.4	68.1	73.6	67.8	72.6	66.8	71.5	65.0	68.9	52.9	55.5	45.4	48.1
Manitoba	71.1	75.4	71.3	75.4	71.0	72.9	68.9	70.8	67.6	69.3	61.9	61.0	46.8	46.4	34.7	34.1
Saskatchewan	73.1	75.5	72.6	75.1	71.6	72.6	69.7	71.0	68.0	67.9	60.1	58.1	41.9	40.6	19.2	27.7
Alberta	69.3	73.3	69.6	73.1	68.3	70.6	67.5	68.8	65.0	66.1	58.9	56.9	43.1	41.1	32.1	29.7
British Columbia	69.9	75.3	72.0	75.2	71.8	74.1	70.1	72.1	68.3	69.8	63.6	65.3	52.4	50.8	43.7	41.8
Yukon(c)	-	-	44.6	29.5	44.8	32.4	44.1	23.6	50.8	29.2	51.9	19.1	51.6	36.2	-	-
Northwest Territories(c)	-	-	28.7	24.5	26.0	21.5	24.9	24.5	22.9	27.8	24.0	27.8	26.6	24.5	-	-

Note: Excludes Newfoundland prior to 1951.

(a) Refers to average age at death.
(b) Figures represent average ages at death over four-year period, 1921-25 and 1931-35.
(c) 1921-25 figures for Canada exclude the Yukon, Northwest Territories, and Quebec and Newfoundland.

Sources: Vital Statistics, 1970, tables D4A, D4B; Canada Year Book, 1969, p.243.

53

TABLE D-5 CRUDE DEATH RATES PER 100,000 CANADIAN POPULATION FROM CERTAIN CAUSES, 1931-1969

Disease	1969	1966	1961	1956	1951	1941	1931	Per Cent Change 1931 to 1969
Cardiovascular-renal disease(a)	367.4	381.4	391.5	403.5	424.2	398.0	276.1	+33.1
Cancer(b)	140.7	134.1	129.7	129.8	127.3	121.2	94.7	+48.6
Accidents	55.5	57.3	52.9	57.7	57.7	64.5	57.7	-3.8
Tuberculosis	2.5	3.3	4.2	7.8	24.8	52.8	73.5	-96.6
Influenza, bronchitis, pneumonia	37.3	37.8	37.6	43.6	58.9	76.2	103.2	-63.9
Four communicable diseases (c)	0.1	0.3	0.8	1.9	3.2	9.7	17.5	-99.4

(a) Includes: diseases of heart (including rheumatic fever) and arteries, intracranial lesions, chronic nephritis.

(b) Hodgkin's disease, leukemia and aleukemia.

(c) Diphtheria, whooping cough, measles, scarlet fever.

Source: Vital Statistics, 1969, table G

54

TABLE D-6 DEATH RATES FOR LEADING CAUSES OF DEATH, BY AGE GROUPS, BY SEX, FOR CANADA SINCE 1931

Cause	1969		1961		1956		1951		1941		1931	
	Male	Female	Male	Female	Male	Female	Male	Female	Male	Female	Male	Female
Under 1												
All causes	2,168	1,687	3,047	2,375	3,499	2,873	4,259	3,390	6,698	5,196	9,439	7,436
Immaturity (a)	320	249	1,251	965	1,326	1,009	1,361	1,053	1,340	1,008	1,993	1,593
Immaturity (b)	-	-	534	424	546	437	602	509	-	-	-	-
Diarrhoea and enteritis	32	20	119	87	155	128	297	227	761	560	1,906	1,410
Influenza, bronchitis(c) and pneumonia	193	143	430	352	580	497	723	594	1,306	1,038	1,360	1,093
Congenital debility	-	-	-	-	-	-	-	-	479	336	857	719
Congenital malformations	410	384	483	437	520	505	548	537	688	628	596	496
Birth injury	65	45	298	231	398	286	462	303	595	376	641	378
Whooping cough	-	-	4	6	16	25	36	37	122	133	197	222
Asphyxia and atelectasis(d)	463	320	373	256	430	295	361	246	185	137	104	78
Meningitis	16	10	28	21	39	40	47	40	93	60	112	89
Accidents, poisonings and violence	99	80	152	108	114	109	128	114	99	103	78	68
1 - 4												
All causes	98	73	127	97	165	141	205	172	468	399	679	612
Influenza, bronchitis(c) and pneumonia	9	8	15	13	25	26	40	39	110	98	159	160
Diarrhoea and enteritis	2	3	4	5	5	5	9	7	52	41	92	70
Accidents, poisonings and violence	44	29	49	32	55	38	61	37	77	49	81	50
Tuberculosis	*	-	1	1	4	2	14	12	32	31	51	45
Diphtheria	-	-	*	-	*	*	1	2	9	11	36	34
Whooping cough	*	-	1	*	1	2	3	5	19	16	21	32
Meningitis	2	2	3	2	5	3	8	7	16	15	22	22
Appendicitis	*	-	1	*	1	1	3	2	14	8	15	9
Poliomyelitis	-	-	*	-	1	1	1	1	1	1	14	8
Measles	*	*	2	2	2	5	5	5	14	12	8	12
Cardiovascular disease	*	*	1	1	2	2	2	1	11	8	7	10
Congenital malformations	11	17	15	11	16	17	11	11	10	15	9	6
Cancer	11	8	13	10	14	11	12	10	10	9	5	5

TABLE D-6 continued

5-14

Cause	1969 Male	1969 Female	1961 Male	1961 Female	1956 Male	1956 Female	1951 Male	1951 Female	1941 Male	1941 Female	1931 Male	1931 Female
All causes	55	34	60	36	70	43	89	59	155	114	185	162
Accidents, poisonings and violence	35	16	35	13	39	18	45	16	48	18	46	15
Tuberculosis	*	*	*	*	1	1	6	8	19	20	23	28
Appendicitis	*	*	1	*	1	*	2	2	15	11	17	16
Influenza, bronchitis(c) and pneumonia	2	1	2	2	2	3	5	5	10	10	14	16
Diphtheria	- -	- -	*	*	*	*	1	1	6	5	11	12
Cardiovascular disease	*	*	1	1	1	1	2	2	5	5	8	11
Meningitis	- -	*	1	1	1	1	1	1	4	5	5	6
Rheumatic fever	*	*	*	*	1	1	2	2	6	5	5	4
Poliomyelitis	- -	- -	*	*	1	*	2	2	1	*	4	4
Nephritis and Nephrosis	*	*	1	1	2	1	2	2	2	2	4	3
Diarrhoea and enteritis	*	*	1	*	*	*	1	1	2	1	4	3
Cancer	8	6	7	5	8	5	7	6	6	4	4	3
Congenital malformations	3	3	3	3	3	2	1	2	2	1	2	1

15 - 24

Cause	1969 Male	1969 Female	1961 Male	1961 Female	1956 Male	1956 Female	1951 Male	1951 Female	1941 Male	1941 Female	1931 Male	1931 Female
All causes	154	52	137	51	148	56	161	92	226	174	284	269
Tuberculosis	*	*	1	1	4	2	18	24	46	69	71	118
Accidents, poisonings and violence	128	33	100	19	106	18	93	18	89	14	96	19
Influenza, bronchitis(c) and pneumonia	2	2	3	2	2	2	5	4	11	7	19	13
Cardiovascular disease	4	2	5	5	5	5	8	7	13	14	14	16
Appendicitis	*	*	1	1	1	*	2	1	11	6	17	10
Maternal causes	- -	*	- -	3	- -	4	- -	9	- -	19	- -	27
Cancer	5	14	10	7	9	7	10	6	8	5	7	7
Nephritis and nephrosis	*	- -	3	2	2	3	3	3	5	6	5	5
Typhoid	- -	- -	*	- -	*	- -	*	*	*	1	6	6
Epilepsy	*	*	2	1	2	1	1	1	2	2	4	3
Rheumatic fever	*	*	1	*	1	*	1	2	3	3	4	2
Congenital malformations	3	1	3	3	3	2	3	2	1	1	1	1

56

TABLE D-6 continued

Cause	1969 Male	1969 Female	1961 Male	1961 Female	1956 Male	1956 Female	1951 Male	1951 Female	1941 Male	1941 Female	1931 Male	1931 Female
25-44												
All causes	218	120	215	122	226	137	252	183	347	318	410	440
Tuberculosis	1	*	3	3	8	6	28	26	65	71	86	110
Accidents, poisonings, and violence	103	29	91	19	95	19	87	16	100	18	102	20
Cardiovascular disease	49	22	57	21	58	25	59	34	54	46	43	48
Cancer	29	38	28	39	27	42	25	45	28	47	25	53
Maternal causes	—	2	—	7	—	10	—	15	—	43	—	69
Influenza, bronchitis[c] and pneumonia	6	5	4	3	4	3	6	5	13	11	31	26
Nephritis and nephrosis	*	*	3	2	4	3	2	6	12	14	15	21
Appendicitis	*	*	1	*	1	1	3	*	8	4	15	7
Ulcer of the stomach or duodenum	1	*	2	*	2	*	3	1	8	1	9	2
Hernia and intestinal obstruction	*	—	1	1	1	1	1	1	3	4	5	5
Typhoid	—	—	—	—	—	*	*	*	2	1	6	3
Epilepsy	2	*	2	2	2	2	2	1	3	1	4	4
Syphilis	—	—	*	*	*	*	1	*	7	2	5	3
Diabetes mellitus	—	2	3	2	3	2	3	2	2	2	4	3
Diarrhoea and enteritis	3	*	1	1	1	1	1	1	1	1	2	2
Anemia	*	*	*	*	*	*	*	*	3	2	1	3
Rheumatic fever	*	4	4	3	3	1	2	3	3	3	1	1
Cirrhosis of the liver	6	4	4	3	3	2	2	1	2	2	1	*
Congenital malformations	2	1	2	2	2	1	2	1	1	1	*	*
45-64												
All causes	1,215	634	1,225	664	1,241	755	1,336	868	1,354	1,040	1,249	1,118
Cardiovascular disease	635	221	656	272	655	324	687	376	528	362	352	319
Cancer	283	246	255	236	251	248	243	266	230	282	202	267
Accidents, poisonings, and violence	122	46	114	32	114	35	120	30	137	34	136	34
Nephritis and nephrosis	5	3	11	8	19	15	30	27	81	84	86	89

TABLE D-6 continued

45-64 (cont'd)

Cause	1969 Male	1969 Female	1961 Male	1961 Female	1956 Male	1956 Female	1951 Male	1951 Female	1941 Male	1941 Female	1931 Male	1931 Female
Influenza, bronchitis(c) and pneumonia	60	24	29	13	29	13	35	25	56	35	89	71
Tuberculosis	7	2	12	3	20	9	48	21	78	40	90	61
Diabetes mellitus	16	16	14	18	12	19	16	20	25	41	20	35
Hernia and intestinal obstruction	4	3	6	4	6	5	7	6	14	13	17	16
Ulcer of the stomach or duodenum	11	2	13	4	15	3	17	3	31	5	24	6
Syphilis	*	*	3	1	5	2	10	3	30	7	23	6
Appendicitis	*	*	1	1	2	1	3	1	11	8	18	12
Anemia	*	1	2	1	2	2	2	3	3	6	10	16
Cirrhosis of the liver	30	15	21	10	20	10	15	7	11	8	12	7
All causes	4,377	2,363	4,388	2,726	4,349	2,888	4,309	3,207	4,591	3,742	4,352	3,835

65-74

Cause	1969 Male	1969 Female	1961 Male	1961 Female	1956 Male	1956 Female	1951 Male	1951 Female	1941 Male	1941 Female	1931 Male	1931 Female
Cardiovascular disease	2,433	1,295	2,597	1,625	2,589	1,730	2,488	1,862	2,219	1,794	1,754	1,532
Cancer	1,008	580	931	590	856	600	783	618	797	694	763	696
Influenza, bronchitis(c) and pneumonia	316	99	148	70	143	65	170	127	199	164	332	366
Nephritis and nephrosis	19	15	37	29	52	57	105	97	376	347	329	338
Accidents,poisoning and violence	158	61	148	55	150	65	168	64	188	104	190	87
Diabetes mellitus	72	92	63	104	59	98	53	98	107	195	77	133
Tuberculosis	21	5	28	10	37	16	72	35	94	52	107	85
Senility	*	*	2	1	4	3	5	8	26	20	64	70
Hyperplasia of the prostate	13	1	24	-	38	-	48	-	116	-	124	-
Anemia	5	5	8	8	8	10	17	18	22	20	52	65
Hernia and intestinal obstruction	16	13	23	23	27	22	27	24	42	27	49	44
Ulcer of the stomach or duodenum	41	12	42	10	46	13	43	11	53	17	42	16
Cirrhosis of the liver	46	22	37	17	34	15	26	18	28	18	29	22
Syphilis	3	2	11	3	15	3	17	4	46	12	29	12

58

TABLE D-6 continued

Cause	1969 Male	1969 Female	1961 Male	1961 Female	1956 Male	1956 Female	1951 Male	1951 Female	1941 Male	1941 Female	1931 Male	1931 Female
All causes	11,476	8,671	11,304	9,462 [75]	11,650	10,215 +(continued)	12,169	11,059	13,060	11,855	11,881	11,635
Cardiovascular disease	7,100	5,902	7,208	6,532	7,342	6,835	7,456	7,085	6,817	6,327	5,247	5,302
Influenza, bronchitis(c) and pneumonia	988	513	637	489	653	542	890	808	882	929	1,142	1,336
Senility	30	50	99	95	165	204	234	273	571	640	1,021	1,205
Cancer	1,856	1,124	1,661	1,076	1,612	1,169	1,446	1,137	1,374	1,121	1,186	1,016
Nephritis and nephrosis	58	50	125	122	223	215	335	357	1,384	1,153	945	824
Accidents, poisonings and violence	304	217	292	280	364	363	362	382	458	540	351	463
Hyperplasia of the prostate	74	--	157	--	220	-	295	-	399	-	477	-
Diabetes mellitus	194	208	136	166	125	163	101	140	187	222	93	132
Hernia and intestinal obstruction	61	49	81	77	67	58	74	57	121	81	128	85
Diarrhoea and enteritis	9	12	30	40	24	33	24	31	29	39	81	97
Tuberculosis	34	16	47	20	60	19	74	43	68	56	81	74
Anemia	30	22	37	33	30	50	54	56	55	51	75	77
Ulcer of the stomach or duodenum	83	38	84	32	78	25	72	26	66	20	47	31

Note: Per 100,000 population; * = less than 1; -- = no cases.
      Newfoundland not included in 1931 and 1941.

(a) All deaths of immature or premature babies.
(b) Deaths for which immaturity was stated to be a subsidiary cause.
(c) Include emphysema and asthma in 1969.
(d) Refer to anoxic and hypoxic conditions.

Sources: Vital Statistics, 1969, tables S3, S4, D9, D13; Dominion Bureau of Statistics, Life Expectancy Trends, 1930-1932 to 1960-1962, (Ottawa: Queen's Printer, 1967),table 7.

59

TABLE D-7 MORTALITY BY NATURAL AND OTHER CAUSES OF DEATH, BY MARITAL STATUS AND SEX, ONTARIO RESIDENTS, 1964-1968.

Age Group	Sex	1966 Census Population Total	Per Cent of S	M	W	D	Deaths: All Natural Causes(a) Number	Average Annual Rate per 100,000 Per Cent Deviation Total	S	M	W	D	Deaths: Accidents, Poisonings, Violence(b) Number	Average Annual Rate per 100,000 Per Cent Deviation Total	S	M	W	D	Male/Female Ratios for all deaths Total	S	M	W	D
1	2	3	4	5	6	7	8	9	10	11	12	13	14	15	16	17	18	19	20	21	22	23	24
0-4	M	382,522	100.0	0.0	0.0	0.0	8,172	427	0	x	x	x	1,127	59	0	x	x	x	1.3	1.3	x	x	x
	F	363,222	100.0	0.0	0.0	0.0	6,089	335	0	x	x	x	762	42	0	x	x	x					
5-24	M	1,290,648	93.3	6.7	0.0	0.0	1,532	24	0	29	600	100	3,998	62	-3	40	1,255	198	2.2	2.2	2.5	1.6	1.7
	F	1,251,923	86.0	13.9	0.0	0.0	1,211	19	0	5	179	100	1,235	20	-5	10	2,825	445					
25-44	M	914,614	14.0	85.2	0.3	0.5	5,555	121	49	-10	121	316	3,839	84	100	-20	281	318	1.8	1.9	1.7	2.5	3.7
	F	908,371	7.9	89.8	1.5	0.9	4,075	90	49	-7	90	69	1,141	25	100	-12	156	204					
45-64	M	641,203	8.9	87.9	2.5	0.7	37,918	1,183	39	-8	87	167	3,654	114	93	-17	142	227	2.0	2.5	2.0	2.6	3.3
	F	640,635	8.0	78.1	12.8	1.0	19,540	610	16	-10	47	57	1,377	43	10	-12	51	140					
65-84	M	236,159	10.9	72.4	17.2	0.4	72,480	6,138	8	-12	40	67	2,196	186	52	-26	63	302	1.6	1.7	1.8	1.9	1.9
	F	293,823	10.5	40.1	49.1	0.3	56,639	3,855	3	-22	17	44	1,459	99	16	-23	15	115					
84+	M	13,993	8.5	36.5	54.9	0.2	14,921	21,326	11	-13	6	36	452	646	39	-39	18	-100	1.2	1.2	1.3	1.3	1.0
	F	23,747	12.3	8.4	79.3	0.1	20,844	17,555	9	-16	0	63	791	666	32	-24	-2	115					

Note: Cols. 4-7 = per cent of col. 3; cols. 10-13 and 15-19 = per cent difference from col. 9 and 14 as 100 per cent; cols. 20-24 = number of male deaths over female deaths. S= single; M= married; W = widowed; D=divorced or separated.

(a) As defined by 1955 I.C.O. Codes 001-795
(b) As defined by 1955 I.C.O. Codes E800-E999.

Source: From tabulations by Dr. W. Cherry, Department of Statistics, University of Waterloo, with permission.

TABLE D-8 EXPECTATION OF LIFE AT SELECTED AGES, BY SEX, FOR CANADIAN REGIONS OR PROVINCES, SINCE 1931

Region or Province and Age	1966 M	1966 F	1961 M	1961 F	1956 M	1956 F	1951 M	1951 F	1941 M	1941 F	1931 M	1931 F
At birth												
Canada	68.89	75.36	68.35	74.17	67.61	72.92	66.33	70.83	62.96	66.30	60.00	62.10
Atlantic Provinces	68.53	75.23	68.58	73.92	67.91	72.89	66.57	70.50	61.69	64.63	60.20	61.91
Quebec	67.88	73.91	67.28	72.77	66.13	71.02	64.42	68.58	60.18	63.07	57.80	56.19
Ontario	68.71	75.53	68.32	74.40	67.80	73.57	66.87	71.85	64.55	68.43	61.30	63.92
Prairie Provinces	70.12	75.66	69.26	75.66	69.26	74.18	68.36	72.28	65.43	68.19	63.47	65.49
British Columbia	69.21	75.84	68.94	75.42	68.14	73.91	66.73	72.37	63.65	68.96	62.15	65.34
Age 1												
Canada	69.70	75.86	69.50	74.98	69.04	73.99	68.33	72.33	66.14	68.73	64.69	65.71
Atlantic Provinces	69.53	75.76	70.06	74.23	69.68	74.23	69.08	72.41	65.68	67.78	64.76	65.44
Quebec	68.77	74.57	68.71	72.56	68.11	72.56	67.19	70.71	64.45	66.28	62.45	62.62
Ontario	69.29	75.87	69.14	74.25	68.76	74.25	68.34	72.91	66.74	70.07	65.05	66.84
Prairie Provinces	70.95	76.78	70.96	75.06	70.48	75.06	69.90	73.43	68.02	70.22	67.24	68.30
British Columbia	69.94	76.33	69.83	74.68	69.19	74.68	67.97	73.32	65.40	70.17	64.55	67.16
Age 20												
Canada	51.69	57.58	51.51	56.65	51.19	55.80	50.76	54.41	49.57	51.76	49.05	49.76
Atlantic Provinces	51.68	57.75	52.17	56.82	51.95	56.01	51.59	54.52	49.36	51.33	49.22	49.62
Quebec	50.81	56.25	50.82	55.54	50.36	54.43	49.76	52.92	48.38	49.85	47.77	47.73
Ontario	51.15	57.45	51.03	56.53	50.81	55.95	50.58	54.76	49.57	52.40	48.79	50.13
Prairie Provinces	52.89	58.45	52.90	58.08	52.55	56.88	52.24	55.53	51.28	53.08	50.98	51.68
British Columbia	51.91	58.01	51.85	57.61	51.32	56.52	50.41	55.51	48.99	53.09	48.68	51.18
Age 40												
Canada	33.26	38.33	32.96	37.45	32.74	36.69	32.45	35.63	31.87	33.99	31.98	33.02
Atlantic Provinces	33.40	38.27	33.76	37.70	33.58	37.03	33.48	35.99	32.22	34.19	32.73	33.70
Quebec	32.33	37.05	32.29	36.38	31.91	35.42	31.54	34.36	30.94	32.72	31.04	32.90
Ontario	32.44	38.17	32.25	37.27	32.24	36.74	32.03	35.75	31.54	34.11	31.56	32.90
Prairie Provinces	34.43	39.27	34.37	38.83	34.12	37.71	33.86	36.63	33.32	34.96	33.34	34.35
British Columbia	33.70	38.98	33.56	38.46	33.11	37.49	32.45	36.72	31.70	35.14	32.17	34.27

TABLE D-8 continued

Region or Province and Age	1966 M	1966 F	1961 M	1961 F	1956 M	1956 F	1951 M	1951 F	1941 M	1941 F	1931 M	1931 F
Age 65												
Canada	13.85	16.85	13.53	16.07	13.36	15.60	13.31	14.97	12.81	14.08	12.98	13.72
Atlantic Provinces	14.14	16.90	14.16	16.35	13.95	15.91	13.90	15.42	13.13	14.50	13.63	14.59
Quebec	13.24	15.79	13.16	15.27	12.88	14.73	12.81	14.17	12.44	13.41	12.60	13.15
Ontario	13.10	16.72	13.05	15.90	12.97	15.56	13.07	14.92	12.63	14.03	12.67	13.47
Prairie Provinces	14.55	17.45	14.22	17.00	14.01	16.20	13.88	15.51	13.35	14.62	13.60	14.40
British Columbia	14.20	17.41	13.98	16.94	13.72	16.15	13.50	15.86	12.96	14.83	13.36	14.60

Note: Newfoundland not included, 1931 and 1941.

Sources: Canada Year Book, 1970, p. 324; Dominion Bureau of Statistics, Life Expectancy Trends 1930-1932 to 1960-1962, table 8.

TABLE D-9 AVERAGE NUMBER OF YEARS ADDED TO LIFE EXPECTANCY BETWEEN 1931 and 1966 AT SELECTED AGES, BY SEX, FOR CANADA AND PROVINCES OR REGIONS.

Provinces and Region	At Birth Male	At Birth Female	1 year Male	1 year Female	20 Years Male	20 Years Female	40 Years Male	40 Years Female	60 Years Male	60 Years Female
Canada	8.8	13.1	4.8	10.0	2.4	7.6	1.0	5.2	0.5	3.4
Atlantic Provinces	-	-	-	-	-	-	-	-	-	-
Quebec	11.7	16.1	6.3	12.0	3.0	8.6	1.3	5.3	0.5	3.2
Ontario	7.4	11.6	4.2	9.1	2.3	7.4	0.8	5.3	0.3	3.7
Prairie Provinces	-	-	-	-	-	-	-	-	-	-
British Columbia	7.0	10.5	5.3	9.1	3.2	6.8	1.5	4.6	0.7	3.3

Source: Vital Statistics, 1969, table N.

BIBLIOGRAPHY

Anderson, T.W., "Oral Contraceptives and Female Mortality
   Trends", Canadian Medical Association Journal 102 (1970):
   1,156-1,160.

Burton, M.M., "A Study of Social Factors Affecting Teenage Multiparae",
   Canadian Journal of Public Health 59 (1968): 10-14.

Dellaportas, G.J., "Birth Weight, Ethnic Origin and Perinatal
   Mortality", Social Biology 18 (1971): 158-163.

Dominion Bureau of Statistics/ Statistics Canada, Vital
   Statistics Handbook Containing International List of Causes
   of Death. Ottawa: Queen's Printer, n.d. (68 pp.)

_____, Canadian Life Tables, 1960-1961. Ottawa:
   Queen's Printer, 1963. (9 pp.)

_____, Leading Causes of Death by Major Age Groupings,
   1921-1955. Ottawa: Queen's Printer, 1963. (31 pp.)

_____, Accident Mortality, 1950-1964. Ottawa: Queen's
   Printer, 1966. (47 pp.)

_____, Infant Mortality, 1950-1964. Ottawa: Queen's
   Printer, 1967. (63 pp.)

_____, Life Expectancy Trends, 1930-1932 to 1960-1962.
   Ottawa: Queen's Printer, 1967. (42 pp.)

_____, Causes of Death, Canada 1958-1964. Ottawa:
   Queen's Printer, 1968. (31 pp.)

Fleury-Giroux, M., "Fécondité et Mortalité en Gaspésie et dans
   le Bas Saint-Laurent". Recherches Sociographiques 9 (1968): 247-264.

George, M.V., Mortality Trends in Canada, 1926-1965. Technical
   Memorandum No.20. Ottawa: Dominion Bureau of Statistics, Census
   Division, 1967.

Neril, L.C., and Day, J.J., "Geographical Distribution of Deaths
   from Arteriosclerotic Heart Disease in Canada", Canadian
   Journal of Public Health 59 (1968): 266-272.

Phillips, A.J., Cancer Mortality Trends in Canada and the
   Provinces, 1944-1963. Toronto: National Cancer Institute of
   Canada, 1965. (44 pp.)

MIGRATION

Canada has received close to ten million immigrants
since Confederation, resulting in a rate of population
increase among the highest for industrialized countries.
Canada's rate of urbanization has been so swift that by 1971
only about one million and a half of her population were
classified as rural farm by the census. Such redistribution
of Canada's population could not have taken place without
substantial migration.

Migration, as a generic term, subsumes all moves of the
population, be they simple changes of residence down the
block, or crossing of a provincial boundary or international
border. Migration is thus a pervasive feature of modern
societies, more so of those which themselves were founded
on massive population transfers and whose population history
is uneven, like that of Canada.

On the average, one out of every two Canadians moves about
once in five years; most just change their location in the
same community, but about every tenth mover goes to another
province. The profile of migrants has been changing together
with the changes in the economic infrastructure. In the past,
most moves were from rural areas to the cities, although the
move may have involved crossing seas; then, migration of some
distance was usually undertaken by single young men, while
young women moved shorter distances to the nearby cities. No
doubt, both sexes were alert and enterprising but both lacked
formal schooling. The contemporary migrant, on the other
hand, is only exchanging one urban residence for another, even
though a change of countries may take place. The contemporary
migrant is educated and married, these characteristics
covarying with the distance moved. This does not mean that
the traditional form of migration has disappeared; at present,
the two types coexist, but the traditional type of migrant is
likely to become more scarce in the future.

In Canada, the migration streams, as one may visualize them,
flow primarily westward. The Maritimes send their population
westward, principally to Ontario, bypassing Quebec. Quebec is
more likely to send its migrants to Ontario but may receive
a fair share in return. Manitoba population generally moves
to Ontario to join, perhaps, the stream of migrants from Ontario
to the west coast, adding new numbers in the Prairies.

There are two major foci of interest in the portrayal of
migration, apart from a host of methodological issues in the
measurement of migration. The first substantive focus is on
immigration and emigration and the second is on the redistribution
of population within the country. As for the latter, the internal
migration is crucial for the well-being of a country like Canada,
which suffers great regional disparities. Unfortunately,
direct data on the internal migration are scarce. On the
other hand, the inflow of immigrants is being monitored by
government agencies fairly accurately, although the necessity
of immigration is no longer demonstrable.

Because of the two-charter group composition of Canada, as
outlined by the British North America Act, governmental
preoccupation with the ethnic origin of Canada's immigrants
and with its native-born population influenced the record
keeping on the immigrants until very recently (the classification
of immigrants by ethnic and racial origins was not discontinued

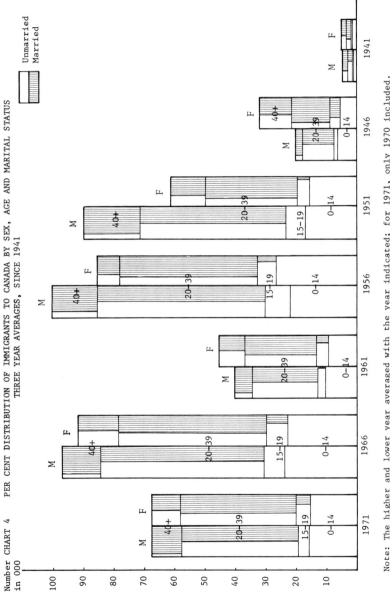

Number CHART 4 PER CENT DISTRIBUTION OF IMMIGRANTS TO CANADA BY SEX, AGE AND MARITAL STATUS
in 000   THREE YEAR AVERAGES, SINCE 1941

Note: The higher and lower year averaged with the year indicated; for 1971, only 1970 included.
Sources: Canada Yearbooks for the corresponding years; 1971 Immigration Statistics Canada. Ottawa: Information
         Canada, 1972. Table 5.

65

until 1967). In the history of the Canadian census and
immigration records, great stress has been laid on proper
ethnic and racial differentiation of the population of Canada.(1)
How accurate such classification is remains a matter of conjecture
(see table M-1). Nonetheless, it serves as a reminder of the
ethnic mix on the one hand and of the de facto dominance by
the population from the British Isles on the other.

What is worth noting is the relative scarcity of French
immigrants, who have only a few times in this century exceeded
10 per cent of those from the British Isles. If it is
assumed that not all those classified as French by ethnic
origin were actually native Frenchmen and that not all
migrated to Quebec, the implications for bilingualism in
Canada become of more than passing interest. In the first
place, the French-speaking population in Canada has managed
quite well on its own in the past, without any appreciable
numerical help from French-speaking immigrants. In the second
place, the direct contribution of all foreign born to the
Canadian birthrate has scarcely exceeded 10 per cent overall;
however, immigration itself contributes about 30 per cent to
the national growth, not including reproduction by the
immigrants. With the recent equalization of the francophone
and anglophone birthrates, the anglophone population is bound
to increase substantially faster than the French-speaking
community, making for difficult administrative decisions.
These in turn will be reflected in the political choices the
country as a whole may have to make.

In addition to the administrative visibility of immigration
issues, the immigrant population has a social visibility as
well, be it by their mode of speech, by their comportment or
by their features. There is at least a twofold implication
of this ethnic and racial mix. Firstly, humanitarian issues
are aired occasionally and their solutions absorbed into the
body politic of Canada. Secondly, a cultural mosaic is being
demonstrated as having no adverse effect on the economic texture
of the Canadian society, thus successfully militating against
simplistic proposals to change the economic system.

The image of cultural pluralism, however, does bear
numerical scrutiny. Even though the number of immigrants
has been steadily decreasing during the past five years
or so, their ethnic and racial diversity has not (see table
P-9). At least one-fourth are now coming from the Third
World, and the traditional immigrant majority from Western
Europe is being well matched by immigrants from Southern
Europe. On the other hand, the new influx of Americans
matches, if not surpasses, the Canadians emigrating to the
United States (see table M-2).

The very persistence of the ethnic mosaic in Canada is brought
about not so much by the fact that the overall proportion
of foreign-born has varied between some 13 and 22 per cent of
the population as by the fact that the foreign-born
population concentrates in some provinces-- especially in
Ontario, where just about every other person was foreign-
born at the time of the 1961 census (see table M-3).

---

(1) The 1952 Immigration Act, for example, favoured British
    subjects, French citizens, and U.S.A. citizens to the
    almost total exclusion of Asians.

That the proportion of foreign-born decreased by the 1971
census is understandable for two reasons: for one, there was a
decline in immigrants for the preceding decade; and secondly,
the foreign-born population is much older than the native-
born population and is dying at a fast rate. Looking to the
future is exceedingly difficult in view of the absence of any
articulated population policy for Canada.

Assuming differing levels of immigration and fertility (see
table M-4), the 1969 projections of Statistics Canada come
up with population-size discrepancies of over two million
within fifteen years. Given the inertia of political and
social institutions, it remains quite probable that immigration
will continue to represent about one-half of 1 per cent of the
annual population increase. Even though one-half a per cent
difference in the national growth rate may not impress a savings
account holder, it may impress a board member of the Bank
of Canada.

The second major focus in the portrayal of migrations is on
internal migration. For the last seventy years, fair records
have been kept of those entering the country to stay but not
of those leaving. Monitoring internal migration, on the other
hand, is quite difficult and usually only indirect; net
estimates of migration tend to omit a variety of in-between
moves. The difference between migrants into a province and
migrants from a province (using the place of birth and place of
residence at each census) represents what is known to
demographers as net migration (see table M-5). If it is
assumed that net migration reflects the minimal migration
history of the provinces(2), it appears that the consistent
gainers are the western provinces of Alberta and British
Columbia and the consistent losers are the Maritime Provinces,
at least during this century. One may also surmise that
Ontario, which remains the key receiving province of the
immigrants, used to send out native-born population in quite
great numbers, presumably westward and south of the border.
However, since the Second World War, its economic centrality
has attracted enough in-migrants, mostly from the Maritimes,
to the offset its losses to the West and South.

Early marriage and childbearing form the first part of the
family life cycle and usually are connected with changing of
residence; thus, one source of data on internal migration
for a substantial proportion of the population is the Family
Allowance payment records. Since the passing of the Family
Allowance Act in 1944, movements of families with children up
to sixteen years of age have been monitored and statistics on
interprovincial movements are a matter of public record.

As recently as 1971, about one-half of all interprovincial
moves by families occurred in and out of Ontario (see table
M-6). This represents about 2 per cent of all families in

---

(2) One of the common measures of migration by indirect methods
is known as lifetime net migration. It estimates the amount
of net migration the difference between the total number
of migrants out of a specified geographic area and the
total number of migrants into that area (e.g., a province)
accruing to each of the provinces at census years, using
information about place of birth and place of residence of
persons as collected at these years. (M.George, Internal
Migration in Canada, p.94).

Ontario, as compared with 3 per cent for British Columbia and
for the nation as a whole. However, when this rate is
cumulated for a five-year period, the migration figures
become quite impressive.

The effect of interprovincial migration on the redistribution
of population across the country is accentuated by the fact that
for the last twenty-five years or so, there were only three
provinces -- namely Ontario, British Columbia and Alberta, in
that order -- that constantly gained in population from the
moves of families (see table M-7). What this means in actual
numbers is that Newfoundland lost some 8,000 families over the
last twenty-five years, Quebec about 22,000 and Saskatchewan
about 38,000. The out-migration was of course not uniform, but
tended to fluctuate over time; the last few years have been
heavy, but some ten years ago the interprovincial movements
of families were light. The heavy population movements of
recent years reflect the coming of age of those born in the
late forties and early fifties now starting their families
and changing their residence. That the losing provinces were
able to sustain a net out-migration loss over such a long
period of time without actually declining in population
indicates that the fertility of their women has been more than
adequate, but not so the capacity of their economy.

The interprovincial migrants represent perhaps less than 10
per cent of all people who change their residence. Since it
appears that migration in our very developed country is mostly
interurban and that youth, marriedness, and education are
attributes of the long-distance movers, then migration should
function as an equalizing force for the redistribution of
talent. If this is the case, the redistributive process
affects migrants who have attained different education more
mobile than those without much formal schooling. On a
nationwide basis, this appears to be true (see table M-8).
About every fifth person with at least some university
education has changed his residence to a different region in
Canada than where his education was received, as compared with
every eighth person with only elementary education who has
moved to another province. Interprovincial migration has
proved to be most advantageous to British Columbia, which has
been able to attract twice as many persons with at least some
university education as it has lost. On the other hand, the
Atlantic Provinces appear net losers for all levels of education.
Corrected, however, for in-migration and for immigration, the
losses are reduced to 10 per cent for the population with at
least some university education. In all, if one views the
role of migration to redistribute talent where it finds its
best application, then the Canadian experience is satisfactory.

The methodological issues inherent in the measurement of
migration become clear as soon as one considers seriously the
few tables at our disposal. The monitoring of entrants into
Canada is reasonably accurate, including the estimates of
illegal immigration. However, estimating emigration is a
difficult procedure at best, relying on the completeness of
immigration records into other countries. An estimate of
internal migration is just that, due to a lack of any complete
population registry like that in the Scandinavian countries,
for instance. All population shifts have to be inferred and
there are several standard ways in which this is done. The
Canadian census, starting with 1961, asked a question on the
place of permanent residence five years prior to the enumeration
day. In 1971, a question on the number of moves during the

preceding five-year period was added. Questions on place of birth and current place of residence by province yield estimates of net interprovincial migration and immigration. An actuarial estimate of net migration is arrived at by subtracting from the new census count the population at the preceding census, together with the difference between births and deaths, the immigrants, and the error statistics for each category. (3)

The real issues in migration methodology are not those of acturial accuracy but those of conceptual clarity as to what migration refers to, whether the length of stay or the intent to stay or "air of permanency" of the migrant become defining criterion. Such issues are best left, however, to those who have particular population problems to solve.

---

(3) There are other sources of migration data, even though for specific populations only: persons or families receiving government transfer payments, e.g. Family Allowance payments, or other social benefit payments; persons registered with provincial or federal agencies, for instance those contributing to Canada Pension Plan. Migration data can also be gathered as a by-product of various national surveys, either labour force surveys or the occasional opinion polls.

TABLE M-1 ETHNIC ORIGIN OF IMMIGRANTS TO CANADA FOR FIVE-YEAR INTERVALS,
SINCE 1901

Origin (a)	1970-1966	Years 1965-1961	1960-1956	1955-1951	1950-1946	1945-1941
British	248,133(b)	155,653	226,300	220,636	196,578	53,256
English (c)	141,299	96,270	135,701	138,200	136,342	34,999
Irish	20,896(d)	22,848	35,710	30,601	19,633	5,768
Scottish	50,259	36,248	54,889	51,835	40,603	12,493
European	377,451	293,811	500,841	454,926	229,098	12,825
Baltic(e)	-	752	2,058	12,217	15,285	24
Belgian(f)	4,073	3,287	7,922	7,878	3,918	114
Czech.(g)	17,887	1,023	1,332	5,542	5,701	171
Dutch	14,681	11,919	40,577	85,721	31,994	905
French	24,550	20,136	18,836	22,209	10,471	4,308
German(h)	42,718	49,121	112,707	163,817	20,958	2,054
Greek	41,767(i)	25,757	26,584	12,793	3,281	118
Hungarian	6,384	4,992	39,419	7,894	4,789	189
Italian	105,374	96,688	137,618	116,035	21,152	400
Jewish(j)	7,011	11,992	17,481	20,845	22,469	1,924
Polish(k)	9,285	13,107	16,855	29,455	45,389	737
Portuguese(1)	54,357	28,856	24,958	10,046	2,438	109
Russian(m)	2,623	1,045	3,624	16,692	26,247	240
Scandinavian(n)	10,493	10,825	31,013	29,553	7,542	1,406
Yugoslavian(o)	32,442	14,311	19,857	14,229	7,464	126
Other	3,806	-	-	-	-	-
Non-European	168,742	48,422	22,109	16,340	4,754	539
Arabian(p)	16,218	4,107	2,256	1,491	387	83
Armenian(q)	4,154	5,119	658	641	117	23
Caribbean(r)	55,146	-	-	-	-	-
Chinese	21,881	11,785	10,407	11,524	2,654	-
Indian(s)	31,878	8,576	2,548	837	356	5
Japanese	3,556	861	868	225	37	5
Negro (t)	-	11,835	4,415	1,260	947	306
South American(u)	9,803	159	149	47	130	38
Other(v)	26,106	5,980	808	317	126	79

(a) Since 1966, country of birth; prior to 1966, "race"; prior to 1926,
nationality.
(b) Includes those from places other than the British Isles; may contain some
Commonwealth non-Europeans.
(c) Includes Welsh and those from Lesser Isles.
(d) Includes those from the Republic of Ireland.
(e) Estonians and Latvians only.
(f) Includes those from Luxembourg.
(g) Czechs, Slovaks, Bohemians, Moravians.
(h) Includes Austrians, Swiss.
(i) Includes those from Cyprus.
(j) Includes those born in Israel (for 1966-1970); Hebrew- nationality
categories for data prior to 1926.
(k) Includes Lithuanians.
(1) Includes Spanish, Maltese, Corsicans.
(m) Includes Ukrainians, Ruthenians; for 1966-1970, those born in U.S.S.R.
(n) Includes Finnish, Icelandic.
(o) Includes a variety of ethnic groups from Southeast Europe: Albanian,
Bosnian, Bukovinian, Croatian, Dalmatian, Galician, Herzegovinian,
Montenegrin, Romanian, Serbian and others.

TABLE M-1 continued

Origin(a)	Years							
	1940-1936	1935-1931	1930-1926	1925-1921	1920-1916	1915-1911	1910-1906	1905-1901(w)
British	32,630	46,048	327,379	273,779	89,587	597,077	375,460	189,810
English (c)	20,856	27,643	181,577	158,010	67,613	427,835	277,628	156,657
Irish	5,228	7,866	58,159	32,713	5,037	38,020	22,518	2,266
Scottish	6,546	10,539	87,643	83,056	16,937	131,121	75,314	33,671
European	40,225	38,802	398,425	136,572	13,008	352,823	197,563	91,044
Baltic(e)	916	34	817	144	-	-	-	5,876(y)
Belgian(f)	630	406	7,090	5,578	1,913	8,790	4,708	3,045(z)
Czech.(g)	4,925	2,500	21,767	5,402	10	-	-	-
Dutch	1,469	1,067	10,675	2,107	644	5,643	3,231	5,005
French	4,623	8,850	21,592	7,597	2,299	10,779	9,190	12,743(aa)
German(h)	5,446	7,387	82,082	1,292	256	38,793	19,399	724
Greek	533	315	3,015	1,510	491	5,019	2,496	-
Hungarian	2,555	2,155	26,247	17,095	-	2,336	3,761	19,827
Italian	1,698	2,200	11,255	19,728	2,549	63,500	35,631	17,288
Jewish(j)	4,367	3,870	22,331	17,120	371	32,214	26,921	35,977(bb)
Polish(k)	2,488	2,675	39,314	679	100	28,951	5,137	-
Portuguese(l)	136	128	505	-	811	-	-	-
Russian(m)	6,341	2,940	61,422	11,563	200	93,572	21,669	12,897
Scandinavian(n)	1,893	2,728	71,873	33,713	3,307	33,655	21,918	17,970
Yugoslavian(o)	2,205	1,547	18,340	9,381	51	29,571	43,505	-
Other	-	-	-	-	-	-	-	12,957(cc)
Non-European	833	1,406	5,089	10,721	1,258	46,370	33,253	7,234
Arabian(p)	134	176	723	985	32	857	1,729	-
Armenian(q)	31	36	276	1,108	28	2,413	2,838	-
Caribbean(r)	-	-	4	315	929	1,940	628	369(dd)
Chinese	1	3	311	5,566	-	25,740	6,037	-
Indian(s)	58	208	-	-	1	101	5,150	-
Japanese	394	595	1,888	2,130	-	3,374	12,331	-
Negro(t)	153	308	1,732	270	250	-	-	-
South American(u)	18	9	61	7	9	-	-	-
Other(v)	44	71	94	19	9	11,945	4,540	6,865

(p) Includes Egyptian, Lebanese, Syrian, other Middle East, but excludes Israeli.
(q) Includes Turkish, Persian; for 1966-1970 includes only those born in Turkey.
(r) West Indies, British Guiana; between 1926-1966, probably included in the Negro category.

TABLE M-1 continued

(s) Older classification as Hindu; includes Pakistani.
(t) See note r; for 1966-1970 included in Other.
(u) Includes Mexican.
(v) Includes American Indian.
(w) The source (Urquhart and Buckley) uses a different grouping of ethnic groups without identifying the component parts.
(x) Includes British from elsewhere than the British Isles.
(y) Probably includes Lithuanians.
(z) Includes Dutch; probably excludes those from Luxembourg.
(aa) Includes those from Luxembourg and Switzerland and Bohemia, Moravia, Slovakia.
(bb) Probably excludes Lithuanians.
(cc) Probably includes those listed as Yugoslavian for other years.
(dd) Includes Japanese.

Sources: Canada Year Book, 1972, p. 225; 1969, p. 209; 1967, p. 221; 1963-64, pp.203-4; 1961, p. 188; 1959, pp. 182-3; 1956, p.185; 1954, p.163; 1952, p.169; 1950, p. 189; 1948-49, p. 179; 1945, p. 171; 1942, p. 156; 1938, pp. 197-8; 1926, pp. 172-3; 1921, p.127; 1915, p.112; 1910, p.411; Urquhart and Buckley, Historical Statistics, Series A316-336.

TABLE M-2 CANADIAN-BORN PERSONS IMMIGRATING INTO THE UNITED STATES,
FROM CANADA AND ELSEWHERE, AND ALL IMMIGRANTS TO THE
UNITED STATES FROM CANADA, SINCE 1946

Year	Canadian Born Entering the U.S.A. From Canada	From Elsewhere	All Persons Entering the U.S.A. from Canada
1970	13,466	338	26,850
1969	18,196	386	29,303
1968	27,189	473	41,716
1967	22,729	713	34,768
1966	27,707	651	37,273
1961	31,312	726	47,470
1956	29,533	-	42,363
1951	20,809	-	25,886
1946	-	-	20,434

Sources: Canada Year Book, 1972, p.232; 1969,p.215; 1960, p.228;
1954, p. 167.

TABLE M-5 LIFETIME INTERPROVINCIAL NET MIGRATION BY PROVINCE AT CENSUS YEARS SINCE 1901.

Province or Territory	Census Years							
	1971(a) No.	1961 No.	1951 No.	1941 No.	1931 No.	1921 No.	1911 No.	1901 No.
Newfoundland	-80,600	-46,007	40,036	-	-	-	-	-
Prince Edward Island	-30,800	-28,486	-21,452	-15,840	-14,621	-15,735	-12,912	- 6,668
Nova Scotia	-122,300	-81,009	-46,246	-31,721	-36,636	-27,919	-21,646	- 7,876
New Brunswick	-107,100	-80,413	-54,162	-26,547	-19,768	-13,851	-12,971	- 3,991
Quebec	-91,400	-45,262	-54,729	-48,139	-75,995	-100,643	-88,307	-62,509
Ontario	365,600	215,776	102,503	-70,321	-169,132	-220,729	-224,208	-69,899
Manitoba	-174,000	-126,681	-91,400	-34,463	-962	35,233	54,361	69,935
Saskatchewan	-368,700	-254,963	-161,505	-10,993	100,272	142,357	140,414	20,398
Alberta	85,800	77,770	49,891	58,136	88,686	103,071	83,477	10,642
British Columbia	517,400	362,354	311,362	177,478	126,778	96,516	81,162	38,818
Yukon and Northwest Territories	5,800	6,921	5,774	2,410	1,388	1,700	630	11,150
Sum of Net Gain or Loss	974,600	662,821	469,530	238,024	317,124	378,877	360,044	150,943
Index of Interprovincial Migration(b)(per cent)	5.3	4.3	3.9	2.5	3.9	5.5	6.4	3.2

Note: For Canadian-born origin. The numbers represent a difference between immigrants and out-migrants.

(a) Preliminary data, randomly rounded.
(b) Net gain divided by the total number of Canadian-born.

Sources: M. George, Internal Migration, table 5.3; Statistics Canada, Census Division, Demographic and Social Characteristics Section, communicated by R. Bradley, 18 July 1973.

TABLE M-6 NUMBER OF CHILDREN TRANSFERRED IN FROM AND OUT TO EACH PROVINCE, WITH PROVINCE OF ORIGIN AND PROVINCE OF DESTINATION, ON BASIS OF 2.27 CHILDREN PER FAMILY 1 JULY 1970 to 30 JUNE 1971

	Nfld.	PEI.	N.S.	N.B.	Que.	Ont.	Man.	Sask.	Alta.	B.C.	Yukon and N.W.T.	Total In	Out
Newfoundland													
In from	-	53	493	242	364	1,598	54	45	102	111	22	3,084	
Out to	-	49	630	327	353	3,085	89	33	118	177	18		4,879
Prince Edward Island													
In from	49	-	354	187	122	482	53	13	62	36	3	1,361	
Out to	53	-	260	258	54	578	42	19	67	67	6		1,404
Nova Scotia													
In from	630	260	-	1,108	763	3,241	218	213	359	465	-	7,257	
Out to	493	354	-	1,107	690	4,609	255	90	453	741	36		8,828
New Brunswick													
In from	327	258	1,107	-	1,399	2,803	354	69	263	226	21	6,807	
Out to	242	187	1,108	-	1,093	3,337	284	84	413	477	15		7,240
Quebec													
In from	353	54	690	1,093	-	7,104	651	181	609	803	67	11,605	
Out to	364	122	763	1,399	-	15,526	641	175	1,032	1,958	125		22,105
Ontario													
In from	3,085	578	4,609	3,337	15,526	-	3,922	2,068	3,935	4,906	182	42,148	
Out to	1,598	482	3,241	2,803	7,104	-	2,340	818	2,955	5,286	198		26,825
Manitoba													
In from	89	42	255	284	641	2,340	-	2,842	1,523	1,357	71	9,444	
Out to	54	53	218	334	651	3,922	-	1,500	2,446	2,563	126		11,867
Saskatchewan													
In from	33	19	90	84	175	818	1,500	-	2,637	1,431	70	6,857	
Out to	45	13	213	69	181	2,068	2,842	-	5,409	3,603	298		14,741
Alberta													
In from	118	67	453	413	1,032	2,955	2,446	5,409	-	6,128	648	19,669	
Out to	102	62	359	263	609	3,935	1,523	2,637	-	8,246	732		18,468

Table M-6 continued

	Nfld.	P.E.I.	N.S.	N.B.	Que.	Ont.	Man.	Sask.	Alta.	B.C.	Yukon and N.W.T.	Total In	Out
British Columbia													
In from	177	67	741	477	1,958	5,286	2,563	3,603	8,246	-	624	23,742	
Out to	111	36	465	226	803	4,906	1,357	1,431	6,128	-	768		16,231
Yukon and Northwest Territories													
In from	18	6	36	15	125	198	126	298	732	768	-	2,322	
Out to	22	3	-	21	67	182	71	70	648	624	-		1,708
TOTAL												134,296	

Note: The number of families can be derived by dividing the number of children by 2.27.
However, the number of children per family in that year varied by province as follows:
Nfld. 2.75; P.E.I. 2.60; N.S. 2.33; N.B. 2.49; Que. 2.29; Ont. 2.19; Man. 2.29; Sask. 2.42;
Alta. 2.31; B.C. 2.16; Yukon and N.W.T. 2.58.

Source: Statistics Canada, Interprovincial Movements of Children in Canada 1970-1971 (October
1971), table 2,3.

78

TABLE M-7 NET NUMBER OF CHILDREN TRANSFERRING INTO AND OUT OF EACH PROVINCE, 1948-1971

Year	Nfld.	P.E.I.	N.S.	N.B.	Que.	Ont.	Man.	Sask.	Alta.	B.C.	Yukon and N.W.T.
1970-71	-1,795	-43	-1,571	-433	-10,500	15,323	-2,423	-7,884	1,201	7,511	614
1969-70	-3,445	-687	-1,783	-2,950	-10,322	18,335	-3,505	-9,334	1,932	11,614	145
1968-69	-949	-369	-764	-1,791	-5,290	5,290	-2,409	-4,983	1,860	8,852	20
1967-68	-1,435	-163	-1,185	-925	-5,391	5,035	-2,696	-2,753	1,516	8,177	-180
1966-67	-2,052	-387	-2,616	-2,497	-3,898	8,526	-4,360	-3,763	-507	12,148	-594
1965-66	-2,465	-517	-3,030	-2,760	-3,412	11,004	-4,746	-3,232	-4,386	14,012	-468
1964-65	-1,346	-521	-3,307	-1,128	-589	6,241	-2,889	-1,913	-2,576	8,419	-909
1963-64	-965	-229	-2,273	-1,655	-208	4,445	-1,541	-1,685	-1,707	6,151	-484
1962-63	-256	-232	217	-1,426	242	593	744	-3,870	815	3,719	-226
1961-62	-18	418	-1,220	-893	2,385	-893	-563	-3,490	2,032	1,293	49
1960-61	-77	99	-925	429	1,757	-1,103	253	-2,441	1,736	314	141
1959-60	-415	70	-1,526	-472	-550	2,457	-627	-3,378	2,344	1,539	60
1958-59	-374	84	-1,058	771	-1,057	1,359	-376	-1,419	2,065	-606	-53
1957-58	-548	-14	-2,172	-18	-184	1,986	-1,589	-2,239	349	2,921	--
1956-57	-385	-489	-3,001	-860	-1,959	5,331	-3,627	-6,266	-1,210	9,082	--
1955-56	-99	-371	-1,860	-1,091	-1,836	5,334	-2,370	-5,345	-1,119	6,801	--
1954-55	54	-495	-769	-676	-705	1,414	-771	-3,142	-370	3,471	--
1953-54	-99	-430	-1,607	-1,431	-1,224	5,154	-1,205	-108	897	2,392	--
1952-53	-9	-343	-1,053	-1,139	-1,803	2,884	-1,481	-2,010	1,888	3,236	--

TABLE M-7 continued

Year	Nfld.	P.E.I.	N.S.	N.B.	Que.	Ont.	Man.	Sask.	Alta.	B.C.	Yukon and N.W.T.
1951-52	-490	-400	-1,382	-1,730	-389	5,863	-1,658	-3,949	101	3,744	--
1950-51	-743	242	-1,569	-2,703	-626	7,970	-1,327	-3,271	1,272	1,162	--
1949-50	-508	21	-807	-1,189	-145	2,378	-610	-3,570	2,647	1,201	--
1948-49	--	-219	-1,679	-596	-224	4,108	-1,332	-5,343	-1,341	4,809	--
1947-48	--	-87	-2,571	-136	-662	3,570	-3,448	-6,817	-729	1,118	--

Note: See note to table M-6. These figures are based on the monthly reports of the Family
      Allowance Division of the Department of National Health and Welfare. These reports
      give the number of families transferring accounts into and out of each province.
      The data are compiled for a census year (June to May) up to and including 1958-59, but
      for the school year (July to June) thereafter.

Source: Statistics Canada, Interprovincial Movements of Children in Canada 1970-71 (October
        1971), table 1.

TABLE M-8 ESTIMATED INTERREGIONAL MIGRATION AND IMMIGRATION OF THE CANADIAN POPULATION 20 YEARS OF AGE AND OVER, BY LEVEL OF EDUCATION AND REGION, JANUARY 1966 (IN THOUSANDS)

Level of Education and Region	Number of Persons Educated in each Region (1)	Outflow to Other Regions (2)	Inflow from Other Regions (3)	Net Inflow(+) or Outflow(-) (3)-(2) (4)	Imm-gration (5)	Net Change(a) (4)+(5) (6)	Percentage Change (6)-(1)x100 (7)
Elementary							
Atlantic	1,127	220	30	-190	34	-156	-13.9
Quebec	2,767	175	159	-15	298	283	10.2
Ontario	2,722	208	397	189	956	1,146	42.1
Prairies	1,723	391	122	-270	323	54	3.1
British Columbia	480	46	332	285	295	581	121.0
Secondary							
Atlantic	622	146	25	-121	24	-97	-15.7
Quebec	1,331	97	130	32	154	187	14.0
Ontario	1,859	156	250	94	445	538	29.0
Prairies	1,092	238	81	-157	134	-23	2.1
British Columbia	398	41	193	152	159	311	78.2
University							
Atlantic	89	25	*	-16	*	-9	-10.0
Quebec	244	30	35	6	45	51	20.8
Ontario	315	45	53	8	82	90	28.8
Prairies	187	40	22	-17	30	13	7.1
British Columbia	88	15	34	19	33	52	59.1

Note: A migrant is defined as a person who obtained a given level of education in one region and who was living in another region at the time of the survey (January 1966); an immigrant is defined as a person who obtained a given level of education in another country and was living in Canada in January 1966. Under this definition, Canadians who have studied abroad and then returned to Canada are considered immigrants. These estimations are based on added questions for the Labour Force Survey, January 1966.

(a) These changes do not take emigration into account since comparable data are not available.

* Estimate of less than 10,000.

Source: M.D.Lagace, Educational Attainment in Canada: Some Regional and Social Aspects, Special Labour Force Study No. 7(Ottawa: Dominion Bureau of Statistics, October 1968), table 7.

BIBLIOGRAPHY

Anderson,I., Internal Migration in Canada, 1921-61. Economic
Council of Canada Staff Study No. 13. Ottawa: Queen's Printer,
1966. (87 pp.)

Buckley, K.A.H., Historical Estimates of Internal Migration in
Canada. Papers for the Canadian Political Science Conference
on Statistics, 1960. Toronto: University of Toronto Press,
1962, pp.1-37.

Charbonneau, H. and Legare, J., "L'Extreme mobilite de la population
urbaine au Canada: l'experience de Montreal entre 1956 et 1961",
Revue de Geographie de Montreal 21 (1967): 235-265.

Cornay,Y., "The Benefits and Costs of Study Abroad and Migration",
Canadian Journal of Economics 3 (1970): 300-308

Courchene, T., "Interprovincial Migration and Economic Adjustment",
Canadian Journal of Economics 3 (1970): 550-557.

Ducherrin, J., "Les Immigrants Francais au Canada", Revue de
l'Universite d'Ottawa 40 (1970): 468-487.

George, M., Internal Migration in Canada. 1961 Census Monograph
Ottawa: Queen's Printer, 1970. (249 pp.).

Gnanasekaran, K., Migration Projections for Canada, 1969-1984.
Analytical and Technical Memorandum No. 6. Ottawa: Dominion Bureau
of Statistics, 1970. (63 pp.)

Kalbach, W., The Impact of Immigration on Canada's Population.
1961 Census Monograph. Ottawa: Queen's Printer, 1970. (465 pp.)

MacDonald, N., Canada: Immigration and Colonization, 1841-1903.
Toronto: Macmillan, 1970. (381 pp.)

McInnis, M., "Age Education and Occupational Differentials in
Interregional Migration: Some Evidence for Canada", Demography
8 (1971); 195-204.

Parai, L., Immigration and Emigration of Professional and Skilled
Manpower During the Post-War Period. Economic Council of Canada
Staff Study No. 1. Ottawa: Queen's Printer, 1965. (248 pp.)

Richmond, A., Post-War Immigrants in Canada. Toronto: University
of Toronto Press, 1967. (320 pp.)

_____, "Return Migration from Canada to Britain", Population
Studies 22 (1968): 263-271.

Samuel, T.J., "Migration of Canadians to the U.S.A.: the Causes",
International Migration Review 7 (1969): 106-116.

_____, The Migration of Canadian-Born Between Canada and
United States of America, 1955 to 1968. Ottawa: Department
of Manpower and Immigration, 1969. (46 pp.)

Stone, L., Migration in Canada: Regional Aspects. 1961 Census
Monograph. Ottawa: Queen's Printer, 1969. (406 pp.)

Vanderkamp, J., "Interregional Mobility in Canada: A Study of the Time Pattern of Migration", <u>Canadian Journal of Economics</u> 1 (1968): 595-608.

_____, "Effect of Out-Migration on Regional Employment", <u>Canadian Review of Economics</u> 3 (1970): 541-549.

Vidder, R., and Gallaway, L., "Settlement Patterns of Canadian Emigrants to the United States, 1850-1960", <u>Canadian Journal of Economics</u> 3 (1970): 476-486.

3 Three Social Institutions

HOUSEHOLDS AND FAMILIES

In the ninety years during which the Canadian census has
included just about all of the present-day territory of Canada,
the number of occupied dwellings(1) has increased about eightfold
as compared with the fivefold increase of the population during
the same period; thus, the number of persons per dwelling has
about halved. The growth in dwellings has been uneven,
registering two peak decades, 1901-1910 and 1951-1960,
corresponding to unusually high immigration periods into Canada.

What such a composite numerical portrait of dwellings and
population betrays is that a very rapid population growth may
force an increase in the number of living quarters but it
forestalls the self-generated construction of living quarters
which takes place in times of slower population growth. In
other words, a discrepancy between the population growth and
the increase in the number of dwelling units could be thought
of as a measure of the standard of living.

The 1960s   reflect a faster social change taking place than
any other previous decade (see table. H-1); the occupied dwellings
increased almost twice as fast as the population, the provinces
of slow growth expanding their housing relatively faster than
the provinces of high population growth. The message in these
data is clear as to the benefits of a slow growth. It should
be borne in mind, though, that those provinces which improved
the most in their ratio of dwellings and population needed
the improvement the most and, one may add, gained their relative
advantage more likely through out-migration than through restraint
in reproduction.

In most instances, dwellings accommodate households which
in turn are primarily one-family households (see table H-2).
Household and family data serve as further indicators of the
social change already suggested by the differential growth rate of
dwellings and population. During the last decade, families(2)
increased by 22 per cent as compared with an increase of 33
per cent for households. The growth in "nonfamily" households(3),
in both the rural and urban areas, accounts for the difference
just noted. In 1971, about 800,000 persons lived alone in
Canada and they represent the bulk of nonfamily households.
No doubt, high-rise apartments in downtown areas of cities

---

(1) The term dwelling, for census purposes, is a "structurally
    separate set of living quarters, with a private entrance
    either from outside the building or from a common hall or
    stairway inside". Houses, apartments, mobile homes and
    sometimes "collective dwellings" like hotels, or institutions
    of various sorts, camps, and similar living arrangements
    are enumerated as dwellings.

(2) Family is defined by Statistics Canada as consisting "either
    of husband and wife with or without children never married
    and living at home, or of a parent with one or more children
    who have never married. In any case, all persons who
    constitute a family must be living in the same dwelling."

(3) The nonfamily household is defined by the census as either
    "one person living alone or a group of two or more persons
    not in families but living together as a household".

84

Chart 5. PERCENTAGE DISTRIBUTION OF NON-FARM FAMILIES AND UNATTACHED
INDIVIDUALS BY INCOME GROUPS, 1955, 1958, 1963 and 1969.

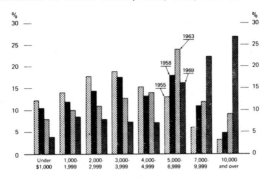

Source: Statistics Canada. Infomat: Weekly Bulletin, July 13, 1973, p. 3.

contain their share of nonfamily households; currently about
every fifth household in urban areas is a nonfamily household.
The sharing of apartments and living alone by the young in the
labour force account for most of the cases.

The proportion of nonfamily households increases as one moves
west; for instance, every fourth rural nonfarm household is a
nonfamily household in the Prairie Provinces. In view of the
dramatic decline of the rural farm population, especially in
Saskatchewan, the substantial number of one-person households
represents the older persons who live alone, in retirement, and
distressingly, often in isolation.

The households with two or more families under one roof have been
steadily declining both in absolute numbers and in proportion to
all households, especially in urban areas. Modern housing
construction does not encourage more than one family per household
and large family homes are already out of reach for the average
Canadian family. Earlier, however, as reflected in the 1951
census, two-or-more-family households were on the increase in
urban areas. Three easily identified social forces can explain
this finding, namely: an increased fertility, an unusual influx
of immigrants not averse to household sharing arrangements, and
a backlog in housing construction. Such a condition was most
pronounced in Ontario, a province continually beset by a fast
population growth.

In view of the recent changes in the Canadian family structure,
it should not come as a surprise that the proportion of families
with fewer than three children (that is, children living at
home and never married, and under twenty-five years of age) has
declined. This decline has been most noticeable in the urban
areas, particularly during the decade of the 1950s and again
at present. At the same time, the proportion of very large
families has increased during the postwar years in just about all
provinces, even though those east of Ontario had more than the
national share of families with many children (six or more)
living at home (see table H-3).

First and foremost, the census puts the population in
historical perspective, actually accounting for the demographic

behaviour in the preceding decades. Thus, the 1951 census
was the last to reflect the traditional Canadian family pattern
in the Province of Quebec, where every fifth family of its
rural population was very large. In contrast, Ontario's rural
farm population showed only every twentieth family as very
large. What is perhaps even more significant, however, was the
great difference between the urban and rural areas in Quebec
with respect to the proportion of large families. In all
other provinces, the rural-urban differences were less
pronounced. But now, a rapid decrease in the family size in
Quebec marks an end to the rustic imagery replete with
stereotypes of the rural Quebec family.

Dealing with aggregate data like those on the number of
families with children at home requires due caution. The
decrease in families with up to two children, which seems to
be reversing as of the 1971 census, may be a result of several
factors: (1) the proportion of families whose children moved
out of home early, due to the early age at marriage; (2) the
proportion of young families just starting their families;
(3) the proportionate increase of the voluntarily childless;
or (4) as was the case for the 1951 census, the proportion of
older couples whose children have left home. The pattern of
bunching births, however, which has been prevalent for the
last twenty years, is likely to increase the number of
families enumerated as with children at home. It will also
reflect the fertility patterns more accurately than the staggered
childbearing pattern where some of the children reach adulthood
while their younger siblings are still at home. The average
number of children in families has to be viewed in this context
as well. However, due to the considerable fertility of the
early sixties, families with fewer than three children at
home are not likely to reflect a proportionate increase until
the next census of 1981.

Families in Canada have increased in number by 12 per cent since
the last quinquennial census of 1966, and the proportion of
never-marrieds among those fifteen years or older has increased
as well, albeit slightly, to reflect the first wave of "baby
boom" children reaching adulthood. Viewed against the total
population, the proportion of single persons decreased to
49.5 per cent from 51.7 per cent in 1966. Thus, over the years
the proportion of population married has been on a steady
increase, the increase being more pronounced west of Ontario
(see table H-4). The sex differential in proportion married
has now pretty much disappeared. It had been quite pronounced
in the western part of Canada, more likely due to the original
sex imbalance (more males than females) than to the age
differences at marriage (males marrying later than females).

The most striking change in the marital-status composition of
the population is the increased proportion of divorced persons,
which occurs in every province. Of course, the population
which has gone through the divorce process is much more numerous
than that listed at any given census.

The legislation in 1968 enabling the provinces to handle
their divorce proceedings accounts for the very steep increase
in the registration of divorces starting with 1969. A summary
of marriages and divorces (see table H-5) shows a fairly steady
marriage rate throughout this century, with some reluctance
to marry registered during the depression decade of the 1930s
and with some undue enthusiasm to marry just after the last
world war. Provincial differences in the marriage rates can be

86

explained by the age structure: the younger population shows a higher marriage rate; thus, out-migration of young persons from the Maritime Provinces accounts for the lower rate of marriage there than elsewhere in Canada. Divorces do not show any signs of abating either. It is quite possible that the exigencies of a modern society will boost the national divorce rate to at least equal that of British Columbia which, in turn, is close to the national rate in the United States.

The enthusiasm with which people marry may be gauged somewhat by the age at first marriage. During the last thirty years the median age at first marriage has decreased by about three years for males, to 23.5, and by about two years for females, to 21.4, narrowing the traditional age gap. One of the social forces which may, perhaps, explain marriage between age peers is the demographic marriage squeeze: young women were marrying men from their own age group because the very rapid expansion of the population base immediately after 1945 brought about an under-supply of potential grooms several years older than the women who were born, for example, in 1949. Very recently, the reverse process has occurred, shrinking the population base so that some twenty years hence there will be an oversupply of eligible and older grooms.

The age at first marriage has shown variations over time. The recent trend has been toward early marriages and a small, if any, age difference between the marriage partners. The interest or disinterest to marry may have fluctuated according to the economic conditions prevailing; differences in age for women to marry used to vary by place of residence, and primarily by education. It is the education which used to predict -- and still does, even though to a lesser degree -- the age at first marriage of Canadian women.

As a matter of historical interest (see table H-4), university-educated women born during the decade of the First World War and marrying during the depression decade married reasonably late (around twenty-seven years of age). Those with only elementary schooling married either some three years earlier, at twenty-four, if they were urban residents or about five years earlier, at twenty-two, if they remained in the country. The recent generations do not show as much difference in their age at first marriage when their level of education is examined. Perhaps education, and marriage and making a living -- the two traditionally incompatible pursuits -- have been reconciled in our wealthy society.

The state of being married is usually the longest phase in one's life cycle and it is associated with a variety of apparent benefits, among them a higher income for men than women. Of course, people remain married for a long time and as they progress through their careers their earnings tend to improve, even though some of the improvement is eroded by inflation. As the family earnings improve, the probability of the wife's employment decreases, explaining the income differential between married men and women (see table H-8). On the other hand, the differential earnings between unmarried men and women are not very pronounced at present, as they might have been not too long ago.

The rightful complaint women have about their earnings being disparagingly low compared to the earnings of men cannot, however, be put to rest from such data.

It may come as a surprise that only about 10 per cent of
married women were employed full time in 1969 (see table H-9).
Thus, most aggregate figures on family earnings are roughly
indicative of the earnings of male heads of households.
A contemporary profile of the income and spending of
Canadian families in 1969 by province shows that in the east,
especially Newfoundland, the larger families (over four persons)
share in a considerably smaller family income (under $6,000),
whereas in the westernmost province smaller families (slightly
under three persons) share in a considerably higher family income
(over $8,000). The age composition of the families does
influence spending, families in the eastern provinces having
more children at home to take care of than those in British
Columbia. For families where the head of the household is over
sixty-five years of age the situation is reversed.

Home ownership is higher in the east than in the west and seems
to be inversely related to the standard of living, as is the
proportion of income spent on food: the higher the proportion
(close to 26 per cent in Newfoundland, close to 18 per cent in
British Columbia) the lower the standard of living.

Spending on reading and education represents a fairly negligible
proportion of all families' income, which means that in the more
prosperous provinces families spend more on education. On the
other hand, smoking and liquor consumption may be similar for all
provinces, as reflected by the fact that the proportion of
family income spent on these goods is higher in the Maritimes
than it is in the prosperous provinces.

Even this small sampling of information on the Canadian family
leads one to believe that this venerable institution continues
to thrive, the occasional rematching of marital partners
notwithstanding.

TABLE H-1 NUMBER OF OCCUPIED DWELLINGS, DECENNIAL INCREASE IN
DWELLINGS AND IN POPULATION, AVERAGE NUMBER OF PERSONS PER
DWELLING, FOR CANADA AND PROVINCES, BY CENSUS YEARS
SINCE 1881

Province	Number	Dwellings Per Cent Increase	Average Persons	Population Per Cent Increase
Canada				
1971	6,034,510	32.5	3.50	18.3
1961	4,480,666	33.8	3.98	30.2
1951	3,349,580	28.9	4.07	18.6
1941	2,597,969	16.7	4.47	10.9
1931	2,227,000	26.2	4.65	18.1
1921	1,764,012	25.2	4.97	22.0
1911	1,408,689	38.4	5.11	35.1
1901	1,018,015	17.6	5.23	12.5
1891	856,607	12.5	5.53	10.9
1881	741,365	-	5.76	-
Newfoundland				
1971	110,440	25.6	4.60	14.0
1961	88,330	24.0	5.07	26.7
1951	71,242	-	5.18	-
Prince Edward Island				
1971	27,880	16.5	3.90	6.7
1961	24,036	6.7	4.35	6.3
1951	22,517	12.1	4.35	3.6
1941	20,079	7.3	4.73	8.0
1931	18,715	0.5	4.70	-0.7
1921	18,628	2.1	4.76	-5.5
1911	18,237	-1.6	5.14	-9.2
1901	18,530	0.8	5.57	-5.3
1891	18,389	3.8	5.93	0.2
1881	17,724	-	6.14	-
Nova Scotia				
1971	207,510	18.4	3.70	7.1
1961	176,132	17.4	4.18	14.7
1951	149,982	21.8	4.28	11.2
1941	123,184	15.3	4.69	12.7
1931	106,854	3.9	4.80	-2.1
1921	102,807	9.6	5.10	6.4
1911	93,784	9.9	5.25	7.1
1901	85,313	7.9	5.39	2.0
1891	79,102	6.7	6.69	2.2
1881	74,154	-	5.94	-

TABLE H-1 continued

Province	Number	Dwellings Per Cent Increase	Average Persons	Population Per Cent Increase
New Brunswick				
1971	157,640	18.8	3.90	6.1
1961	133,368	16.6	4.48	15.9
1951	114,353	24.5	4.51	12.7
1941	91,881	14.9	4.98	12.0
1931	79,976	13.6	5.10	5.2
1921	70,428	15.6	5.51	10.2
1911	60,936	4.6	5.78	6.3
1901	58,226	6.4	5.69	3.1
1891	54,718	6.9	5.87	0.0
1881	51,166	-	6.28	-
Quebec				
1971	1,604,780	34.7	3.70	14.6
1961	1,197,295	38.8	4.39	29.7
1951	862,599	33.9	4.70	21.7
1941	644,529	20.2	5.17	15.9
1931	536,383	34.7	5.36	21.8
1921	398,267	17.1	5.93	17.7
1911	346,196	16.7	5.90	21.6
1901	291,427	18.2	5.66	10.8
1891	246,644	14.0	6.04	9.5
1881	216,432	-	6.28	-
Ontario				
1971	2,225,495	35.6	3.40	23.5
1961	1,647,707	39.2	3.78	35.6
1951	1,183,448	30.1	3.88	21.4
1941	909,394	14.8	4.17	10.4
1931	792,047	24.2	4.33	17.0
1921	637,552	20.5	4.60	16.1
1911	529,190	18.8	4.78	15.8
1901	445,310	9.4	4.90	3.3
1891	406,948	13.3	5.20	9.7
1881	359,293	-	5.36	-
Manitoba				
1971	288,370	20.3	3.30	7.2
1961	240,861	18.7	3.82	18.7
1951	202,968	24.0	3.83	6.4
1941	163,655	12.4	4.46	4.2
1931	145,577	23.8	4.81	14.8
1921	117,541	37.1	5.19	32.2
1911	85,720	72.2	5.38	80.8
1901	49,784	61.7	5.13	67.3
1891	30,790	140.5	4.95	144.9
1881	12,803	-	4.86	-

Province	Number	Dwellings Per Cent Increase	Average Persons	Population Per Cent Increase
Saskatchewan				
1971	267,565	9.0	3.40	0.1
1961	246,712	11.0	3.75	11.2
1951	222,235	7.3	3.74	-7.2
1941	207,173	4.9	4.32	-2.8
1931	197,572	20.7	4.67	21.7
1921	103,661	38.4	4.63	53.8
1911	118,283	570.4	4.16	439.5
1901	17,645	-	5.17	-
Alberta				
1971	464,610	32.8	3.40	22.2
1961	351,488	39.5	3.78	41.8
1951	251,891	30.4	3.73	18.0
1941	193,246	12.6	4.12	8.8
1931	171,670	26.1	4.26	24.3
1921	136,125	55.3	4.32	57.2
1911	87,672	490.7	4.27	412.6
1901	14,842	-	4.92	-
British Columbia				
1971	667,545	45.3	3.20	34.1
1961	463,067	36.4	3.51	39.8
1951	339,587	54.3	3.43	42.5
1941	220,014	23.5	3.72	17.8
1931	178,206	49.6	3.90	32.3
1921	119,003	59.4	4.41	33.7
1911	74,677	102.2	5.26	119.7
1901	36,938	84.5	4.84	82.0
1891	20,016	104.4	4.90	98.5
1881	9,793	-	5.05	-

Note: Canada summary excludes Newfoundland and Yukon and Northwest
Territories. 1961 count includes collective-type dwellings. 1971
figure randomly rounded; excludes collective-type dwellings. Per
cent change for Canada refers to data including Newfoundland and Yukon
and Northwest Territories. For 1971, average persons for dwellings
are average persons per household.

Sources: 1971 Census of Canada, Advance Bulletin AH-1 (December 1972), table
1; 1961 Census of Canada, Bull. 7.2-4, tables I and II; 1951
Census of Canada, vol. III, table 1; "Summary Housing
Characteristics 1971". Statistics Daily (August 1972), p.2.

TABLE H-2 HOUSEHOLDS BY PROPORTION URBAN, RURAL NONFARM AND RURAL FARM, FOR CANADA AND PROVINCES, SINCE 1921

Province	All Households			Proportion of One-Family Households			Proportion of Two-or-More Family Households			Proportion of Non-Family Households		
	Urban	RNF	RF	U	RNF	RF	U	RNF	RF	U	RNF	RF
Canada												
1971	4,743,280	970,595	327,425	79.6	81.9	88.5	2.0	2.2	2.0	19.5	15.8	9.5
1966	3,941,459	811,776	427,238	81.3	82.4	87.9	2.5	2.4	2.8	16.3	15.2	9.4
1961	3,280,682	824,501	449,553	82.6	83.0	87.1	2.8	2.8	3.9	13.6	14.7	9.0
1951	2,155,035	624,475	629,785	81.5	81.6	84.1	3.9	3.9	5.8	10.7	14.5	10.1
1941	1,521,413	469,940	714,736	82.1	80.6	82.3	5.5	4.3	5.4	12.4	15.1	12.3
1931	1,240,715	1,012,014		93.7	93.7		6.3	6.3				
1921	958,371	938,856		–	–	–						
Newfoundland												
1971	64,850	44,705	915	86.2	84.6	83.1	5.6	6.5	9.8	8.2	8.9	7.7
1966	52,627	42,354	1,651	87.3	85.5	85.2	6.4	7.0	9.5	6.3	7.5	5.3
1961	44,534	41,736	1,670	86.5	85.7	83.2	7.7	7.2	9.4	5.9	7.1	5.6
1951	29,735	38,355	2,890	82.8	83.5	85.1	11.8	9.9	10.7	5.4	6.6	4.2
Prince Edward Island												
1971	11,090	12,165	4,640	79.9	79.1	84.7	2.3	3.0	5.7	17.9	17.8	9.7
1966	9,566	9,174	6,620	82.6	79.6	84.5	2.5	3.3	6.3	14.9	17.5	9.3
1961	7,911	8,543	7,488	82.8	79.3	81.9	4.2	3.3	7.8	13.0	17.4	10.3
1951	5,575	6,230	10,650	80.8	83.6	79.9	7.7	3.2	8.1	11.5	13.2	12.0
1941	5,122	1,491	13,819	82.7	82.7	80.8	8.3	6.2	8.4	9.0	11.1	10.8
1931	4,259	14,475		91.3	91.4		8.7	8.6				
1921	4,105	14,696		–	–	–						
Nova Scotia												
1971	120,010	82,190	6,225	80.1	80.7	84.2	2.7	3.2	4.6	17.2	16.1	11.2
1966	106,624	67,929	10,692	82.9	80.8	82.8	3.6	3.5	5.3	13.6	15.7	11.9
1961	94,307	68,349	12,685	82.7	81.5	82.4	5.1	3.9	6.6	12.1	14.6	10.9
1951	78,430	45,375	25,750	81.6	81.0	79.2	8.7	5.3	8.9	9.7	13.7	11.9
1941	58,237	39,047	31,357	84.3	80.5	76.0	8.6	7.1	7.1	7.1	12.4	16.9
1931	47,842	60,832		92.0	91.3		8.0	8.7				
1921	45,440	63,283		–	–	–						

TABLE H-2 continued

Province		All Households			Proportion of One-Family Households			Proportion of Two-or-More Family Households			Proportion of Non-Family Households		
		Urban	RNF	RF	U	RNF	RF	U	RNF	RF	U	RNF	RF
New Brunswick	1971	94,165	58,580	5,350	81.7	82.6	85.8	2.5	4.1	5.6	15.8	13.3	8.6
	1966	76,008	55,586	10,167	83.6	84.0	85.1	2.6	4.1	7.4	13.8	12.0	7.6
	1961	65,675	55,308	11,732	84.5	84.1	83.4	3.7	4.6	9.5	11.8	11.3	7.1
	1951	51,785	34,360	27,865	83.1	84.1	81.6	6.3	5.6	11.1	10.6	10.3	7.3
	1941	32,321	33,270	29,008	82.5	87.0	87.8	7.2	8.1	11.6	10.3	4.9	2.6
	1931	27,516	52,776		92.4	90.0		7.6	10.0		-	-	-
	1921	25,880	51,069		-	-		-	-		-	-	-
Quebec	1971	1,346,310	203,470	55,965	79.8	85.0	91.5	1.6	2.1	3.1	18.6	12.9	5.5
	1966	1,142,228	162,254	89,633	83.1	86.2	90.5	1.9	2.6	4.6	15.0	11.3	5.0
	1961	936,802	161,761	92,906	85.1	86.2	89.2	3.0	3.4	6.3	12.0	10.4	4.5
	1951	603,400	125,460	129,925	84.6	85.6	86.4	7.1	4.5	8.6	8.3	9.9	5.0
	1941	444,773	65,593	153,060	85.2	83.7	88.3	5.8	5.2	7.0	9.0	11.1	4.7
	1931	357,178	178,294		93.8	91.2		6.2	8.8		-	-	-
	1921	261,407	180,949		-	-		-	-		-	-	-
Ontario	1971	1,865,970	274,080	88,110	78.6	83.2	89.4	2.4	1.7	2.3	19.0	15.1	8.4
	1966	1,531,937	228,370	116,238	80.7	83.2	88.4	3.4	1.6	2.8	15.7	15.2	8.8
	1961	1,290,551	229,808	120,522	81.3	83.5	87.4	5.1	2.0	3.4	13.5	14.5	8.5
	1951	840,255	173,915	166,955	79.0	81.7	84.0	10.1	3.6	6.0	10.9	14.7	10.0
	1941	606,009	180,335	182,923	82.3	82.7	82.5	5.8	4.0	5.2	11.9	13.3	12.3
	1931	501,109	309,048		92.8	94.0		7.2	6.0		-	-	-
	1921	400,987	280,642		-	-		-	-		-	-	-
Manitoba	1971	209,725	47,495	31,500	77.2	77.6	88.1	1.4	1.8	1.2	21.4	20.6	10.7
	1966	180,611	39,836	38,833	80.8	78.6	87.8	2.0	1.9	1.6	17.2	19.6	10.7
	1961	158,301	41,063	40,390	82.3	79.6	88.2	3.7	2.0	2.6	14.0	18.4	9.7
	1951	118,710	32,745	50,945	83.9	81.2	86.4	6.0	2.3	3.6	10.1	16.5	10.0
	1941	84,364	34,970	57,608	82.1	82.0	84.3	5.3	3.6	5.0	12.6	14.4	10.7
	1931	69,516	79,074		93.6	94.7		6.4	5.3		-	-	-
	1921	57,169	71,815		-	-		-	-		-	-	-

93

TABLE H-2 continued

Province	All Households U	RNF	RF	Proportion of One-Family Households U	RNF	RF	Proportion of Two-or-More Family Households U	RNF	RF	Proportion of Non-Family Households U	RNF	RF
Saskatchewan												
1971	148,850	60,150	58,845	76.5	74.0	87.4	1.0	1.1	1.0	22.6	25.0	11.6
1966	134,282	57,565	68,975	79.1	76.1	87.1	1.0	1.0	1.2	19.9	23.0	11.6
1961	108,856	61,987	74,581	81.7	76.9	86.6	2.2	1.3	1.8	16.0	21.8	11.6
1951	69,705	51,780	99,970	81.6	78.5	88.0	4.1	1.7	3.1	14.3	19.8	19.0
1941	77,592	13,108	124,239	77.0	74.0	80.2	3.1	2.2	3.9	19.9	23.8	15.9
1931	67,183		132,202	96.5	–	95.0	3.5	5.0	–	–	–	–
1921	50,146		118,409	–	–	–	–	–	–	–	–	–
Alberta												
1971	353,185	53,905	57,850	78.7	76.9	86.7	1.1	1.3	1.3	20.2	21.8	12.0
1966	280,422	45,267	68,018	80.6	76.9	86.2	1.9	1.4	1.5	18.2	21.7	12.3
1961	228,960	52,647	68,209	82.3	77.8	85.7	2.2	1.6	2.2	15.4	20.5	12.1
1951	125,425	40,230	85,095	81.2	77.6	81.8	4.5	1.8	3.2	14.3	20.6	15.0
1941	83,587	21,411	96,798	78.3	73.7	77.5	3.7	2.3	3.7	18.0	24.0	18.8
1931	67,730		105,772	96.1	–	95.8	3.9	4.2	–	–	–	–
1921	53,055		88,135	–	–	–	–	–	–	–	–	–
British Columbia												
1971	521,660	128,640	18,005	74.6	81.8	87.9	1.6	1.5	1.8	23.8	16.7	10.3
1966	422,940	98,747	21,388	77.4	81.5	87.6	1.5	1.4	1.6	21.1	17.1	10.8
1961	341,557	98,620	19,357	79.8	80.4	86.7	2.5	1.8	2.2	17.7	17.8	11.1
1951	232,015	76,025	29,740	80.6	77.6	82.7	4.8	2.3	3.2	14.6	20.1	14.1
1941	129,408	80,715	25,924	74.7	73.3	72.3	4.0	2.8	3.7	21.3	23.9	24.0
1931	98,382	99,541		95.5	96.3	–	4.5	3.7	–	–	–	–
1921	60,182	69,858		–	–	–	–	–	–	–	–	–

TABLE H-2 continued

Provinces	All Households			Proportion of One-Family Households			Proportion of Two-or-More Family Households			Proportion of Non-Family Households		
	Urban	RNF	RF	U	RNF	RF	U	RNF	RF	U	RNF	RF
Yukon and Northwest Territories												
1971	7,465	5,215	15	76.4	79.2	-	1.5	4.3	-	22.2	16.3	-
1966		8,931			80.2			3.4			16.4	
1961		7,920			79.7			4.0			16.4	

Note: Nonfamily households 1951 and earlier residual category. Newfoundland not included before 1951. Yukon and Northwest Territories not included for 1941 and earlier. For 1941, one-family households represent the "normal family", consisting of husband and wife and children, if any. About 95 per cent of one-family households were "normal families". For 1931, one-family households include one-person families. For Yukon and Northwest Territories all households are given. Figures for 1971 randomly rounded.

Sources: Statistics Canada, User Inquiry Service, unpublished materials (1971); 1966 Census of Canada, vol. ii (2-5), table 29; 1961 Census of Canada, Bull. 2.1-2, table 8; 1951 Census of Canada, vol. III, table 48; 1941 Census of Canada, vol. V, table 4; 1931 Census of Canada, vol. 5, table 61; 1921 Census of Canada, vol. III, table 2.

TABLE H-3 FAMILIES, BY NUMBER OF CHILDREN 24 AND UNDER AT HOME, URBAN, RURAL NONFARM AND RURAL FARM, FOR CANADA AND PROVINCES, SINCE 1951

Province	All Families			Per Cent with 0-2 Children			Per Cent with 6+ Children			Average Number of Children per 100,000			
	Urban	RNF	RF	U	RNF	RF	U	RNF	RF	Urban	U	RNF	RF
Canada													
1971(a)	3,923,380	842,150	305,150	74.3	67.4	60.3	2.4	6.4	7.9	1.6	1.7	2.0	2.3
1966	3,413,178	713,202	399,886	71.3	63.3	58.9	3.6	8.8	10.6	1.6	1.8	2.2	2.4
1961	2,985,055	733,581	428,808	73.3	63.7	59.7	1.5	8.6	10.4	1.6	1.7	2.2	2.4
1951	2,123,540	562,222	601,622	80.2	70.3	64.1	2.8	6.2	9.6	-	1.5	1.9	2.3
Newfoundland													
1971(a)	65,380	43,825	935	61.7	58.5	61.0	8.4	10.4	12.8	-	2.3	2.6	2.4
1966	52,966	42,315	1,730	58.8	55.4	58.3	11.5	15.5	16.5	-	2.5	2.8	2.7
1961	45,653	41,876	1,738	57.7	55.5	55.5	12.0	15.9	16.0	-	2.6	2.8	2.8
1951	31,808	39,984	3,066	62.6	60.5	57.0	9.5	10.3	15.3	-	2.3	2.4	2.7
Prince Edward Island													
1971(a)	9,390	10,405	4,465	68.8	66.7	62.6	4.9	7.9	10.0	-	1.9	2.1	2.2
1966	8,427	7,873	6,428	65.4	62.9	61.0	5.8	10.5	11.0	-	2.0	2.3	2.3
1961	7,289	7,363	7,317	67.7	61.9	63.9	2.7	10.3	9.7	-	2.0	2.3	2.2
1951	5,477	5,661	10,243	73.6	66.5	66.8	4.5	7.9	8.3	-	1.7	2.1	2.1
Nova Scotia													
1971(a)	103,145	71,755	5,820	71.7	69.2	66.9	5.6	3.8	6.4	1.7	1.8	1.9	2.0
1966	96,430	59,803	10,004	67.9	66.0	67.4	5.5	7.3	7.9	2.0	2.0	2.1	2.0
1961	88,352	61,343	12,199	68.8	66.0	68.0	5.2	7.1	7.6	-	1.9	2.1	2.0
1951	78,875	41,468	24,784	74.0	69.4	69.5	4.4	6.2	6.9	-	1.8	2.0	1.8
New Brunswick													
1971(a)	81,910	53,315	5,210	69.5	64.1	59.7	4.6	9.0	10.6	-	1.9	2.2	2.4
1966	67,790	51,344	10,173	66.6	59.2	57.8	5.9	12.5	14.6	-	2.0	2.5	2.6
1961	60,685	51,897	12,071	67.7	58.6	58.5	5.9	13.0	14.0	-	2.0	2.6	2.6
1951	49,849	32,796	28,994	75.1	63.8	69.5	4.2	9.4	14.1	-	1.7	2.3	2.6

TABLE H-3 continued

Provinces	All Families			Per Cent with 0-2 Children			Per Cent with 6+ Children			Average Number of Children			
	Urban	RNF	RF	U	RNF	F	U	RNF	RF	U	Urban	RNF	RF
Quebec													
1971(a)	1,119,980	182,505	54,695	72.0	62.8	46.7	3.3	9.1	17.7	1.8	1.7	2.3	3.2
1966	995,614	149,330	84,357	67.8	57.7	44.8	5.3	13.0	23.3	2.0	1.8	2.6	3.5
1961	857,132	151,973	94,717	68.4	56.6	44.2	5.6	14.1	24.5	2.0	1.8	2.6	3.5
1951	603,096	119,084	133,861	72.7	61.4	47.4	5.6	11.4	22.6	1.8	-	2.4	3.4
Ontario													
1971(a)	1,561,040	238,025	82,770	76.2	70.1	63.8	1.8	4.3	5.7	1.6	1.5	1.8	2.1
1966	1,350,017	198,527	109,389	73.8	66.6	69.2	2.5	5.5	6.7	1.7	1.6	2.0	2.1
1961	1,192,608	203,352	115,518	76.6	67.3	66.5	2.0	5.5	5.9	1.6	1.5	2.0	2.0
1951	848,660	154,218	159,894	84.4	76.1	72.5	1.3	3.5	4.8	1.3	-	1.6	1.8
Manitoba													
1971(a)	168,055	38,770	29,175	76.5	69.0	63.0	1.8	7.0	4.4	1.5	1.5	1.9	2.1
1966	153,834	33,384	35,517	73.6	65.1	62.3	2.4	9.3	6.9	1.6	1.6	2.1	2.2
1961	143,394	34,635	37,802	76.5	65.8	62.9	1.8	7.4	6.8	1.6	1.5	2.0	2.2
1951	115,266	28,053	47,949	85.0	73.1	67.0	1.0	5.2	6.2	1.3	-	1.8	2.1
Saskatchewan													
1971(a)	116,825	45,995	52,945	74.1	71.3	63.9	2.4	5.7	5.2	1.6	1.6	1.8	2.1
1966	109,331	45,396	61,947	71.8	68.4	61.9	2.9	6.6	6.5	1.7	-	1.9	2.2
1961	94,607	49,755	67,414	74.2	69.7	63.0	2.2	5.3	5.5	1.6	1.6	1.8	2.1
1951	63,552	42,567	90,069	82.1	75.3	68.3	1.6	3.3	5.6	1.4	-	1.6	2.0
Alberta													
1971(a)	286,400	43,085	52,625	72.9	67.2	62.0	2.0	6.1	5.6	1.7	1.7	2.0	2.1
1966	233,252	37,001	60,905	69.7	64.3	61.1	2.7	7.9	7.0	1.8	1.8	2.1	2.2
1961	200,249	43,139	62,283	72.9	65.4	62.2	2.1	6.0	6.4	1.7	1.7	2.1	2.2
1951	114,474	32,636	76,216	82.8	72.7	66.6	1.2	3.9	5.6	1.4	-	1.8	2.0
British Columbia													
1971(a)	407,310	109,820	16,500	77.4	71.7	62.8	1.3	3.2	4.7	1.5	1.4	1.7	2.1
1966	341,880	83,999	19,418	75.2	67.0	62.6	1.8	4.9	6.1	1.6	1.5	2.0	2.1
1961	292,308	83,981	17,734	77.6	68.2	64.7	1.3	4.4	5.2	1.5	1.4	1.9	2.0
1951	211,387	61,928	26,530	86.6	77.8	71.7	0.7	2.7	4.1	1.2	-	1.5	1.8

TABLE H-3 continued

Province	All Families			Per Cent with 0-2 Children			Per Cent with 6+ Children			Average Number of Children		
	Urban	RNF	RF	U	RNF	F	U	RNF	RF	U	UrbanRNF 100,000	RF
Yukon and Northwest Territories												
1971(a)	5,955	4,665		67.3	53.1		5.1	13.8		2.0	-	2.8
1966	3,637	4,248		61.0	52.3		14.0	12.0		2.3	-	2.8
1961	2,778	4,282		65.9	57.9		5.8	8.7		2.1	-	2.5

(a) 1971 figures randomly rounded.

Sources: 1971 Census of Canada, vol.II-part 2 (Bull.2.2-3), tables 20,23; 1971 Census of Canada, vol. II, part 1 (Bull.2.1-4), table 2; 1971 Census of Canada, "Summary of Household and Family Characteristics", Advance Bulletin AH-1, table 2; 1966 Census of Canada, vol. II (2-10), table 58; 1961 Census of Canada, vol. II (2.1-5), table 49; 1951 Census of Canada, vol. X, table 81; Statistics Canada, Census Division, Housing and Families Section, 1971 figures on families by number of unmarried children at home (informal release).

TABLE H-4 PER CENT DISTRIBUTION OF THE POPULATION 15 YEARS AND OVER BY
MARITAL STATUS, FOR CANADA AND PROVINCES, FOR CENSUS YEARS
SINCE 1901

	Population(b) 15 years and over		Single		Married		Widowed		Divorced	
	Male	Female	M	F	M	F	M	F	M	F
Canada(a)										
1971	7,531,895	7,655,520	31.6	25.0	64.9	63.9	2.5	9.8	1.0	1.3
1966	6,681,497	6,741,626	31.4	24.7	65.2	64.7	2.9	10.0	0.4	0.6
1961	6,052,802	5,993,523	29.9	23.0	66.4	66.8	3.3	9.7	0.4	0.5
1956	5,488,060	5,367,521	30.8	23.6	65.4	66.3	3.5	9.6	0.3	0.4
1951	4,920,815	4,837,897	32.1	25.7	63.8	64.5	3.8	9.4	0.3	0.4
1941	4,281,237	4,026,867	39.8	33.0	56.1	58.0	4.0	9.8	0.2	0.2
1931	3,715,527	3,379,504	41.0	34.0	54.9	57.3	4.0	8.5	0.1	0.1
1921(c)	3,004,173	1,875,898	39.2	32.0	56.7	59.2	4.0	8.6	0.1	0.1
1911	2,619,818	2,210,306	45.1	34.8	51.4	56.9	3.4	8.2	0.1	0.1
1901	1,816,139	1,708,593	44.8	38.2	51.1	52.9	4.1	8.8	(d)	(d)
Newfoundland										
1971	166,750	160,765	34.6	27.0	62.6	64.3	2.7	8.4	0.2	0.3
1966	150,535	143,778	35.1	27.5	61.6	63.8	3.2	8.6	(d)	0.1
1961	137,647	128,645	34.4	25.6	61.9	65.7	3.6	8.7	(d)	(d)
1956	128,719	117,445	34.7	25.4	61.4	65.5	3.8	9.1	(d)	(d)
1951	113,333	106,693	34.6	24.4	61.0	64.9	4.4	9.7	(d)	(d)
Prince Edward Island										
1971	38,155	38,080	35.7	26.9	60.4	60.5	3.4	12.1	0.6	0.6
1966	35,806	35,096	36.3	26.7	59.7	61.3	3.8	11.8	0.1	0.2
1961	34,239	32,689	35.5	25.0	60.5	63.3	3.8	11.5	0.1	0.2
1956	32,764	31,887	35.6	26.1	59.6	62.2	4.7	11.5	0.1	0.2
1951	33,433	32,131	37.1	27.4	58.0	61.2	4.8	11.3	0.1	0.1
1941	34,649	31,725	44.0	33.6	51.5	55.6	4.5	10.7	(d)	(d)
1931	31,116	28,811	43.5	33.9	51.1	54.5	5.4	11.6	(d)	(d)
1921	30,202	29,620	42.9	35.8	51.9	52.8	5.1	11.3	(d)	(d)
1911	31,365	31,736	46.3	41.8	48.8	47.8	4.8	10.4	(d)	(d)
1901	33,187	33,598	48.5	43.7	47.2	46.6	4.4	9.7	(d)	(d)
Nova Scotia										
1971	273,085	275,115	32.9	25.1	63.2	62.6	3.1	11.3	0.8	1.0
1966	250,249	251,236	32.8	25.2	63.3	62.9	3.4	11.4	0.4	0.5
1961	243,047	237,632	32.6	23.9	63.4	64.8	3.7	10.9	0.3	0.4
1956	232,938	226,208	33.0	24.4	62.7	64.4	4.0	11.0	0.3	0.3
1951	218,251	214,846	34.1	25.8	61.4	62.8	4.3	11.1	0.2	0.3
1941	210,303	198,819	41.7	32.9	53.7	56.2	4.5	10.8	0.1	0.1
1931	178,426	167,421	42.3	33.3	52.8	55.4	4.8	11.2	0.1	0.1
1921	176,203	170,048	41.2	33.9	53.9	55.0	4.8	11.0	0.1	0.1
1911	166,773	159,454	43.7	36.6	52.1	53.0	4.2	10.4	(d)	(d)
1901	154,680	149,468	46.0	38.7	49.7	50.6	4.3	10.6	(d)	(d)
New Brunswick										
1971	215,110	216,345	33.8	26.8	62.8	62.1	2.8	10.3	0.7	0.8
1966	196,470	198,256	33.8	27.1	62.7	62.2	3.2	10.2	0.3	0.4
1961	186,341	184,408	32.3	25.4	64.0	64.4	3.5	9.8	0.3	0.4
1956	175,118	174,227	32.6	26.5	63.4	63.6	3.8	9.6	0.3	0.4
1951	165,553	166,230	32.9	27.0	62.9	65.2	4.0	9.5	0.2	0.3
1941	160,627	150,983	42.0	33.9	53.7	56.7	4.2	9.3	0.1	0.1
1931	135,339	128,160	41.5	34.3	53.6	56.0	4.8	9.7	0.1	0.1
1921	126,727	121,470	40.2	33.5	55.1	56.8	4.7	9.6	0.1	0.1
1911	116,544	110,755	42.8	36.2	52.8	54.3	4.3	9.4	0.1	0.1
1901	108,474	104,868	44.9	38.5	50.5	51.8	4.4	9.7	(d)	(d)

| | Population(b) 15 years and over | | Single | | Proportion Married | | Widowed | | Divorced | |
	Male	Female	M	F	M	F	M	F	M	F
Quebec										
1971	2,082,025	2,160,210	35.0	30.7	62.2	60.1	2.4	8.5	0.5	0.7
1966	1,890,915	1,946,357	35.2	31.2	61.9	60.3	2.8	8.4	0.1	0.2
1961	1,680,630	1,715,186	33.9	30.2	62.9	61.6	3.2	8.0	0.1	0.2
1956	1,492,531	1,514,261	34.7	31.1	61.9	60.8	3.4	8.0	0.1	0.1
1951	1,326,263	1,363,310	35.7	33.2	60.5	58.8	3.7	7.9	0.1	0.1
1941	1,136,897	1,132,172	43.2	40.2	52.7	52.2	4.1	7.6	(d)	0.1
1931	933,331	918,506	42.5	40.1	53.0	52.1	4.5	7.7	(d)	(d)
1921	730,024	730,849	39.5	37.2	55.9	54.8	4.5	7.9	0.1	0.1
1911	626,201	607,921	40.5	36.9	55.2	55.3	4.2	7.7	0.1	0.1
1901	503,590	507,168	40.5	37.9	55.1	53.9	4.4	8.2	(d)	(d)
Ontario										
1971	2,709,805	2,784,795	29.2	22.6	67.2	65.5	2.5	10.4	1.0	1.5
1966	2,351,298	2,405,497	28.4	21.6	68.3	67.0	2.9	10.8	0.4	0.7
1961	2,106,048	2,122,295	26.4	19.6	69.9	69.3	3.3	10.5	0.4	0.6
1956	1,895,622	1,890,886	27.3	20.2	68.8	68.7	3.6	10.6	0.3	0.5
1951	1,680,363	1,677,865	29.0	22.5	66.9	66.5	3.8	10.6	0.3	0.5
1941	1,452,190	1,411,222	36.1	29.8	59.6	59.9	4.2	10.1	0.2	0.2
1931	1,262,289	1,210,401	37.8	32.0	58.0	58.1	4.1	9.8	0.1	0.1
1921	1,033,669	1,014,566	36.9	31.9	58.8	58.2	4.2	9.8	0.1	0.1
1911	925,168	860,886	42.4	36.0	53.9	54.7	3.7	9.2	0.1	0.1
1901	749,117	748,599	44.1	39.4	51.8	51.3	4.1	9.3	(d)	(d)
Manitoba										
1971	348,430	353,020	31.4	23.4	64.8	64.1	2.8	11.2	1.0	1.3
1966	327,227	328,660	31.3	23.1	65.1	65.0	3.2	11.3	0.4	0.6
1961	315,107	306,473	29.9	21.1	66.4	68.0	3.4	10.4	0.4	0.5
1956	297,416	288,281	30.0	21.6	66.0	67.9	3.7	10.0	0.3	0.5
1951	280,919	272,908	31.3	23.8	64.7	66.4	3.7	9.3	0.3	0.5
1941	280,978	257,787	40.2	32.0	56.0	59.7	3.7	8.0	0.2	0.3
1931	257,114	224,184	42.9	34.1	53.6	58.5	3.4	7.3	0.1	0.1
1921	207,105	178,903	40.0	29.3	56.8	63.7	3.1	6.9	0.1	0.2
1911	172,533	130,013	47.9	32.4	49.7	61.7	2.3	5.8	0.1	0.1
1901	88,858	68,526	48.7	33.4	48.3	60.8	3.1	5.8	(d)	(d)
Saskatchewan										
1971	327,575	318,235	32.4	22.3	63.9	65.5	3.0	11.3	0.8	0.9
1966	324,891	309,504	32.2	21.5	64.2	67.3	3.2	10.7	0.3	0.4
1961	318,314	291,953	31.7	20.0	64.6	69.9	3.5	9.8	0.3	0.3
1956	311,928	281,967	32.6	21.0	63.6	69.7	3.6	9.0	0.2	0.3
1951	304,326	272,150	34.6	23.1	61.6	68.3	3.6	8.3	0.2	0.3
1941	341,337	286,579	43.1	31.3	53.4	62.0	3.4	6.6	0.1	0.1
1931	334,479	260,806	44.8	31.1	52.1	63.2	3.0	5.7	0.1	0.1
1921	260,954	195,661	42.4	24.8	54.6	69.7	2.9	5.4	0.1	0.1
1911	206,257	118,479	53.0	25.6	44.8	69.7	2.1	4.7	0.1	0.1
1901	31,470	24,190	45.7	28.0	51.1	65.4	3.2	6.6	(d)	(d)
Alberta										
1971	564,685	548,690	30.6	21.9	65.4	67.1	2.3	8.8	1.6	2.2
1966	484,502	467,935	30.5	21.0	66.1	68.7	2.7	9.3	0.7	1.0
1961	448,820	413,800	29.8	18.7	66.6	71.8	2.9	8.7	0.6	0.8
1956	394,845	355,436	31.4	19.6	65.1	71.3	3.1	8.5	0.4	0.6
1951	346,247	306,448	33.7	21.7	62.6	69.6	3.3	8.1	0.4	0.6
1941	310,860	256,857	41.2	28.6	55.1	64.2	3.4	7.0	0.3	0.3
1931	279,370	213,257	43.6	29.0	53.0	64.6	3.2	6.2	0.2	0.2
1921	215,591	159,141	42.3	24.5	54.4	69.3	3.1	6.0	0.2	0.2
1911	161,733	91,572	53.7	26.3	44.1	68.6	2.1	4.9	0.1	0.1
1901	26,425	18,094	47.6	25.9	49.7	68.0	2.6	6.0	(d)	(d)

	Population(b) 15 years and over		Single		Proportion Married		Widowed		Divorced	
	Male	Female	M	F	M	F	M	F	M	F
British Columbia										
1971	789,070	785,570	29.1	20.9	66.3	66.1	2.6	10.6	2.0	2.5
1966	655,215	644,189	29.2	19.9	66.6	67.4	3.2	11.3	1.0	1.4
1961	569,041	550,898	26.9	17.8	68.5	69.9	3.6	11.2	0.9	1.2
1956	513,580	479,019	28.3	17.6	67.2	70.2	3.8	11.1	0.7	1.0
1951	441,951	418,872	28.0	19.2	67.3	69.1	4.0	10.7	0.7	1.1
1941	346,364	296,364	36.5	26.5	59.0	63.0	4.0	9.9	0.5	0.6
1931	298,599	224,487	40.0	28.7	56.2	62.2	3.6	8.8	0.3	0.3
1921	218,180	156,944	38.8	25.5	57.7	66.0	3.3	8.2	0.3	0.3
1911	205,240	95,986	56.6	28.2	41.3	65.0	2.1	6.6	0.1	0.2
1901	91,210	42,951	57.2	32.0	39.9	60.7	2.8	7.2	0.1	0.1
Yukon and Northwest Territories(e)										
1971	17,210	14,675	35.4	25.6	61.1	69.0	2.1	4.3	1.5	1.2
1966	14,389	11,118	39.7	25.1	56.9	68.0	2.6	6.1	0.8	0.9
1961	13,570	9,544	40.0	22.3	53.7	71.0	3.7	5.9	0.8	0.8
1956	12,599	7,904	45.3	23.2	51.2	70.2	2.9	6.0	0.6	0.7
1951	10,176	6,444	43.8	20.9	51.7	70.7	3.8	8.0	0.7	0.5
1941	7,032	4,359	45.8	19.5	49.3	70.1	4.6	10.3	0.3	0.1
1931	5,465	3,471	43.8	18.0	50.2	70.0	5.6	9.3	0.4	0.2
1921	5,033	3,264	47.5	20.7	46.7	64.6	5.3	14.5	0.5	0.2
1911	8,004	3,504	58.8	20.3	37.1	68.5	3.7	10.5	0.5	0.7
1901	29,428	11,131	70.1	43.7	27.0	50.1	2.5	6.1	0.1	0.1

(a) Excludes Newfoundland prior to 1951.
(b) Represents all population minus singles of under 15 years of age.
(c) Includes the 485 members of the Royal Canadian Navy.
(d) Less than 0.05 per cent.
(e) Combined.

Sources: 1971 Census of Canada, Population by Marital Status and by
Sex, Advance Bulletin AP-6, table 1; 1966 Census of Canada
Bull. 5-401, tables XIX, 7; Statistics Canada, Census Division
Demographic and Social Characteristics Section, "Population
by Marital Status and Sex, Canada and Provinces, 1971"
(informal release).

TABLE H-5 MARRIAGES, (NUMBERS AND RATES) AND DIVORCES,(NUMBERS AND RATES) PER 1,000 MARRIAGES, FOR CANADA, AT FIVE YEAR INTERVALS SINCE 1901, AND MARRIAGE AND DIVORCE RATES FOR PROVINCES, FOR SELECTED YEARS SINCE 1951

| | MARRIAGES | | DIVORCES | |
	No.	Rate/1000 Population	No.	Rate/1000 Marriages
Canada(a)				
1971	189,240	8.7	29,626	156.6
1970	188,428	8.8	29,063	154.2
1969	182,186	8.7	26,079	143.1
1968	171,766	8.3	11,343	66.0
1967	165,879	8.1	11,165	67.3
1966	155,596	7.8	10,239	65.8
1961	128,475	7.0	6,563	51.1
1956	132,713	8.3	6,002	45.2
1951	128,408	9.2	5,270	41.0
1946	137,398	10.9	7,757	56.5
1941	124,644	10.6	2,462	19.8
1936	82,941	7.4	1,570	18.9
1931	68,239	6.4	700	10.3
1926	68,378	7.0	608	8.9
1921	71,254	7.9	558	7.8
1916	64,000(b)	8.0	-	-
1911	63,000(b)	8.6	-	-
1906	47,000(b)	7.5	-	-
1901	38,000(b)	6.9	-	-

(a) Excludes Newfoundland prior to 1950, Yukon and Northwest Territories for 1921-46.

		1971(c)	1970	1969	Rates 1968	1967	1966	1961	1951
Nfld.	M(d)	9.0	8.6	8.3	8.4	8.0	7.6	7.2	7.0
	D(d)	32.0	31.1	24.1	3.5	2.7	3.0	6.0(e)	4 0(e)
PEI	M	8.6	8.3	7.9	6.8	7.4	6.9	6.0	5.9
	D	61.4	71.2	117.5	26.7	22.4	23.9	8.0(e)	10 0(e)
N.S.	M	8.7	8.9	8.6	8.3	8.2	7.7	7.2	7.9
	D	104.8	114.1	120.4	79.1	63.7	69.6	46.3	36.7
N.B.	M	9.7	9.1	9.1	8.6	8.8	8.4	7.5	8.5
	D	78.5	66.4	64.2	26.5	53.6	30.0	43.1	35.6
Que.	M	8.2	8.2	7.9	7.8	7.9	7.7	6.8	8.8
	D	104.5	97.5	61.6	13.2	15.7	22.2	9.7	8.1
Ont.	M	9.0	9.0	9.0	8.5	8.2	7.8	7.1	9.8
	D	175.2	173.2	176.4	81.1	74.5	75.1	61.6	46.7
Man.	M	9.2	9.2	9.1	8.5	8.2	7.6	7.1	9.5
	D	150.1	136.1	150.2	56.1	60.1	71.7	47.9	49.0
Sask.	M	8.4	7.8	8.0	8.1	7.9	7.3	6.6	8.2
	D	104.1	115.9	114.8	49.6	52.6	45.9	40.8	33.2
Alta.	M	9.6	9.6	9.5	8.9	8.7	8.1	7.9	9.9
	D	223.9	245.1	231.5	140.5	134.5	131.9	99.2	63.3
B.C.	M	9.3	9.4	8.8	8.4	8.2	7.8	6.7	9.7
	D	242.4	252.7	231.0	131.3	170.6	144.5	127.4	118.8

(b) Estimates
(c) Preliminary
(d) Marriages per 1000 Population; Divorces per 1000 Marriages.
(e) Absolute numbers.

Sources: Vital Statistics 1971: Preliminary Annual Report, tables 11,15.
Vital Statistics 1970, tables M1, M10; Urquhart and Buckley,
Historical Statistics for Canada, Series B75-81, B82-91.

TABLE H-6 MEDIAN AGE AT FIRST MARRIAGE BY SEX, FOR CANADA AND PROVINCES, FOR SELECTED YEARS SINCE 1940

Years

	1970		1968		1966		1961		1956		1951		1946		1940	
	M	F	M	F	M	F	M	F	M	F	M	F	M	F	M	F
Canada	23.5	21.4	23.5	21.3	23.7	21.2	24.0	21.1	24.5	21.6	24.8	22.0	25.4	22.5	26.4	23.2
Nfld.	23.0	20.7	22.8	20.6	23.2	20.5	23.6	20.4	23.9	20.8	24.4	21.3	-	-	-	-
P.E.I.	23.2	21.3	23.1	20.8	23.4	20.7	23.3	20.7	24.3	21.1	25.1	21.6	26.0	22.6	26.2	22.7
N.S.	22.8	21.2	23.0	21.0	23.2	20.9	23.3	20.5	23.8	21.0	24.8	21.6	25.2	22.0	25.9	22.6
N.B.	23.0	20.9	22.8	20.7	23.0	20.5	23.3	21.8	23.9	20.8	24.4	21.0	25.0	21.7	25.9	22.3
Que.	24.0	22.1	24.0	21.9	24.1	21.9	24.6	21.8	25.0	22.4	25.1	22.6	25.8	23.1	26.8	23.9
Ont.	23.4	21.3	23.3	21.2	23.5	20.9	23.8	21.0	24.3	21.5	24.4	21.9	24.9	22.2	26.0	23.0
Man.	23.3	21.1	23.3	21.0	23.6	21.0	23.9	20.9	24.4	21.4	25.0	21.9	25.8	22.6	26.6	23.1
Sask.	22.9	20.6	22.9	20.6	23.4	20.6	23.9	20.7	24.7	21.2	25.2	21.7	25.9	22.3	26.5	22.4
Alta.	23.0	20.8	23.2	20.8	23.5	20.7	24.0	20.7	24.5	21.2	24.8	21.6	25.7	22.0	26.5	22.4
B.C.	23.4	21.1	23.6	21.1	23.7	21.0	24.2	21.0	24.6	21.5	24.9	22.1	25.6	22.7	26.8	23.4
Yukon	23.9	20.6	24.1	21.9	25.5	21.2	26.6	22.4	26.4	22.7	24.7	22.8	-	-	-	-
N.W.T.	23.0	20.5	24.5	21.0	23.5	20.1	24.3	20.9	23.7	20.7	23.2	19.4	-	-	-	-

Note: Data not available for years prior to 1940.

Sources: Vital Statistics, 1970, table M4
         Vital Statistics, 1968, table M3

TABLE H-7 AVERAGE AGE AT FIRST MARRIAGE, BY MARITAL STATUS AND EDUCATION, FOR WOMEN BORN BETWEEN 1911 and 1916, BY PLACE OF RESIDENCE, FOR CANADA IN 1961

Marital Status and Education	Place of Residence: Metropolitan Areas City	Metropolitan Areas Suburbs	Cities of 5,000-29,999	Rural Nonfarm	Rural Farm
Married					
Husband Present					
Elementary	24.1	24.0	23.0	23.7	22.5
Secondary	25.3	25.0	24.5	24.0	23.9
Some University	26.6	26.5	27.1	26.2	26.3
University	27.4	27.3	27.9	28.2	27.2
Husband Absent					
Elementary	22.6	22.4	21.5	21.9	22.2
Secondary	24.0	23.9	23.3	23.1	22.4
Some University	24.9	25.5	-	-	-
University	28.0	25.8	-	-	-
Widowed					
Elementary	22.7	23.0	21.7	21.7	21.7
Secondary	24.0	23.9	23.2	23.9	23.0
Some University	24.6	27.9	-	-	-
University	25.3	25.3	-	-	-
Divorced					
Elementary	22.2	21.2	22.9	18.4	18.4
Secondary	22.9	22.5	22.4	21.9	26.4
Some University	25.9	24.0	-	-	-
University	25.4	21.7	-	-	-

Note: Tabulation from the 1961 Census.

Source: J. Henripin, Tendances et Facteurs, 1961 Census Monograph (Ottawa: Queen's Printer, 1968), table 5.7.

TABLE H-8 PROPORTION OF POPULATION IN INCOME GROUPS BY MARITAL STATUS AND SEX, FOR CANADA IN 1970

Income	Single		Married		Widowed Divorced(a)		Unstated(b)	
	M	F	M	F	M	F	M	F
	1,374,235	890,689	3,902,483	1,617,912	219,583	433,072	276,203	167,889
	100.0	100.0	100.0	100.0	100.0	100.0	100.0	100.0
Less than $2,500	44.7	42.2	12.3	42.6	27.4	35.1	25.2	45.7
2,500-5,000	27.0	33.8	18.4	35.4	24.5	36.0	20.0	34.9
5,000-7,000	15.2	14.1	20.3	13.7	16.9	15.6	19.0	12.8
7,000-10,000	9.8	6.9	27.3	6.4	18.1	8.8	22.5	4.9
10,000-15,000	2.7	2.4	15.2	1.5	9.3	3.1	10.3	1.3
15,000-20,000	0.5	0.4	3.5	0.3	2.0	0.8	1.9	0.3
20,000-25,000	0.1	0.1	1.2	0.1	0.8	0.3	0.6	0.1
25,000 and over	0.1	0.1	1.7	0.1	1.1	0.5	0.7	0.1

Note: The population proportions are calculated from an expanded stratified random sample of individual income tax returns for the taxable year of 1970. Marital status is listed as reported in the T1 Short Form even though the respondents were taxed as single or married, depending on the taxation criteria.

(a) Includes separated.
(b) Marital status not reported on the T1 Short Form.

Source: Department of National Revenue, Taxation: Taxation Statistics, 1972 (Ottawa: Information Canada, 1972), table 7B.

TABLE H-9 PATTERNS OF EXPENDITURE OF FAMILIES AND UNATTACHED INDIVIDUALS FOR CANADA AND PROVINCES 1969

	Canada	Nfld.	P.E.I.	N.S.	N.B.	Que.	Ont.	Man.	Sask.	Alta.	B.C.
				Family Characteristics							
Number of families in sample	15,140	1,012	269	1,419	986	2,959	3,469	969	1,108	1,480	1,469
Estimated no. of families in population	5,881,821	110,650	27,183	204,522	151,437	1,546,385	2,197,856	281,715	282,294	444,491	635,288
				Average							
Family size	3.28	4.18	3.65	3.44	3.75	3.54	3.18	3.13	3.01	3.12	2.93
No. of children under 5	.30	.56	.31	.36	.39	.31	.29	.29	.28	.31	.27
No. of children 5-15	.83	1.26	1.04	.90	1.04	.94	.78	.76	.74	.79	.68
No. of adults 16-17	.13	.17	.15	.14	.16	.14	.11	.13	.12	.13	.11
No. of adults 18-64	1.79	2.00	1.75	1.77	1.85	1.94	1.77	1.67	1.57	1.72	1.62
No. of adults 65 and over	.28	.26	.47	.34	.36	.25	.27	.34	.33	.23	.31
No. of full-time earners	.80	.63	.63	.75	.72	.82	.87	.75	.72	.82	.67
Age of head	47.2	45.5	51.3	48.5	48.6	46.4	46.8	49.0	50.3	46.2	48.4
Net Income before taxes ($)	8,026.5	5,701.7	5,530.8	6,389.6	6,282.8	7,789.6	8,987.5	7,244.3	5,994.0	7,916.4	8,059.4
Other money receipts ($)	195.7	124.5	68.8	180.8	83.0	146.0	221.3	193.5	215.2	212.7	257.5
Net change in assets and liabilities ($)	137.7	99.4	-112.9	17.1	-53.9	41.4	211.3	219.1	19.3	51.9	296.3
				Percentage							
Homeowners	58.1	73.4	68.9	65.4	65.1	44.5	61.7	64.2	69.1	63.5	60.1
Car and Truck Owners	71.5	55.5	69.1	69.4	69.0	63.3	74.6	75.5	75.3	77.8	76.6
With head Canadian-born	75.4	93.0	95.1	93.4	95.7	88.4	67.4	73.2	74.4	68.4	62.8
With wife employed full-time	10.0	7.9	10.0	9.2	9.0	8.2	12.6	7.8	7.9	11.7	7.4

Note: These calculations are based on a 1970 sample of 15,140 families and unattached individuals in all areas of Canada, both rural and urban, excluding Yukon and Northwest Territories.

107

TABLE H-9 continued

	Canada	Nfld.	P.E.I.	N.S.	N.B.	Que.	Ont.	Man.	Sask.	Alta.	B.C.
				Percentage Distribution							
Total Expenditure ($)	100.0 8,161.1	100.0 5,792.0	100.0 5,784.3	100.0 6,623.8	100.0 6,510.9	100.0 7,937.7	100.0 9,112.2	100.0 7,281.9	100.0 6,208.2	100.0 8,185.2	100.0 8,058.8
Food	18.7	25.8	23.1	21.2	21.9	20.9	17.3	18.8	19.0	16.8	17.6
Shelter	15.2	13.1	14.9	14.9	13.7	15.1	15.5	14.6	15.6	14.7	15.5
Household Operation	4.1	4.0	4.7	4.4	4.3	4.0	4.2	3.6	3.9	4.0	4.1
Furnishings and equipment	4.6	4.6	3.7	4.2	3.9	4.1	4.7	4.2	4.7	5.1	5.0
Clothing	8.1	10.6	9.2	8.4	9.1	8.9	7.8	8.1	7.9	8.2	7.1
Personal Care	2.1	2.0	2.3	2.2	2.4	2.2	2.2	2.0	2.0	2.0	1.9
Medical and Health Care	3.4	1.7	3.4	2.3	3.3	3.5	3.6	3.4	3.4	3.1	2.9
Smoking and Alcoholic beverages	3.8	5.1	4.3	4.1	3.8	4.5	3.5	3.6	3.6	3.0	3.5
Travel and Transportation	13.1	11.9	13.8	14.4	14.8	12.1	13.0	13.7	13.6	14.3	13.9
Recreation	3.4	3.0	2.9	3.1	2.7	2.8	3.6	3.6	3.4	4.0	4.1
Reading	.6	.4	.6	.6	.5	.7	.6	.6	1.0	.6	.7
Education	.9	1.1	1.0	.8	.6	.8	.8	1.1	1.5	1.2	.9
Miscellaneous expenses	1.6	1.2	1.5	1.5	1.5	1.5	1.5	1.6		1.8	1.9
Total Current Consumption	79.5	84.6	85.4	82.0	82.5	81.1	78.2	78.7	80.0	78.8	79.0
Personal Taxes	13.5	9.3	8.1	10.3	10.0	12.7	14.6	13.7	11.8	13.7	14.0
Security	4.3	3.4	3.7	4.8	4.6	4.3	4.3	4.6	4.5	4.5	4.2
Gifts and Contributions	2.7	2.6	2.9	2.8	2.9	2.0	2.9	3.1	3.7	3.0	2.8

Source: Statistics Canada Daily (January 28, 1972), pp. 2,3,5.

BIBLIOGRAPHY

A number of bibliographic references listed under "Fertility" contain data and interpretation applicable to this section.

Carisse, C., "Fécondité et Famille au Canada Francais", Revue de l'Institut de Sociologie (Brussels) 1 (1968): 53-66.

Dominion Bureau of Statistics/Statistics Canada, Incomes of Nonfarm Families and Individuals in Canada, Selected Years 1951-1965. Ottawa: Queen's Printer, 1969. (92 pp.)

_____, Socio-Economic Characteristics of the Population Aged 14-24, 1967. Ottawa: Information Canada, 1972. (67 pp.)

_____, Household Facilities by Income and Other Characteristics 1968. Ottawa: Information Canada, 1972. (180 pp.)

_____, Family Incomes (Census Families), 1969. Ottawa: Information Canada, 1972. (24 pp.)

Illing, W.M., Population, Family Household and Labour Force Growth to 1980. Staff Study No. 19. Ottawa: Economic Council of Canada, 1967. (101 pp.)

Ivison, C., Trends in Marriage and Illegitimacy: A Comparative Study of Canada, the Provinces, and the Economic Regions of Ontario. Demography and Educational Planning. Edited by B. MacLeod. Toronto: Ontario Institute for Studies in Education, 1970, pp. 183-204.

Newcombe, H.B., and Smith, M.E., "Changing Patterns of Family Growth: The Value of Linked Vital Records as a Source of Data", Population Studies 24 (1970): 193-203

Pelletier, A.S., Thompson, F.D., and Rochon, A., The Canadian Family. 1931 Census Monograph. Seventh Census of Canada, 1931. Vol. X. Ottawa: King's Printer, 1942, pp.3-214.

Schlesinger, B., and MacRae, A., "Remarriages in Canada: Statistical Trends", Journal of Marriage and the Family 32 (1970): 300-303.

EDUCATION

From among the social institutions to which sociologists pay their customary attention, education is perhaps the most descriptive of social structure. The educational process streamlines and socializes the population in several ways: first, a good proportion of children and young adults are kept at routine tasks in school; second, they are exposed to a fairly standardized set of information and training and mental discipline; third, the students are rated by some agreed-upon academic performance criteria; and, finally, the students are effectively grouped into broad categories with prespecified life chances. In all these instances, the school experience usually precedes a job experience, and from the latter a smaller and smaller proportion of the adult population is now exempt.

Even a summary tabulation of a population in school will suggest, over time, the magnitude of the social change which has taken place. The proportion of the Canadian population aged five to twenty-four attending school has about doubled since 1911 (see table E-1). This increase reflects first the increase in secondary-school enrollment and, more recently, in post-secondary school enrollment, the latter accounting for the renewed edge of males over females at school.

The sex difference in school attendance shows interesting variations across the provinces. Earlier in this century, a balance of the sexes prevailed for the provinces east of Manitoba but in schools west of Ontario, more females than males remained in school, a feature even now of the farm populations and of lower income groups across North America. An explanation for this lies in the job market conditions: boys were encouraged to get "a job" and lack of schooling did not matter; in recent decades, however, young women can get work easily with only a secondary-school education. This may be due to the rapid expansion of the white-collar service jobs which are sometimes defined as temporary either by the primarily female job seekers or the employers or both.

The customary age for attendance at the elementary grades is five through thirteen years. In view of the fact that not all five-year-olds are at school and that some children older than thirteen are still in elementary grades, and that the number of those enrolled in elementary schools has exceeded the number of five-to-thirteen year olds for the last decade or so, two conclusions can be drawn: (1) elementary education has become universal in this country; and (2) some pupils repeat one or two grades (see table E-2).

The very rapid increase in secondary-school enrollment is the most remarkable and the most significant change in Canadian education. The enrollment in the postsecondary schools and in the universities, of course, has been increasing at an extremely fast rate, but the numbers involved in secondary schooling and their proportion in the appropriate age group (fourteen to seventeen years) indicate that before long secondary as well as elementary education will be universal. This universality is partly due to the effect of compulsory school attendance, in general up to the sixteenth birthday, and partly due to the labour-market conditions, which seem to offer the young very few provisions for apprenticeship. Furthermore, the institutionalization of school attendance may very well account for the voluntary extension of one's stay at school, even though the motivation to learn may not always be demonstrable.

Chart 6. Funds for Providing Instruction, Sources and Expenditures Canada 1972-73

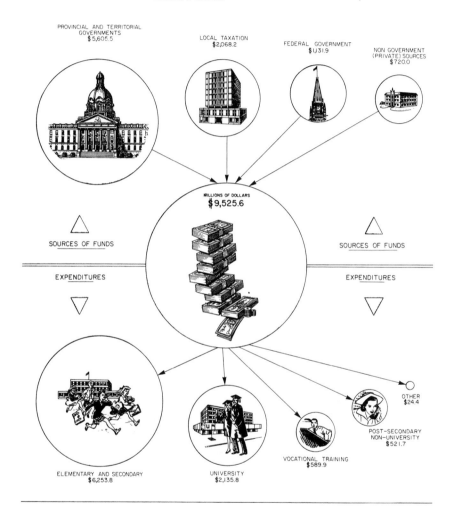

MILLIONS OF DOLLARS

PROVINCIAL AND TERRITORIAL
GOVERNMENTS
$5,605.5

LOCAL TAXATION
$2,068.2

FEDERAL GOVERNMENT
$1,131.9

NON GOVERNMENT
(PRIVATE) SOURCES
$720.0

MILLIONS OF DOLLARS
$9,525.6

SOURCES OF FUNDS

SOURCES OF FUNDS

EXPENDITURES

EXPENDITURES

ELEMENTARY AND SECONDARY
$6,253.8

UNIVERSITY
$2,135.8

VOCATIONAL TRAINING
$589.9

POST-SECONDARY
NON-UNIVERSITY
$521.7

OTHER
$24.4

Source: Statistics Canada. Advance Statistics of Education 1972-73. Ottawa:
Information Canada. 1973. Chart 2, page 23.

111

The opening of C.E.G.E.P. (Colleges d'enseignement général et professionel) explains Quebec's lead, even though temporary, in the proportion of eighteen-to twenty-four-year olds at school Such a development was not really predictable from the economic infrastructure of the province and requires an explanation. The language and other cultural self-identification does not encourage out-migration and thus it is quite possible to understand the politicization of the young, whose education may be ample enough to redefine traditional thinking while not specialized enough to fit into the occupational structure. The power of the traditional value system is perhaps most evident in the preponderance of the general programmes (for an eventual transfer to universities) over the technical programmes, by a factor of 1.3 (as of fall 1970) for all students. For male students the factor is 1.5. When it comes to graduating from the two streams of postsecondary institutions, the general programmes produce over twice as many graduates as the technical programmes. In comparison, the enrollments in Ontario C.A.A.T.s (Colleges of Applied Arts and Technology) are predominantly (over 70 per cent) male, technically oriented and producing close to three times as many technical-stream graduates as C.E.G.E.P.s. Of course, Ontario's capacity to absorb technical graduates easily exceeds Quebec's.

All in all, Ontario retains its lead in Canadian postsecondary education by having the highest number of undergraduate and of graduate students. During the academic year 1971-72, 41 and 45 per cent of all undergraduate and graduate students in Canada were enrolled in Ontario universities and colleges (see table E-3). For Canada as a whole, the increase in the number of undergraduate students in the last fifty years has been about elevenfold. Graduate students have increased by a factor of about 85 during the same period. During those fifty years, the ratio of undergraduate to graduate students has changed from 54 to 1 to about 7 to 1, reflecting a remake of the Canadian university to parallel the American model rather closely.

Two qualitative changes in the composition of the undergraduate enrollment by faculties (see table E-4) reflect an alteration in societal needs on one hand and the prevailing power of interest groups on the other. In the first place, the proportion of undergraduate majors in arts and sciences as well as in education has increased substantially, no doubt to man the rapidly expanding secondary-school teaching positions and to accommodate an increasing number of women students, who usually study in the sex-typed "gentle" disciplines, like languages and fine arts. In the second place, the diminished proportion of students in the traditional faculties of medicine, law and theology cannot but imply some self-imposed strictures on admissions on the part of medicine and law faculties, the attrition in theology being more likely a case of disinterest.

The number of postsecondary degrees received by men and women documents the role sex has played in Canadian postsecondary, especially university, education. Some fifty years ago, one in five recipients of Bachelor of Arts degrees was a woman, a ratio which held until about twenty years ago. Only very recently are women approaching an equal share in university first degrees (see table E-5). When it comes to graduate training, the proportion of women receiving a Master of Arts degree (or equivalent) still remains close to a 1 to 5 ratio. The ratio increased during the 1950s, a decade which combined an enthusiasm for motherhood with a promise of prosperity in a suburban environment. The share of women receiving doctorates has remained fairly negligible throughout the history of Canadian graduate education, making

women's liberation demands for parity of representation on
Canadian faculties somewhat unreasonable and the present rank and
salary difference between the sexes explainable.

Another feature of Canadian university enrollment is the
increased visibility of foreign students on the campuses across the
country, mostly due to featured coverage by the mass media. One
factor which may very well account for this visibility is the fact
that close to 30 per cent of all graduate students are foreign
students, making their support from Canadian taxes quite a salient
issue. On the other hand, the proportion of foreign students among
all university students in Canada has been stabilized very closely
around 6 per cent for the past fifty years (see table E-6).
Considering citizenship alone, close to 90 per cent of full-time
university students were Canadian citizens during the 1968-69 academic
year. As a matter of fact, about the same number of Canadians
study abroad as foreigners study in Canada, which appears a fair
exchange in terms of tax support and tax benefits. Interestingly
enough, about three times as many Canadians study in the United
States as Americans study in Canada, the supposed disaffection of
American youth with their government and the supposed affection of
Canadian youth for their nation notwithstanding. The American
tradition on Canadian campuses has had a long history; for instance,
during the depression years 75 per cent of the foreign students in
Canada were Americans and there were more of them in Canada than
Canadian students in the United States.

Over the past twenty years, rapidly expanding Canadian
universities have had to depend on recruiting a large number of
professors from abroad. This accounts for the present situation
in the universities and colleges, where in 1971, only 62 per cent
of all teaching and administrative posts were held by Canadians.
Fifteen per cent were held by American citizens and 10 per cent
were held by British citizens. The issue of citizenship of professors
in Canada tends to be more perplexing than in other countries,
where foreign-born or foreign-trained academics are bona fide
immigrants seeking citizenship in the host country.

The social background of Canadian university students is
often a subject of concern to taxpayers. No doubt the Canadian
student ranks during the past decade and a half have included
children of social classes which previous to that time had not
taken part in postsecondary, particularly university, education.
Referring to a sample survey undertaken in 1969 (see table E-8),
we notice that about one-half of all students have fathers in
executive and professional occupations. These occupations,
however, do not amount to more than one-quarter of all the labout
force. Statistically, there will be more students in the sample
whose father had a large family and a high income than there will
be students whose father had a small family and a moderate income.
Discounting this sampling bias, there are still more students at
universities who come from a socially advantaged background than
would be their due in the working of a randomly distributive
justice. As a rule of thumb, one may assume that students in law,
medicine and arts come from families with a higher socioeconomic
status than do students enrolled in a variety of "applied"
faculties, including education and engineering. Women, especially
in arts, are more likely to be from privileged homes than their
male classmates.

The already referred-to survey shows another interesting
finding. Those students who report their father working for an
employer fall into two distinct groups. On the one hand, the
students who define their social background by classifying their

113

fathers in "labouring" occupations represent a higher proportion of all students than those who classify their fathers in clerical or service or other semiskilled occupations. In view of the fact that the census classification of "labourers" represents but a small fraction of the labour force, one may wonder whether this designation of one's social background does not reflect more some fashionable "ism" and an exaggerated class consciousness than an "objective" situation. Curiously enough, in Quebec, where the C.E.G.E.P. were established to draw from the working classes, the "labouring" designation of the father's occupation is the least frequent, whereas east of that province, it is quite strong. Were one to surmise that geographical or perceived marginality is conducive to political polarization, then the survey findings become understandable. On the other hand, political polarization in Quebec, however strong it may be, is more likely along language lines than along social-class lines.

A good number of the graduates of Canadian universities return to classrooms to teach the six million or so pupils in the schools throughout the country. In the last twenty years, the number of elementary and secondary-school teachers has close to tripled for Canada as a whole, and some provinces, like Ontario and British Columbia, have experienced an even faster rate of growth (see table E-7). The baby-boom population "bulge" is still travelling upwards through the secondary schools and into the universities, but the decrease in the elementary-school-age population in absolute numbers should allow for a better pupil-teacher ratio than the overcrowded classrooms have afforded until now.

The statistical profile of elementary and secondary school teachers continues to show a high women-to-men ratio; this ratio is being equalized, though, especially as one moves away from the eastern seaboard. Similarly, as one moves away from the Maritimes the number of teachers with university training increases, and so does the length of teaching experience of males. This, among other things, elevates the mean salaries of all teachers. Those teaching in secondary schools are twice as likely to be university trained as those teaching in elementary grades, but this gap also narrows as one moves westward.

Although not everybody attends school, about one-third of all Canadians seem to be involved full time in education, at a cost of about one-fifth of all taxes collected, or close to 10 per cent of the Gross National Product. Those not in school are more likely than not to be in the labour force with whatever formal education they may have attained (see table E-10). The proportion of the population not at school but with some higher education is still low when compared, for instance, with the United States. The giant strides in educational attainment in the last thirty years have benefited the vigorous provinces more than those not central to the Canadian economy.

One of the features of the educated members of the population is that they become quite mobile (see table E-11), leaving their places of education and training for those of better jobs and higher wages. Such losses in manpower are at least partially compensated for by the federal tax-equalization programme.

Whether there are too many years of formal training or whether the educational attainment of the Canadian population is still too low remain difficult questions of social accounting. Just recently, for example, 15 per cent of the twenty-one-year-olds were at school, leaving 85 per cent for the labour force. A well-trained labour force can be highly efficient, even though a well-

educated one need not be. A highly efficient labour force can
easily carry the cost of educating its university minority;
whether the cost seems excessive depends on the value placed on
education. There is no doubt that the institution of education
must be preserved, even though those who benefit from it at
present may not be the most meritorious but only the most
fortunate. The question then remains whether a trained and educated
population will create jobs for itself or whether such jobs must
be there first to justify the taxpayer's burden.

TABLE E-1   SCHOOL-AGE POPULATION 5-24 YEARS OF AGE, BY PROPORTION ATTENDING SCHOOL, BY SEX, FOR CANADA AND PROVINCES, FOR CENSUS YEARS SINCE 1911

Provinces and Sex	1971 Population(a)	1971 % at School	1961 Population	1961 % at School	1951 Population	1951 % at School	1941 Population	1941 % at School	1931 Population	1931 % at School	1921 Population	1921 % at School	1911 Population	1911 % at School
Canada(b)	8,568,495	73.5	6,551,726	65.6	4,675,221	52.2	4,299,158	50.5	4,157,576	51.8				
Males	4,350,085		3,328,174	67.1	2,355,710	53.0	2,168,564	50.3	2,104,409	51.6	1,744,263	49.2	1,487,055	37.0
Fems.	4,218,410		3,223,552	64.1	2,316,511	51.4	2,130,594	50.7	2,053,167	52.1	1,730,676	49.3	1,383,172	41.4
Nfld.	237,145	71.5	197,935	65.2	139,680	54.9	-	-	-	-	-	-	-	-
Males	120,095		100,106	66.0	70,524	54.8	-	-	-	-	-	-	-	-
Fems.	117,050		97,829	64.5	69,156	54.9	-	-	-	-	-	-	-	-
P.E.I.	46,205	71.1	39,699	65.4	34,505	56.8	36,594	52.0	34,929	52.1				
Males	23,505		20,324	64.2	17,601	55.6	18,852	49.8	18,069	49.8	17,757	48.7	19,971	45.3
Fems.	22,700		19,375	66.6	16,904	58.0	17,742	54.4	16,860	54.5	17,126	49.2	19,378	44.3
N.S.	319,695	73.8	278,639	67.5	224,755	58.2	222,456	51.8	210,244	54.6				
Males	163,370		143,226	67.5	113,387	58.2	112,845	50.4	107,884	52.7	107,251	48.5	99,834	44.4
Fems.	156,325		135,413	67.4	111,368	58.3	109,611	53.3	102,360	56.6	105,520	49.6	101,225	44.7
N.B.	271,575	70.0	239,560	65.0	188,454	54.7	186,480	49.2	174,368	51.1				
Males	138,930		121,883	65.3	93,721	55.5	94,838	47.5	88,948	49.9	81,400	44.7	74,618	42.0
Fems.	132,645		117,677	64.7	94,733	53.8	91,642	51.0	85,420	52.3	80,673	46.5	72,357	43.4
Que.	2,475,720	72.3(c)	2,029,198	61.3	1,502,987	47.8	1,364,808	47.5	1,236,807	47.5				
Males	1,253,370		1,025,521	63.2	752,163	49.6	681,374	48.5	614,672	48.4	508,418	48.3	431,102	42.7
Fems.	1,122,350		1,003,677	59.3	750,824	46.0	683,434	46.5	622,135	46.6	518,614	47.2	436,396	42.1
Ont.	2,958,740	76.1	2,091,405	68.9	1,392,637	53.3	1,289,424	52.3	1,261,268	54.4				
Males	1,501,880		1,062,701	70.6	707,396	53.8	653,226	51.8	641,341	54.2	538,699	50.4	491,927	41.4
Fems.	1,456,860		1,028,704	67.2	685,241	52.7	636,198	52.7	619,927	54.6	538,367	50.1	471,059	42.4
Man.	383,205	73.5	322,347	66.6	248,677	53.7	271,986	50.5	293,615	52.6				
Males	194,635		164,342	67.8	124,834	54.3	137,325	50.2	148,513	52.3	125,481	50.6	97,567	35.4
Fems.	188,570		158,005	65.3	123,845	53.0	134,661	50.9	145,102	52.9	123,064	51.2	88,199	38.8
Sask.	365,875	73.6	331,019	66.6	286,492	56.1	364,229	52.6	404,173	53.4				
Males	186,810		169,341	67.0	145,316	55.5	185,975	51.4	207,591	51.8	158,316	49.0	113,630	26.8
Fems.	179,065		161,678	66.1	141,176	56.7	178,254	53.9	196,582	55.1	150,157	50.4	84,727	34.5

Provinces and Sex	1971 Popu- lation	1971 % at School	1961 Popu- lation	1961 % at School	1951 Popu- lation	1951 % at School	1941 Popu- lation	1941 % at School	1931 Popu- lation	1931 % at School	1921 Popu- lation	1921 % at School	1911 Popu- lation	1911 % at School
Alta.	666,030	71.2	477,594	65.6	319,428	54.5	305,523	53.0	299,837	53.9	-	-	-	-
Males	338,040		243,012	66.9	162,751	54.1	154,482	51.8	153,549	52.3	117,809	49.1	82,056	27.5
Fems.	327,990		233,582	64.4	155,677	54.8	151,041	54.1	146,288	55.5	110,675	51.3	63,127	33.8
B.C.	820,810	71.3	530,233	67.9	328,555	55.0	251,488	51.7	237,115	53.6	-	-	-	-
Males	417,490		270,248	69.3	166,008	55.7	126,429	55.5	121,124	52.7	87,439	51.0	74,001	27.5
Fems.	403,320		259,985	66.5	162,547	54.4	125,059	51.9	115,991	54.5	85,618	52.2	52,185	38.1
Y. and N.W.T.	23,425	62.5	14,097	49.2	9,051	22.3	6,170	13.1	5,220	10.6	-	-	-	-
Males	11,960		7,470	47.3	5,011	20.8	3,218	11.8	2,718	9.8	-	-	-	-
Fems.	11,465		6,627	51.4	4,040	24.1	2,952	14.6	2,502	11.5	-	-	-	-

Note: Proportion at school based on the Fall enrollment in 1970. Includes public, federal and private schools but not private kindergartens and nurseries. Includes vocational high schools under Public School Board Administration. For Northwest Territories and Yukon, excludes Arctic Quebec.

(a) Figures for Canada include Newfoundland since 1951 only.
(b) Population figures for 1971 randomly rounded.
(c) Preliminary.

Sources: Statistics Canada, Education Division, Advance Statistics of Education, 1972-73 (Ottawa: Information Canada, August 1972), table 3; Statistics Canada, Census Division, "Demographic and Social Characteristics, Population by Five Year Age Groups and Sex, Canada and Province, 1971" (informal release); Urquhart and Buckley, Historical Statistics, Series V43-53; D.B.S. Census of Canada, 1961 General Review, Bull.7.1.-10, table 1; Canada Year Book, 1931, table 27; 1921 Census of Canada, vol. II, table 12.

117

TABLE E-2 SCHOOL ENROLLMENT BY LEVEL OF SCHOOLING AND BY PERCENTAGE OF POPULATION AT SCHOOL FROM THE CORRESPONDING AGE GROUPS, FOR CANADA AND PROVINCES, FOR SELECTED YEARS, SINCE 1951

Province and Academic Years	Number of Students			Per Cent in Age Groups		
	Primary	Secondary	Post-Secondary	5-13	14-17	18-24
Canada(a)						
1971-1972(b)	3,926,420	1,872,697	501,126	95.4	106.1	18.6
1965-1966	3,922,000	1,205,000	252,500	101.6	79.6	12.4
1960-1961	3,413,000	789,000	144,600	97.6	66.2	8.6
1955-1956	2,784,000	508,000	89,900	97.2	53.5	5.7
1951-1952	2,230,000	394,000	73,900	95.9	46.3	4.9
Newfoundland						
1971-1972(b)	130,635	32,929	8,628	108.7	65.1	13.0
1965-1966	121,961	24,986	3,565	105.3	68.1	5.9
1960-1961	109,630	19,287	1,238	100.4	66.7	2.7
1955-1956	90,528	12,205	577	97.2	53.8	1.4
1951-1952	73,715	9,983	379	97.1	51.6	1.0
Prince Edward Island						
1971-1972(b)	22,484	8,154	2,340	98.2	82.4	17.4
1965-1966	21,579	6,836	924	98.1	70.5	7.8
1960-1961	20,645	4,621	638	94.7	59.2	6.7
1955-1956	19,093	3,576	321	95.9	51.1	3.4
1951-1952	17,105	3,075	315	95.8	44.2	3.3
Nova Scotia						
1971-1972(b)	161,813	54,937	19,183	105.1	82.0	19.4
1965-1966	163,039	42,923	10,236	107.0	67.6	11.9
1960-1961	155,841	30,672	6,344	105.9	57.2	8.8
1955-1956	138,973	24,028	4,773	105.1	52.3	6.9
1951-1952	124,293	19,017	3,857	107.2	44.6	5.8

TABLE E-2 continued

Province and Academic Years	Number of Students			Per Cent in Age Groups		
	Primary	Secondary	Post-Secondary	5-13	14-17	18-24
New Brunswick						
1971-1972(b)	127,205	49,861	13,307	97.5	85.3	16.1
1965-1966	129,731	37,795	7,760	96.1	65.1	10.9
1960-1961	127,706	27,570	4,645	96.7	59.7	8.3
1955-1956	110,891	18,387	2,935	95.3	46.9	5.4
1951-1952	93,151	15,582	2,117	93.4	43.4	4.0
Quebec						
1971-1972(b)	966,727	671,982	151,056	82.5	129.6	19.3
1965-1966	1,044,403	415,812	92,225	100.9	88.3	14.0
1960-1961	930,315	261,622	54,722	97.6	65.4	10.3
1955-1956	806,550	146,105	32,704	98.8	46.4	6.7
1951-1952	653,199	104,337	27,575	95.0	38.3	5.8
Ontario						
1971-1972(b)	1,461,898	620,288	184,596	104.5	104.6	19.5
1965-1966	1,323,743	467,164	72,293	104.6	78.3	11.3
1960-1961	1,121,909	300,912	41,913	100.3	68.2	7.7
1955-1956	865,330	199,793	27,625	99.7	57.6	5.5
1951-1952	657,542	155,056	22,798	99.3	49.6	4.7
Manitoba						
1969-1970	172,600	70,827	25,977	104.5	91.7	22.3
1965-1966	179,219	59,923	11,858	98.3	81.9	12.2
1960-1961	164,302	41,282	6,830	96.4	70.1	8.1
1955-1956	144,262	28,004	4,903	99.6	56.9	6.1
1951-1952	119,734	23,075	4,414	98.8	50.3	5.4

TABLE E-2 continued

Province and Academic Year	Number of Students			Per Cent in Age Groups		
	Primary	Secondary	Post-Secondary	5-13	14-17	18-24
Saskatchewan						
1969-1970	178,045	72,366	20,806	104.4	90.6	18.6
1965-1966	182,337	65,224	11,271	95.0	84.6	11.8
1960-1961	170,685	47,689	6,732	95.1	76.8	8.1
1955-1956	151,412	37,294	3,892	95.2	65.4	4.5
1951-1952	143,562	31,073	2,999	101.7	55.4	3.4
Alberta						
1969-1970	300,488	121,195	43,989	103.0	96.9	24.8
1965-1966	276,741	95,986	17,505	92.2	89.5	12.4
1960-1961	236,358	68,848	8,179	93.2	84.9	6.6
1955-1956	186,840	45,128	4,389	95.1	69.2	3.9
1951-1952	150,231	36,102	3,015	96.8	61.1	2.9
British Columbia						
1969-1970	326,535	189,810	45,522	106.0	94.5	19.4
1965-1966	302,275	149,779	24,921	97.3	74.9	14.5
1960-1961	238,620	108,413	13,382	89.7	73.0	9.8
1955-1956	187,007	73,188	7,829	89.4	66.8	6.8
1951-1952	141,734	53,225	6,484	88.9	59.9	6.0

Note: Provinces are only roughly comparable due to variations in their definition of grade
      level. Population figures are as of 1 June, preceding the specified academic year.

(a) Excludes Yukon, Northwest Territories, and students overseas.
(b) Excludes schools for the blind and the deaf; includes kindergartens with elementary-school
    enrollment.

Sources: Statistics Canada, Education Division, Advance Statistics of Education,1972-73
         (Ottawa: Information Canada, 1972), table 3; Statistics Canada, Census Division,
         Demographic and Social Characteristics Section,"Population by Single Years of Age,
         1971" (informal release); Dominion Bureau of Statistics, Education Division,
         Survey of Education in the Western Provinces, 1969-1970 (Ottawa: Information Canada, 1971),
         tables 5,6,11,17,20; W. Illing and Z.Zsigmond, Enrollment in Schools and Universities,
         tables A1, 2,6,7,11,12,17,21,22,26,27,31,32,36,37,41,42,46,47,and B1,2.

TABLE E-3 NUMBER AND PER CENT OF TOTAL UNDERGRADUATE AND GRADUATE ENROLLMENT IN CANADIAN UNIVERSITIES DURING THE REGULAR SESSION FOR CANADA AND PROVINCES, FOR SELECTED ACADEMIC YEARS SINCE 1920-1921

Canada and Provinces School Level	1971-72(a) No.	%	1967-68 No.	%	1965-66 No.	%	1960-61 No.	%	1955-56 No.	%	1950-51 No.	%	1940-41 No.	%	1930-31 No.	%	1920-21 No.	%
Canada																		
Undergrad.	413,274	100.0	237,020	100.0	188,692	100.0	107,339	100.0	69,310	100.0	64,036	100.0	34,817	100.0	31,576	100.0	22,791	100.0
Grad.	52,438	100.0	34,833	100.0	24,920	100.0	9,120	100.0	5,013	100.0	4,559	100.0	1,569	100.0	1,350	100.0	423	100.0
Nfld.																		
Undergrad.	10,167	2.5	4,324	1.8	3,106	1.7	1,205	1.1	573	0.8	380	0.6	-	-	-	-	-	-
Grad.	621	1.2	174	0.5	62	0.3	33	0.4	4	0.1	-	-	-	-	-	-	-	-
P.E.I.																		
Undergrad.	2,968	0.7	1,369	0.6	924	0.5	563	0.5	263	0.4	270	0.4	128	0.4	102	0.3	107	0.5
Grad.	-	-	-	-	-	-	-	-	-	-	-	-	-	-	-	-	-	-
N.S.																		
Undergrad.	18,231	4.4	9,821	4.1	8,997	4.8	5,664	5.3	4,385	6.3	3,879	6.1	1,964	5.6	1,968	6.2	1,660	7.3
Grad.	1,498	2.9	911	2.6	586	2.4	182	2.0	81	1.6	119	2.6	60	3.8	40	3.0	18	4.3
N.B.																		
Undergrad.	14,876	3.6	7,383	3.1	5,998	3.2	3,973	3.7	2,497	3.6	2,020	3.2	1,011	2.9	903	2.9	487	2.1
Grad.	744	1.4	721	2.1	400	1.6	91	1.0	47	0.9	32	0.7	9	0.6	5	0.4	6	1.4
Que.																		
Undergrad.	87,910	21.3	74,948	31.6	61,506	32.6	35,862	33.4	22,792	32.9	19,819	31.0	10,930	31.4	9,090	28.8	7,157	31.4
Grad.	14,100	26.9	11,829	33.9	10,018	40.2	3,122	34.2	1,602	32.0	1,465	32.1	419	26.7	369	27.3	113	26.7
Ont.																		
Undergrad.	168,687	40.8	69,307	29.2	52,124	27.6	29,501	27.5	21,088	30.4	21,268	33.2	11,693	33.6	11,414	36.2	9,050	39.7
Grad.	23,106	44.1	13,829	39.6	8,925	35.8	3,446	37.8	2,371	47.3	1,939	42.5	717	45.7	633	46.9	190	44.9
Man.																		
Undergrad.	22,806	5.5	12,631	5.3	10,469	5.6	6,001	5.6	4,218	6.1	4,411	6.9	2,483	7.1	2,608	8.3	1,644	7.2
Grad.	2,332	4.5	1,142	3.3	1,091	4.4	516	5.7	245	4.9	174	3.8	68	4.3	50	3.7	30	7.1

121

TABLE E-3 continued

Canada and Provinces School Level	1971-72 No.	%	1967-68 No.	%	1965-66 No.	%	1960-61 No.	%	1955-56 No.	%	1950-51 No.	%	1940-41 No.	%	1930-31 No.	%	1920-21 No.	%
Sask.																		
Undergrad.	15,937	3.7	12,051	5.1	10,300	5.5	5,442	5.1	3,004	4.3	2,575	4.0	1,945	5.6	1,755	5.7	647	2.8
Grad.	1,252	2.4	874	2.5	556	2.2	229	2.5	111	2.2	168	3.7	49	3.1	62	4.6	10	2.4
Alta.																		
Undergrad.	34,358	8.3	17,764	7.5	13,445	7.1	6,918	6.5	3,873	5.6	3,015	4.7	1,939	5.6	1,490	4.7	989	4.3
Grad.	4,616	8.8	2,543	7.3	1,640	6.6	491	5.4	201	4.0	239	5.2	84	5.4	84	6.2	41	9.7
B.C.																		
Undergrad.	37,334	9.0	27,422	11.6	21,833	11.6	12,210	11.4	6,617	9.6	6,399	10.0	2,724	7.8	2,246	7.1	1,050	4.6
Grad.	4,169	8.0	2,860	8.2	1,642	6.6	1,010	11.1	351	7.0	423	9.3	163	10.4	107	7.9	15	3.6

Note: Undergraduate category includes only full-time undergraduates enrolled in the regular session for specified years; excludes Normal School students and nurses studying for R.N.Graduate category includes full-time and part-time students enrolled in the regular session for specified years. Percentages may not total 100 due to rounding.

(a) Preliminary figures for the winter session.

Sources: Statistics Canada, Education Division, Advance Statistics of Education, 1972-73 (Ottawa: Queen's Printer, 1972), table 10; Dominion Bureau of Statistics, Education Division, Survey of Higher Education, 1967-68 (Ottawa: Queen's Printer, 1969), part II, table 14; Dominion Bureau of Statistics, Education Division, Survey of Higher Education, 1954-61 (Ottawa: Queen's Printer, 1964), table 15.

TABLE E-4 PER CENT OF FULL-TIME UNDERGRADUATE ENROLLMENT IN TRADITIONAL FACULTIES IN CANADIAN UNIVERSITIES, FOR SELECTED ACADEMIC YEARS SINCE 1920-21.

Faculty	Academic Year							
	1971-72	1965-66	1960-61	1955-56	1950-51	1940-41	1930-31	1920-21
All enrollment	368,998	188,692	107,346	69,310	64,036	34,817	31,576	22,791
Agriculture	0.9	1.3	1.8	1.8	2.6	3.9	2.8	3.8
Arts and Sciences	54.6	56.9	48.9	44.7	46.5	50.6	53.3	41.1
Commerce	4.9	5.5	6.1	5.7	5.3	3.4	2.8	1.6
Dentistry(a)	0.7	0.7	1.0	1.2	1.5	-	-	-
Education	15.7	11.3	9.7	4.8	3.6	1.9	2.0	0.7
Engineering	5.7	8.8	13.6	16.2	13.1	12.6	11.3	12.5
Household Science(a)	1.7	1.2	1.4	1.7	2.3	-	-	-
Law	2.4	2.2	2.3	3.9	3.6	2.0	2.7	4.9
Medicine	2.1	2.4	4.0	6.3	6.9	8.4	9.3	14.2
Pharmacy(a)	1.0	0.9	1.5	1.7	2.2	-	-	-
Theology	0.7	1.5	3.1	4.5	4.3	7.0	7.1	9.4
Other	9.8	7.3	6.6	7.5	7.9	10.2	8.7	11.8

Note: Enrollment figures prior to 1950-51 exclude Newfoundland.

(a) Prior to 1940-41 dentistry, pharmacy, and household science included with "other".

Sources: Statistics Canada, Education Division, Service Bulletin, vol. 1, no. 8 (October 1972), table 3; Dominion Bureau of Statistics, Education Division, Survey of Higher Education 1967-1968 (Ottawa: Queen's Printer, 1969), tables 3,4,14.

TABLE E-5 NUMBER OF DEGREES GRANTED BY CANADIAN UNIVERSITIES, BY TYPE OF DEGREE, FOR SELECTED ACADEMIC YEARS SINCE 1920-21

Academic Year	Bachelor and First Professional Degrees(a)		Master and License(b)		Doctorates (earned)		Doctorates (honorary)	
	Total	% Earned by Women	Total	% Earned by Women	Total	% Earned by Women	Total	% Earned by Women
1970-71	67,200	38.1	9,638	22.0	1,625	9.3	-	-
1965-66	38,470	32.9	5,233	19.0	697	10.9	254	7.9
1960-61	20,240	25.8	2,447	19.0	305	8.5	285	4.9
1955-56	13,770	22.9	1,459	20.8	366	4.6	200	7.5
1950-51	15,754	20.3	1,632	13.9	202	5.5	188	5.9
1945-46	8,192	26.9	877	11.3	104	11.5	134	6(c)
1940-41	6,576	24.1	673	10.6	75	5(c)	83	6(c)
1930-31	5,290	25.3	468	21.4	46	7(c)	95	-
1920-21	3,627	18.3	218	22.0	24	1(c)	58	-

(a) Includes equivalent diplomas, as, for example, in theology, and honours degrees.
(b) The license in the French-language universities is the next degree after the Bachelor, as the Masters degree is in the English-language universities. This category excludes Masters and license degrees (i.e., in law, optometry) which are in reality the first professional degree and which are included in that column.
(c) Absolute numbers.

Sources: Statistics Canada, Education Division, Advance Statistics of Education, 1972-73 (Ottawa: Information Canada, 1972), table 11; Dominion Bureau of Statistics, Education Division, Survey of Higher Education, 1968-69 (Ottawa: Queen's Printer, 1970), part II, table 3; Survey of Higher Education, 1967-68 (1969), part II, table 8; Survey of Higher Education 1961-62 (1964), table 8.

TABLE E-6 STUDENTS IN CANADIAN UNIVERSITIES FROM OTHER COUNTRIES, AND CANADIAN STUDENTS IN THE UNITED STATES AND THE UNITED KINGDOM, FOR SELECTED ACADEMIC YEARS SINCE 1920-21

Academic Year	Total Full-Time Enrollment in Canada	Students with residence in - U.S.	U.K.	Brit. W. Indies	Nfld(a)	Other Countries	Total Enrollment from Other Countries in Canada	% of students from outside Canada of total enrollment in Canada	Canadians studying in U.S.(b)	U.K.(c)
1971-72	323,026	5,820	5,542	1,811(d)		15,582	28,758	8.9	13,318(e)	992(e)
1967-68	261,207	3,910	1,042	1,115		9,401	15,356	5.9	12,144	784
1965-66	205,888	3,395	886	1,064		5,939	11,284	5.5	9,755	660
1960-61	113,857	2,362	582	1,210		3,097	7,251	6.4	6,058	502
1955-56	72,732	1,773	281	635		1,696	4,385	6.0	4,990	404
1950-51	68,306	1,758	164	251		1,014	3,188	4.7	4,528	372
1945-46	63,550	1,116	167	263	303	507	2,356	3.7	1,636	-
1940-41	36,319	1,478	41	74	174	289	2,056	5.7	1,458	-
1935-36	35,108	2,018	156	32	133	237	2,576	7.3	1,075	262
1930-31	32,926	1,506	333	54	175	236	2,304	7.0	1,313	212
1925-26	25,698	934	133	64	130	236	1,497	5.8	123	156
1920-21	23,139	-	-	-	-	-	1,306	5.6	-	-

(a) Newfoundland prior to 1949 was considered to be a country outside of Canada.
(b) Data from the Institute of International Education, New York, U.S.A.
(c) Data from the Association of Universities of the British Commonwealth, London, England, Newfoundland is included with Canada for all years.
(d) Students classified by citizenship under British West Indies all from the Caribbean.
(e) For 1969.

Sources: Statistics Canada, Fall enrollment in Universities and Colleges 1971-72 (1973), tables 1A, 10, 11A; UNESCO Statistical Yearbook 1971 (1972), table 2.22; Dominion Bureau of Statistics, Education Division, Survey of Higher Education, 1967-68 (1969), part II, table 7; Survey of Higher Education, 1954-61 (1964), table 8.

TABLE E-7 NUMBER OF ELEMENTARY- AND SECONDARY-SCHOOL TEACHERS, BY PROPORTION OF WOMEN, MEDIAN SALARY AND EXPERIENCE, SEX, AND PROPORTION WITH UNIVERSITY DEGREES, FOR CANADA AND PROVINCES, FOR SELECTED ACADEMIC YEARS SINCE 1950-51

Province and Year	Number of Teachers(a)	Proportion Females	Median Experience in Years(b)		Median Salary in $(c)	Proportion with Univ. Degrees(d)
			M	F		
Canada						
1969-1970	249,078	63.0	7.1	7.4	7,124(e)	43.1
1965-1966	197,775	65.4	6.2	7.1	5,215(f)	33.2
1960-1961	152,530	70.9	7.9	8.0	4,247	25.7
1955-1956	115,645	73.2	7.7	8.0	2,979	-
1950-1951	89,682	73.2	7.9	7.2	2,050	-
Newfoundland						
1969-1970	6,315	62.0	5.3	5.2	5,102	26.3
1965-1966	5,545	63.3	4.3	4.0	3,326	14.0
1960-1961	4,317	63.1	3.2	3.8	2,421	10.7
1955-1956	3,106	66.3	4.9	3.8	1,402	-
1950-1951	2,499	66.1	3.8	3.5	919	-
Prince Edward Island						
1969-1970	1,486	73.8	5.3	9.6	4,787	24.6
1965-1966	1,209	80.3	4.2	9.2	2,998	12.1
1960-1961	969	85.0	5.4	7.7	2,294	7.2
1955-1956	822	84.1	7.0	6.4	1,532	-
1950-1951	719	83.6	6.5	5.3	1,135	-
Nova Scotia						
1969-1970	9,443	71.4	5.8	10.3	6,013	39.1
1965-1966	7,897	76.4	6.8	11.5	3,717	30.0
1960-1961	6,664	81.1	8.1	10.5	2,992	24.7
1955-1956	5,586	83.2	7.1	9.3	1,939	-
1950-1951	4,436	84.0	6.5	8.2	1,595	-
New Brunswick						
1969-1970	7,822	69.7	5.4	8.5	5,826	32.9
1965-1966	6,812	75.2	5.7	9.1	3,637	19.9
1960-1961	5,866	78.5	5.4	8.6	2,735	14.5
1955-1956	4,636	81.9	6.0	8.1	1,946	-
1950-1951	3,907	84.2	4.7	7.2	1,493	-

Note:The Yukon and Northwest Territories are not included in these data.

(a) Elementary teachers include all those who teach grades 1-6 but no grade above 6. Secondary teachers include all those who teach grades 9-13 but no grade below 9. Teachers whose appointment does not fall within the above categories are classified as secondary if they are in a junior high school or junior/senior school or if they teach in more than one school; otherwise they have been counted as elementary.
(b) Teaching experience as of the opening of school in September; excludes Quebec; also excludes Ontario up to 1959-60 and in 1968-69 and 1969-70, and Saskatchewan in 1965-66.
(c) Excludes one-room, rural school teachers; also excludes Quebec.
(d) Excludes Quebec, Yukon and Northwest Territories; includes principals.
(e) Excludes Saskatchewan.
(f) Excludes Ontario.

TABLE E-7 continued

Province and Year	Number of Teachers	Proportion Females	Median Experience in Years M	Median Experience in Years F	Median Salary in $	Proportion with Univ. Degrees
Quebec(g)						
1969-1970	70,700(h)	68.7	-	-	-	-
1965-1966	56,701(i)	72.4	-	-	-	-
1960-1961	45,694	79.0	-	-	-	-
1955-1956	35,301	81.1	-	-	-	-
1950-1951	26,651	79.2	-	-	-	-
Ontario(j)						
1969-1970	89,929(h)	59.8	-	-	-	-
1965-1966	68,602	60.5	5.7	6.0	5,489	33.7
1960-1961	49,292	66.9	7.4	7.2	4,496	32.0
1955-1956	35,560	69.5	-	-	3,236	-
1950-1951	26,202	69.8	-	-	2,217	-
Manitoba						
1969-1970	11,194	62.6	7.0	5.7	6,883	37.7
1965-1966	9,232	63.6	6.5	7.0	4,420	29.3
1960-1961	7,460	66.6	6.9	8.0	3,946	24.5
1955-1956	6,080	71.3	7.3	7.7	2,667	-
1950-1951	4,990	71.8	7.3	7.4	1,782	-
Saskatchewan						
1969-1970	11,553(h)	60.6	7.6	7.8	7,143	34.0
1965-1966	10,500	62.4	7.9(k)	8.6(k)	4,854(k)	22.8(k)
1960-1961	8,638	66.0	10.1	8.7	4,070	18.0
1955-1956	7,624	66.5	8.5	7.6	2,863	-
1950-1951	7,218	69.1	6.9	5.9	1,748	-
Alberta						
1969-1970	19,821	60.5	7.1	8.3	7,564	52.8
1965-1966	15,518	63.1	7.4	9.9	5,618	38.4
1960-1961	11,762	65.8	10.4	9.7	4,585	29.6
1955-1956	8,391	69.1	10.1	9.4	3,258	-
1950-1951	6,788	67.4	10.5	8.5	2,376	-
British Columbia						
1969-1970	20,815	55.0	8.4	6.5	7,978	53.7
1965-1966	15,759	56.3	9.1	7.4	6,068	44.2
1960-1961	11,868	56.6	9.0	8.4	5,416	37.4
1955-1956	8,539	57.4	7.3	8.2	3,785	-
1950-1951	6,272	60.8	10.4	8.6	2,770	-

(g) Teachers in schools under provincial control only.
(h) Estimate.
(i) Reflects a change in definition of secondary grades.
(j) Includes full-time itinerant teachers from 1960-61 on.
(k) 1964-65.

Source: Dominion Bureau of Statistics, Education Division, Salaries and Qualifications of Teachers in Public, Elementary and Secondary Schools, 1969-1970 (Ottawa: Queen's Printer, 1971), tables 1,5.

TABLE E-8 ESTIMATED NUMBER AND PROPORTION OF POST-SECONDARY SCHOOL
STUDENTS, BY THE OCCUPATIONAL CLASSIFICATION OF PARENTS,
FOR CANADA, ACADEMIC YEAR 1968-1969

Present or Past Occupation of Parent	Father No.	Father %	Mother No.	Mother %
Total	387,242	100.0	387,242	100.0
Self-employed	118,403	30.6	26,180	6.5
Farm	33,920	8.8	7,209	1.8
Business	59,493	14.1	11,839	3.1
Profession	24,990	6.5	6,132	1.6
Keeps home only	2,086	0.5	238,416	61.6
Works for employer	242,681	62.7	101,640	26.3
Executive and Managerial	40,607	10.5	2,120	0.5
Professional and technical	36,063	9.3	18,018	4.7
Adminstrative and supervisory	42,539	11.0	6,155	1.6
Clerical, secretarial, sales	24,279	6.3	43,564	11.2
Service	21,683	5.6	9,338	2.4
Processing, machining, assembling	22,868	5.9	4,433	1.1
Labouring	35,603	9.2	6,932	1.8
Other	18,839	4.9	11,080	2.9
No response(a)	24,273	6.3	22,006	5.7

Note: Estimates based on an 8 per cent sample of the post-secondary
student population of all eligible institutions, during the
academic year 1968-1969.

(a) Number of students sampled who did not respond projected to the
total postsecondary student population.

Source: Dominion Bureau of Statistics, Education Division, Post-
Secondary Student Population Survey, 1968-69 (Ottawa: Queen's
Printer, 1970), table 23.

TABLE E-9 ESTIMATED NUMBER AND PROPORTION OF POST-SECONDARY SCHOOL STUDENTS BY THE OCCUPATIONAL CLASSIFICATION, PRESENT OR PAST, OF THEIR FATHERS WORKING FOR AN EMPLOYER, FOR CANADA AND PROVINCES FOR THE ACADEMIC YEAR 1968-1969.

Occupation of Father	Canada No.	Canada %	Nfld. %	PEI. %	N.S. %	N.B. %	Que. %	Ont. %	Man. %	Sask. %	Alta. %	B.C. %
All employed	242,681	100.0	4,100	847	9,288	6,488	67,707	91,768	10,022	8,140	18,171	24,353
Executive and managerial	40,607	16.7	10.1	8.3	19.9	14.2	13.5	20.0	16.8	17.7	17.3	15.3
Professional and technical	36,063	14.9	13.2	19.6	13.9	10.5	13.3	16.2	15.8	14.3	14.3	16.3
Administrative and supervisory	42,539	17.5	16.6	20.1	17.3	20.6	16.7	17.0	20.0	18.2	18.8	19.1
Clerical, secre-tarial, sales	24,279	10.0	8.4	8.2	10.0	8.9	11.8	9.2	7.1	10.9	9.9	10.0
Service	21,683	8.9	8.6	11.0	8.3	10.2	9.0	8.1	9.3	11.5	11.2	9.4
Processing, mach-ining, assembling	22,868	9.4	8.3	8.0	6.6	5.4	11.0	10.7	8.4	3.5	6.1	7.5
Labouring	35,603	14.7	22.5	22.1	18.6	17.5	13.8	13.5	15.6	17.3	15.8	16.1
Other	18,839	1.8	12.4	8.7	8.4	12.6	11.1	5.4	7.0	6.7	6.8	6.3

Source: Dominion Bureau of Statistics, Education Division, Post-Secondary Student Population Survey, 1968-69, table 23.

129

TABLE E-10 LEVEL OF EDUCATIONAL ATTAINMENT OF THE POPULATION 15 YEARS AND OVER AND NOT ATTENDING SCHOOL, BY HIGHEST LEVEL OF SCHOOLING, BY SEX, FOR CANADA AND PROVINCES, FOR CENSUS YEARS SINCE 1941.

| Province and Year | Population 15 Years and Over Not at School | | Highest Level of Schooling (a) — Per Cent with | | | | | | | | | |
| | | | No Schooling | | Elementary | | Secondary | | University — Some | | University — Graduated | |
	M	F	M	F	M	F	M	F	M	F	M	F
CANADA												
1971(d)	13,168,025		–		37.2		53.0		5.1		4.7	
1961	5,498,252	5,548,353	1.7	1.5	48.3	42.2	42.5	51.7	3.3	2.9	4.2	1.7
1951(b)	4,542,977	4,500,496	–	–	57.4	49.4	34.0	42.4	8.6	8.2	–	–
1941	4,018,283	3,788,893	–	–	62.8	55.2	30.7	38.6	6.4	6.2	–	–
NEWFOUNDLAND(c)												
1971	280,865				48.9		20.2		4.3		2.1	
1961	124,300	117,045	6.5	4.4	55.7	49.5	34.3	43.2	2.3	2.5	1.2	0.4
1951	207,413				70.7		26.8		2.5		–	
PRINCE EDWARD ISLAND												
1971	65,135				42.1		49.0		5.9		3.0	
1961	31,485	29,812	1.2	0.6	55.7	37.9	38.1	57.8	2.7	3.0	2.3	0.7
1951	61,876				55.0		40.7		4.4		–	
1941	62,760				60.6		36.5		2.9		–	
NOVA SCOTIA												
1971	470,080				35.5		55.8		4.7		4.0	
1961	220,685	217,782	1.8	1.1	46.7	34.7	45.6	59.8	2.8	2.8	3.1	1.6
1951	406,793				50.1		44.0		5.9		–	
1941	383,107				55.9		39.3		4.8		–	
NEW BRUNSWICK												
1971	366,875				49.1		45.2		4.3		3.3	
1961	168,244	167,959	3.5	2.0	59.3	48.3	31.8	45.7	2.7	2.9	2.7	1.0
1951	312,235				62.5		33.2		4.3		–	
1941	292,777				67.1		29.5		3.4		–	

130

TABLE E-10 Continued

Province and Year	Population 15 Years and Over Not at School		Highest Level of Schooling (a)									
			No Schooling		Per Cent with Elementary		Per Cent with Secondary		University Some		Graduated	
	M	F	M	F	M	F	M	F	M	F	M	F
QUEBEC												
1971	3,679,040				47.1		36.8		4.6		4.5	
1961	1,522,969	1,594,611	1.1	0.9	55.6	52.9	35.8	42.4	3.2	2.2	4.3	1.6
1951	2,566,126		-	-	63.1		30.9		6.0		-	-
1941	2,151,229		-	-	67.1		28.3		4.6		-	-
ONTARIO												
1971	4,766,015				32.8		57.1		5.0		5.1	
1961	1,920,232	1,975,220	1.2	1.1	45.8	39.7	45.0	54.7	3.1	2.5	4.9	2.0
1951	3,191,383		-	-	48.7		39.9		11.4		-	-
1941	2,700,632		-	-	54.3		37.2		8.5		-	-
MANITOBA												
1971	610,345				36.8		53.7		5.1		4.4	
1961	285,744	283,189	2.7	3.1	44.1	36.7	45.7	55.3	4.0	3.3	3.5	1.6
1951	524,102		-	-	53.1		40.9		6.0		-	-
1941	502,194		-	-	58.5		36.6		4.9		-	-
SASKATCHEWAN												
1971	557,555				41.0		49.9		5.6		3.4	
1961	288,034	265,591	2.9	3.3	51.8	41.2	39.7	50.8	2.9	3.5	2.7	1.2
1951	537,932		-	-	58.2		35.4		6.4		-	-
1941	578,022		-	-	65.0		30.2		4.8		-	-
ALBERTA												
1971	958,220				28.4		60.5		5.8		5.3	
1961	406,097	378,635	1.8	2.2	42.0	32.8	48.6	58.4	3.4	4.8	4.2	1.8
1951	610,158		-	-	48.0		44.0		8.0		-	-
1941	524,249		-	-	56.6		37.0		6.4		-	-

TABLE E-10 continued

Province and Year	Population 15 Years and Over Not at School		Highest Level of Schooling (a)									
			No Schooling		PerCent with Elementary		PerCent with Secondary		University			
									Some		Graduated	
	M	F	M	F	M	F	M	F	M	F	M	F
BRITISH COLUMBIA												
1971	1,385,400		-		26.2		61.9		6.9		4.9	
1961	517,487	509,502	1.6	1.5	35.8	28.3	53.1	62.9	5.0	5.2	4.5	2.1
1951	816,602		-		40.5		49.2		10.3		-	
1941	601,177		-		47.3		44.7		8.0		-	

(a) For 1951 and 1941 data was collected on the number of years of schooling. Elementary school classification includes those with 8 or fewer years of schooling, secondary school classification includes those with 9 to 12 years of schooling, and the summary postsecondary classification includes those with 13 or more years of schooling. No data available prior to 1941.
(b) Includes Yukon and Northwest Territories but excludes Newfoundland.
(c) For provinces for the years 1951 and 1941 no information is available by sex and educational attainment.
(d) For 1971, last digit randomly rounded. Preliminary data, no breakdown for sex. No separate data for no schooling.

Sources: 1971 Census, internal tabulation, unpublished; 1961 Census of Canada, Bull.7.1-10, 12.5; 1951 Census of Canada, vol. X, tables 11,13.

TABLE E-11 ESTIMATED CANADIAN POPULATION 20 YEARS OF AGE AND OVER, BY LEVEL OF EDUCATION, REGION IN WHICH THAT LEVEL WAS ATTAINED AND RESIDENCE IN JANUARY 1966.

Level of Education and Region in Which That Level was Attained	Total (in 000)	Residence in 1966				British Columbia (%)
		Atlantic (%)	Quebec (%)	Ontario (%)	Prairies (%)	
Elementary						
Atlantic	1127	80.5	4.5	11.7	1.6	1.7
Quebec	2767	0.4	93.7	4.8	0.6	0.5
Ontario	2721	0.4	3.2	92.4	2.4	1.6
Prairies	1723	*	1.0	6.6	77.3	14.8
British Columbia	480	*	*	3.9	4.9	90.3
Secondary						
Atlantic	662	76.5	6.0	13.8	2.0	1.7
Quebec	1331	*	92.7	5.4	*	0.8
Ontario	1856	0.6	4.1	91.6	2.2	1.5
Prairies	1092	*	1.4	6.9	78.2	13.2
British Columbia	398	*	*	4.2	5.1	89.8
University						
Atlantic	89	71.9	*	14.5	*	*
Quebec	244	*	87.9	7.5	*	*
Ontario	315	*	6.7	85.7	3.7	3.0
Prairies	187	*	*	8.2	78.9	10.4
British Columbia	88	*	*	*	*	83.3

Note: These calculations are based on added questions to the Labour Force Survey, January 1966.

* Based on estimate of less than 10,000.

Source: M.D.Lagace, Educational Attainment in Canada, tables 6,F5.

BIBLIOGRAPHY

A number of bibliographical references listed with other sections deal with education.

Bertram, G., The Contribution of Education to Economic Growth. Staff Study No. 12. Ottawa: Economic Council of Canada, 1966. (146 pp.)

Cousin, J., Fortin, J.P., and Wenaas, C.S., Some Economic Aspects of Provincial Educational Systems. Staff Study No. 27. Ottawa: Economic Council of Canada, 1971. (232 pp.)

Illing, W., and Zsigmond, Z., Enrollment in Schools and Universities 1951-52 to 1975-76. Staff Study No.20. Ottawa: Economic Council of Canada, 1967. (161 pp.)

Lagace, M., Educational Attainment in Canada: Some Regional and Social Aspects. Special Labour Force Studies, No.7. Ottawa: Queen's Printer, 1968. (53 pp.)

Macleod, B., ed., Demography and Educational Planning: Papers from a Conference on Implications of Demographic Factors for Educational Planning and Research. Toronto: Ontario Institute for Studies in Education, 1970. (274 pp.)

Ostry, S., ed., Canadian Higher Education in the Seventies. Ottawa: Economic Council of Canada, 1972. (310 pp.)

Zsigmond, Z., and Wenaas, C., Enrollment in Educational Institutions by Province, 1951-52 to 1980-81. Staff Study No. 25. Ottawa: Economic Council of Canada, 1970. (306 pp.)

EMPLOYMENT

The three social institutions of family, education and work
are closely interconnected. Families supply entrants into the
work force, the schools impart the required skills, competence
and persuasion to work, and the employment structure and
opportunities in turn influence family formation and education
practices. A number of government agencies keep track of the
ever-changing employment patterns, issuing a wealth of
statistical information on the numbers and composition of the
Canadian labour force. The classification categories in use
seem to be quite straightforward, using the area of work and
the level of work as the two major criteria of classification.
For instance, extractive industries like mining or quarrying
define the areas of work, whereas clerical or managerial
occupations denote the level at which such work may be pursued.
It is only a close look at the data that reveals difficulties in
interpretation.

Three major sets of difficulties are associated with
interpreting the statistical information on the Canadian labour
force and its occupational structures. In the first place, there
is the interest which such data serve; are they to identify
areas of activities in which work is performed, the type of
industries which employ people, or the level of competence which
the workers have? In the second place, there is the change which
has taken place and which has radically transformed the
Canadian labour force: how comparable are the occupational
categories over time and how much of an approximation of the
real change are the time series at our disposal? For instance,
the censuses in 1951, 1961 and 1971 have collected information
using differing description and classification of occupational
groups. In the third place, there is the difficulty with the
comprehensiveness of the concept of labour force itself; how
much is the change in employment patterns a statistical
artifact resulting from a restrictive or an all-inclusive use of
the definition? For instance, at the present time, all those
are counted in the labour force who are fifteen years of age
or over, not in school and either employed or unemployed but
looking for employment. Prior to the 1951 census, however, only
those gainfully employed were included in the labour-force
statistics, and, as another example, women working on farms as
members of the farm households were omitted from the
agricultural labour force.

Inasmuch as the economic sectors in which people work are
ceding their importance to the level of competence at which
they work, so does the informativeness of older occupational
statistics lose its one other than historical value. However, at
least at the present time, most information available on the
development and growth of the Canadian labour force is of the
traditional variety, that is, with an emphasis on the areas and
not levels of work. Accepting such a limitation still allows
us to gain a fair picture of the employment patterns of
Canadians during this century.

There are two main facets of social change reflected in
the government statistics on the labour force: one is the
increasing proportion of nonmanual occupations, which represent
close to one-half of the labour force; the second is the increasing
proportion of women in the labour force, representing now about
one-third of the total. Other changes, such as the occupational
integration of the immigrants,the distribution of income to
various occupational groups, and the increase in the educational

135

Chart 7.   Education Levels in the Labour Force and Among the Unemployed, Canada, April 1972

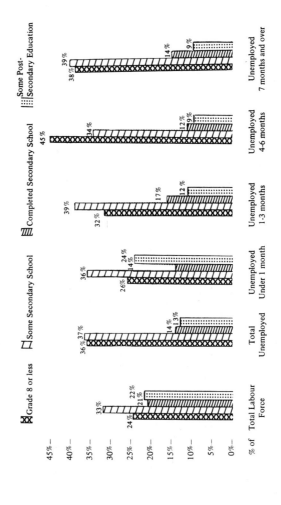

Note: Data from a special survey added to the regular labour force survey, April 1972.

Source: Statistics Canada Daily, March 29, 1973, page 3.

136

attainment of the labour force are but concomitants of the overriding feature of modern economic systems, namely a high level of administrative organization.

There are close to nine million persons in today's labour force, about three times as many as there were at the beginning of the century. In terms of a proportion of population fifteen years of age and over, there has been hardly any change, but there has been a considerable redistribution in the proportion by sex. In 1911, roughly 16 per cent of women were gainfully employed, while in 1971, 37 per cent of women were in the labour force, a proportion as high as in just about any industrial country. Considering that there are slightly fewer women than men in postsecondary schools, that women outlive men by a fair margin, that some do not work because of family obligations and others because they feel they don't have to, one should not expect the proportion of women working to go over 40 per cent. Even though it appears that women have been entering the labour force at a rapid rate, a realistic evaluation of the data would show that female employment has not been as low as the figures indicate (see table J-1), nor is it presently as high as it seems. The discrepancy is due to the enumeration of gainfully occupied in the census preceding 1951, to the underreporting of female farm employment ending after 1941, and to the present inclusion into the labour force of those seeking work but currently not working. This last group may include a fair number of married women who are "seeking" work, although unenthusiastically, but appear in the labour force statistics nonetheless.

The proportion of men fifteen years of age and over in the labour force has shown a slight decrease since 1911; the decrease can be attributed about equally to extended schooling, especially after World War II, and to the institutionalization of retirement from work, an arrangement brought about by an improvement in longevity and the resulting pressures for social provisions. The drop registered by the 1941 census was due, of course, to the participation in Active Service.

Across the provinces west of Quebec, the labour force represents a higher proportion of the population fifteen years old and over and for both sexes than it does east of Ontario. This may be explained in part by the provincial age and sex structures -- western provinces are younger on the whole; in part, by the differing school attendance -- a higher school participation implies an ensuing higher labour-force participation, and vice versa; in part, by the history of employment -- underemployment and unemployment may encourage people to discount themselves from inclusion into the labour force by not declaring themselves as seeking work, as is probably the case in the Atlantic Provinces.

If the attendance at school cuts into labour-force participation, then it would apply most to persons between the ages of fifteen and nineteen and to a fair extent to those between the ages of twenty and twenty-four. Furthermore, since secondary-school education in Canada has become practically universal, sex equalization in the labour-force participation rates should become evident. Sex equalization has shown some gains since the 1941 census and has recently become even more pronounced (see table J-2). Men show their highest participation in the labour force after the age of twenty-five; women, before that age, childbearing and the comfortable income of their husband contributing to their eventual withdrawal from the labour

137

force. Furthermore, one should not forget that the custom of the land has not encouraged women to work outside the home, even though household jobs have become less demanding due to a variety of technological innovations. On the other hand, such a cultural lag in the preparedness to work may turn into a blessing, as we are coming to a time where leisure activities will occupy more and more of our time.

The institutionalization of retirement from work and the availability of a variety of private and government pension plans explain the decreasing employment of those sixty-five and over. With the exception of Prince Edward Island, the eastern provinces show a lower labour-force participation rate of older persons than is the case in the western provinces. For those over sixty-five, Newfoundland and British Columbia show the lowest participation rates, each for different reasons: Newfoundland, because of lack of employment, and British Columbia, because of the retired population.

As of 1971, the greatest disparity between the sexes in employment is in the Atlantic region, where among those twenty-five years and older almost three times as many men as women are in the labour force. The sex ratio in employment is the lowest (2.2) in Ontario, and the Prairies and British Columbia are somewhere in between. Only some thirty years ago, however, the sex ratio for the labour force participation was close to 6 for Canada and about 11 for Saskatchewan. In that province a substantial portion of the labour force was in agriculture, which explains the male bias in enumeration. Consequently, this ratio for Saskatchewan has declined to the Ontario level as of the 1971 census.

At the turn of the century, close to one-half of all gainfully occupied males were in agriculture, whereas less than 4 per cent of the female labour force were enumerated as being agriculturally employed (see table J-3). On the other hand, slightly over 40 per cent of all women workers were enumerated in domestic service and another 30 per cent in manufacture, accounting for the majority of working women being employed at quite menial tasks. In actual numbers, of course, there were three times as many men as women working in factories, even though they represented only 14 per cent of the male labour force. The third major category which attracted women employees was that of professions. In 1901, 15 per cent of the female labour force were in that category, compared to only 3 per cent of the males in the labour force.

Although the proportion of the female labour force in professional occupations has not changed very much in 1971 from the original 15 per cent in 1901, the proportion of professional workers in the male labour force has increased close to four times in that seventy-year period. No doubt the category of professions includes everybody from grade-school teachers or health workers to medical doctors and physicists, disparate occupations to be sure, at least in terms of financial rewards. In any case, every fourth male and every fifth female in the labour force derived their income from a professional or managerial occupation in 1971, although the distribution favoured those in the most economically developed provinces like Ontario and British Columbia.

The expansion of the labour force in the last two decades was possible through tapping three sources of manpower: women, immigrants and, of late, the expanded "baby boom" cohorts. All

138

three groups appear to be educationally advantaged over the rest of the labour force. The older women entrants have, on the average, more education than the men in their age group; the new selective immigration process directly encourages immigrants with high educational attainment; and the young entrants into the labour force have gone through the expanded and upgraded Canadian educational system.

Survey data on the educational attainment of the labour force (see table J-4) demonstrate for both sexes the interrelatedness of occupational standing and education. Males, who have an edge in university enrollments and graduation are correspondingly represented in the white-collar occupations. Of the males in that broad occupational classification, about 29 per cent have at least some university training, as compared with about 18 per cent of females in the same category. Of course, some women in the white-collar sector are in professional occupations, mostly teaching and health professions, but the majority are in clerical and secretarial jobs. This may explain the sex difference in educational attainment. On the other hand, for all occupations, women have higher educational attainment than men.

In a way, the immigrants, especially the recent immigrants of the past decade or so, tend to "behave" like women with respect to their entry into the labour force; that is, they tend to have a higher average education than the native-born in similar employment. The entry into the Canadian labour market by the recent immigrants is bimodal; that is, the professions on the one hand and the crafts on the other are enjoying more than their proportionate share of the Canadian newcomers (see table J-5); in both cases there may have been more vacancies than native-born applicants.

The occupational differentiation of the labour force is reflected in a differentiation of rewards which are, to a great extent, translated into income. It is with regard to income that the uses of broad occupational categories in the Canadian censuses and labour force surveys understate the real differences in jobs. Using the data from the 1970 income tax returns, we can discern three major groups of income recipients: professionals whose income is not tied to working for an employer; a large group of employees in middle-range occupations be it sales, clerical or a variety of manual employment, or public employment in teaching, health services and administration; and those who are more or less outside of the labour force and whose income depends on pensions, annuities, small-scale farming and small business. In the last group the sex difference in incomes is small, in the middle group males are listed as earning about twice as much as females, and in the professions males earn about four times as much as the females (see table J-6). However, when one looks at the last category in more detail (see table J-7), the professions, including medical practitioners, lawyers, accountants and consulting engineers and architects, have clearly higher salaries than any other group in the labour force and these tend to be dominated by males.

The specialized professional occupations which require independent decision about individual clients are usually those which require university training. Of course, there are a host of jobs which require an equal amount of training - for instance, most of the teaching and health-assistance professions- but such jobs are tied to an employer, have fairly definite routines, and do not command a large salary. The skilled crafts on the other hand, which parallel the professional self-

139

employed occupations in being contractual between the client
(that is, customer) and the craftsman, offer a better income
than that earned in routinized professional employment. As in
the past, formal education still explains the differences in
earnings, even though the differences are being slowly eroded
by redistributive taxation and financial concessions to the
disadvantaged. The rosy prediction of only a few years back,
that youth would seek entry to higher education in ever-
increasing numbers in order to benefit from better jobs, now
appears unwarranted. It may be for no other reason than that
the modern occupational structure does not need as many new
entrants as are brandishing their newly acquired knowledge
or diplomas. After all, for efficiency's sake most tasks
performed to earn a living must become routinized and thus
uninteresting. This applies even to those occupations which
are service oriented to their clientele, like social work or
counselling. Sooner or later their practitioners come to
realize how alike people are in their responses to similar
situations, a lesson which the demographers have always imparted
to their students.

TABLE J-1 NUMBER AND PERCENTAGE OF THE POPULATION 15 YEARS AND OVER IN THE LABOUR FORCE BY SEX FOR CANADA AND PROVINCES AT CENSUS YEARS SINCE 1911

PROVINCES AND SEX	1971 No.	1971 %	1961 No.	1961 %	1951 No.	1951 %	1941(a) No.	1941(a) %
CANADA								
Male	5,760,245	76.4	4,694,294	77.73	4,114,407	83.79	3,352,428	78.43
Female	3,053,095	39.9	1,763,862	29.48	1,162,232	24.06	831,129	20.66
Total	8,813,340	58.0	6,458,156	53.71	5,276,639	54.16	4,183,557	50.42
NEWFOUNDLAND								
Male	109,490	65.6	88,702	64.44	89,384	78.87	—	—
Female	42,115	26.2	23,608	18.35	17,027	15.96	—	—
Total	151,600	46.3	112,310	42.18	106,411	48.36	—	—
PRINCE EDWARD ISLAND								
Male	28,855	75.3	26,068	76.14	28,093	84.03	26,001	75.04
Female	14,715	38.7	8,080	24.72	5,957	18.54	5,099	16.07
Total	43,565	57.0	34,148	51.02	34,050	51.93	31,100	46.86
NOVA SCOTIA								
Male	198,360	72.6	178,559	73.47	177,905	81.51	153,712	73.09
Female	93,770	34.1	58,260	24.52	42,680	19.87	36,952	18.59
Total	292,130	53.3	236,819	49.27	220,585	50.93	190,664	46.60
NEW BRUNSWICK								
Male	153,565	71.4	132,549	71.13	134,728	81.38	118,794	73.96
Female	74,175	34.3	45,806	24.84	34,034	20.47	27,358	18.12
Total	227,740	52.8	178,355	48.11	168,762	50.87	146,152	46.90
QUEBEC								
Male	1,488,095	71.4	1,289,425	76.72	1,126,696	84.95	922,292	81.12
Female	745,740	35.0	478,694	27.91	340,591	24.98	259,312	22.90
Total	2,233,835	53.0	1,768,119	52.07	1,467,287	54.55	1,181,604	52.07

TABLE J-1 continued

PROVINCES AND SEX	CENSUS YEARS					
	1931		1921		1911	
	No.	%	No.	%	No.	%
CANADA						
Male	3,244,788	87.46	2,658,463	88.66	2,341,437	89.65
Female	663,329	19.65	485,140	17.60	357,044	16.18
Total	3,908,117	55.15	3,143,603	54.62	2,698,481	56.00
NEWFOUNDLAND						
Male	–	–	–	–	–	–
Female	–	–	–	–	–	–
Total	–	–	–	–	–	–
PRINCE EDWARD ISLAND						
Male	27,613	88.74	26,788	88.70	27,853	88.80
Female	4,316	14.98	3,995	13.49	3,913	12.33
Total	31,929	53.28	30,783	51.46	31,766	50.34
NOVA SCOTIA						
Male	152,632	85.54	155,740	88.39	147,864	88.66
Female	27,811	16.61	28,528	16.78	23,997	15.05
Total	180,443	52.17	184,268	53.22	171,861	52.68
NEW BRUNSWICK						
Male	117,008	86.46	111,874	88.28	102,669	88.09
Female	21,927	17.11	19,647	16.17	16,237	14.66
Total	138,935	52.73	131,521	52.99	118,906	52.31
QUEBEC						
Male	813,323	87.14	634,587	86.93	546,537	87.28
Female	200,850	21.87	136,900	18.73	98,429	16.19
Total	1,014,173	54.77	771,487	52.81	644,966	52.26

TABLE J-1 continued

PROVINCES AND SEX	1971 No.	%	1961 No.	%	CENSUS YEARS 1951 No.	%	1941(a) No.	%
ONTARIO								
Male	2,178,005	80.3	1,700,567	80.75	1,438,110	85.58	1,137,584	78.34
Female	1,232,825	44.3	478,694	32.63	340,591	26.49	314,487	22.28
Total	3,410,830	62.1	2,393,015	56.59	1,882,508	56.06	1,452,071	50.71
MANITOBA								
Male	270,770	77.6	246,198	78.13	231,899	82.55	215,180	76.58
Female	149,135	42.3	96,444	31.47	66,135	24.23	49,764	19.30
Total	419,905	59.9	342,642	55.12	298,034	53.81	264,944	49.18
SASKATCHEWAN								
Male	252,235	76.9	248,479	78.06	250,709	82.38	272,823	79.93
Female	124,585	39.2	77,110	26.41	50,936	18.72	42,681	14.89
Total	376,820	58.2	325,589	53.35	301,645	52.33	315,504	50.25
ALBERTA								
Male	455,080	80.5	361,961	80.65	290,931	84.02	247,456	79.60
Female	243,520	44.4	127,550	30.82	62,566	20.42	40,375	15.72
Total	698,605	62.7	489,511	56.75	353,497	54.16	287,831	50.70
BRITISH COLUMBIA								
Male	612,570	75.5	421,786	74.12	345,952	78.28	258,586	74.66
Female	317,460	40.4	155,862	28.29	97,908	23.37	55,101	18.59
Total	930,030	59.0	577,648	51.58	443,860	51.56	313,687	48.81

143

TABLE J-1 continued

PROVINCES AND SEX	CENSUS YEARS					
	1931		1921		1911	
	No.	%	No.	%	No.	%
ONTARIO						
Male	1,094,008	86.67	917,826	88.79	829,200	89.63
Female	200,850	20.58	136,900	19.08	98,429	17.62
Total	1,343,103	54.32	1,111,369	54.26	980,911	54.92
MANITOBA						
Male	224,885	87.47	183,703	88.70	154,917	89.79
Female	44,812	20.00	31,444	17.58	21,749	16.73
Total	269,697	56.04	215,147	55.74	176,666	58.39
SASKATCHEWAN						
Male	300,740	89.91	239,743	91.87	194,606	94.35
Female	37,409	14.34	24,588	12.57	12,926	10.91
Total	338,149	56.80	264,331	57.89	207,532	63.91
ALBERTA						
Male	252,315	90.32	194,497	90.22	149,147	92.22
Female	33,425	15.67	21,087	13.25	11,664	12.74
Total	285,740	58.00	215,584	57.53	160,811	63.49
BRITISH COLUMBIA						
Male	262,264	87.83	193,705	88.78	188,644	91.91
Female	43,684	19.46	25,408	16.19	16,418	17.10
Total	305,948	58.49	219,113	58.41	205,062	68.08

Notes: The "Gainfully occupied: rather than the "Labour Force" concept was used prior to 1951 for
determining the labour force status. Canada Summary excludes Yukon and Northwest Territories.
1971 includes Yukon and Northwest Territories.

(a) Excludes persons on active service on June 2nd, 1941.

Sources: Statistics Canada, Information; 1971 Labour Force Data. (1974), page 1 and table 1;
1961 Census of Canada Bull. 3.1-1, table 1.

144

TABLE J-2 PER CENT OF THE POPULATION 15 YEARS OF AGE AND OVER IN THE LABOUR FORCE, BY AGE GROUP AND SEX, FOR CANADA AND PROVINCES, BY CENSUS YEARS SINCE 1941

CENSUS YEARS

Province and Age Group	1971 Population 15 Years and Over		Per Cent in Labour Force(a)		1961 Population 15 Years and Over		Per Cent in Labour Force	
	M	F	M	F	M	F	M	F
CANADA	7,531,895	7,655,520	76.4	39.9	6,039,232	5,983,979	77.7	29.5
15-19 years	1,074,435	1,039,915	46.6	37.0	727,748	702,347	39.5	33.0
20-24 years	941,775	947,630	86.5	62.8	585,192	595,106	86.6	49.3
25-34 years	1,461,580	1,427,960	92.6	44.5	1,254,194	1,219,952	93.9	29.5
35-44 years	1,285,815	1,240,585	92.8	43.9	1,188,277	1,196,861	94.2	31.0
45-54 years	1,132,315	1,159,265	90.3	44.4	956,643	918,936	91.8	33.3
55-64 years	854,110	877,625	80.1	34.4	653,708	634,162	81.7	24.4
65 +	781,865	962,545	23.6	8.2	673,470	716,615	28.4	6.7
NEWFOUNDLAND	166,750	160,765	65.6	26.2	137,645	128,645	64.4	18.4
15-19	30,085	29,539	31.6	28.1	21,941	21,888	28.4	28.0
20-24	22,075	22,525	79.0	46.2	15,288	14,950	77.8	37.2
25-34	31,730	30,675	88.2	28.6	27,332	24,958	83.3	16.3
35-44	25,735	23,490	86.1	25.2	25,814	23,150	82.0	14.5
45-54	23,430	21,365	79.5	23.1	20,983	18,360	77.4	14.9
55-64	18,400	16,410	64.9	18.5	12,734	11,997	64.7	11.2
65 +	15,300	16,775	11.5	4.8	13,553	13,342	16.0	3.3
PRINCE EDWARD ISLAND	38,155	38,080	75.3	38.7	34,239	32,689	76.1	24.7
15-19	5,855	5,695	56.1	34.1	4,583	4,292	48.7	28.7
20-24	4,680	4,570	91.9	64.5	3,292	3,052	85.6	43.6
25-34	6,190	5,930	94.1	45.0	5,732	5,317	91.5	23.5
35-44	5,535	5,195	91.8	42.4	5,712	5,695	91.8	26.0
45-54	5,295	5,295	89.3	47.3	5,528	4,973	90.9	30.4
55-64	4,915	4,740	79.8	38.6	4,117	3,705	82.2	24.0
65 +	5,685	6,670	27.6	9.2	5,275	5,655	38.9	6.9

TABLE J-2 continued

CENSUS YEARS

Province and Age Group	1951 Population 15 Years and Over		1951 Per Cent in Labour Force		1941(b) Population 15 Years and Over		1941(b) Per Cent in Labour Force	
	M	F	M	F	M	F	M	F
CANADA	4,910,639	4,831,453	83.8	24.1	4,274,205	4,022,508	78.4	20.7
15-19	531,186	524,923	57.1	37.2	564,548	554,190	50.9	25.8
20-24	535,897	550,190	92.3	46.8	517,145	513,846	68.9	41.8
25-34	1,062,471	1,106,592	96.4	24.2	918,060	889,720	86.8	24.8
35-44	947,408	917,067	96.7	21.8	743,692	690,256	91.6	16.1
45-54	726,839	678,475	94.5	20.4	647,412	577,972	93.8	12.9
55-64	556,129	519,539	85.7	14.5	493,095	419,865	89.3	10.9
65 +	550,709	534,667	38.6	5.1	390,253	376,659	47.2	5.5
NEWFOUNDLAND	113,333	106,693	78.9	16.0	---	---	---	---
15-19	15,358	15,045	50.0	32.5	---	---	---	---
20-24	13,412	13,306	90.5	34.3	---	---	---	---
25-34	25,335	23,536	92.8	13.3	---	---	---	---
35-44	21,911	19,506	92.9	10.5	---	---	---	---
45-54	14,369	13,514	89.9	10.2	---	---	---	---
55-64	10,932	10,312	81.1	7.3	---	---	---	---
65 +	12,016	11,474	32.6	2.2	---	---	---	---
PRINCE EDWARD ISLAND	33,433	32,131	84.0	18.5	34,649	31,725	75.0	16.1
15-19	4,176	4,120	64.1	32.0	4,678	4,506	54.0	23.0
20-24	3,345	3,212	93.3	39.8	4,472	3,790	58.2	35.5
25-34	6,390	6,349	96.2	17.9	7,326	6,165	77.5	19.3
35-44	6,085	5,556	96.8	15.3	5,242	4,732	87.0	11.4
45-54	4,734	4,251	93.8	15.5	4,690	4,489	91.6	9.4
55-64	3,890	3,749	87.7	12.3	3,755	3,573	92.5	9.5
65 +	4,813	4,894	50.0	5.3	4,486	4,470	64.0	5.2

TABLE J-2 continued

CENSUS YEARS

Province and Age Group	1971 Population 15 Years and Over M	F	1971 Per Cent in Labour Force M	F	1961 Population 15 Years and Over M	F	1961 Per Cent in Labour Force M	F
NOVA SCOTIA	273,085	275,105	72.6	34.1	243,047	237,632	73.5	24.5
15-19	41,140	39,060	40.3	30.6	33,166	31,073	38.1	28.3
20-24	34,645	33,785	86.0	57.0	25,543	23,768	86.9	43.0
25-34	48,600	46,905	93.4	38.2	44,021	43,295	91.3	23.7
35-44	40,835	40,540	93.1	38.0	44,491	45,127	91.3	24.8
45-54	40,425	41,400	88.4	38.5	39,601	36,280	88.0	28.3
55-64	34,690	33,715	75.1	30.4	25,838	25,059	76.8	21.8
65 +	32,750	39,705	19.8	7.9	30,387	33,030	27.0	6.3
NEW BRUNSWICK	215,110	216,345	71.4	34.3	186,341	184,408	71.1	24.8
15-19	35,405	34,365	39.4	29.0	27,437	26,077	35.7	26.5
20-24	28,875	27,685	84.3	54.6	18,777	18,642	82.9	43.4
25-34	37,865	36,055	91.7	38.6	33,593	33,884	89.6	24.0
35-44	31,380	31,580	91.2	38.5	34,818	34,991	89.4	25.8
45-54	31,075	31,570	87.4	39.3	29,310	27,366	87.0	29.5
55-65	25,595	25,295	77.1	33.3	19,589	19,348	75.6	22.0
65 +	24,910	29,795	19.7	7.6	22,817	24,100	24.8	5.5
QUEBEC	2,082,025	2,160,210	71.4	35.0	1,680,630	1,715,186	76.7	27.9
15-19	315,040	306,225	37.4	32.5	235,792	231,634	37.8	36.8
20-24	271,985	277,425	80.8	61.4	181,076	188,557	83.4	51.0
25-34	430,165	427,135	87.8	39.9	366,057	369,768	92.8	26.9
35-44	358,755	360,820	87.3	34.4	329,279	366,455	92.9	24.7
45-54	303,995	317,715	84.3	33.8	256,145	255,189	90.1	26.6
55-64	221,515	238,420	73.4	26.4	167,581	171,982	79.8	20.2
65 +	180,570	232,440	21.5	9.0	144,700	161,601	27.4	7.3

147

TABLE J-2 continued

CENSUS YEARS

Province and Age Group	1951 Population 15 Years and Over		1951 Per Cent in Labour Force		1941(b) Population 15 Years and Over		1941(b) Per Cent in Labour Force	
	M	F	M	F	M	F	M	F
NOVA SCOTIA	218,251	214,846	81.5	19.9	210,303	198,819	73.1	18.6
15-19 years	25,867	25,666	49.9	29.8	28,523	27,898	42.0	23.6
20-24	22,941	23,334	93.0	40.2	27,934	27,031	60.2	37.4
25-34	45,936	47,340	95.8	19.5	47,719	42,785	79.4	22.2
35-44	43,105	39,807	95.7	17.7	32,681	30,511	87.1	14.5
45-54	29,618	28,204	92.8	17.2	28,084	26,544	92.5	11.4
55-64	23,562	22,292	84.8	13.7	22,036	20,350	90.7	10.2
65 +	27,222	27,703	40.0	4.9	23,326	23,700	54.1	5.2
NEW BRUNSWICK	165,553	166,230	81.4	20.5	160,627	150,983	74.0	18.1
15-19	21,088	21,762	53.9	32.0	24,679	23,765	46.2	21.0
20-24	17,217	19,342	90.6	40.2	22,026	20,281	60.1	36.8
25-34	35,357	36,810	95.1	19.1	34,916	31,920	81.5	21.5
35-44	31,717	29,859	95.5	17.3	24,733	23,902	89.6	14.4
45-54	22,446	21,701	93.4	18.1	21,497	20,156	93.7	11.5
55-64	18,134	17,317	85.3	13.0	16,362	14,939	92.1	9.9
65 +	19,594	19,439	38.0	4.6	16,414	16,020	50.8	5.1
QUEBEC	1,326,263	1,363,310	85.0	25.0	1,136,897	1,132,172	81.1	22.9
15-19	167,765	169,736	61.9	39.7	175,941	175,252	57.7	26.6
20-24	164,499	176,403	91.0	46.2	148,355	155,882	76.0	42.2
25-34	304,810	324,500	96.4	23.9	266,195	266,555	91.5	27.5
35-44	257,952	260,464	96.6	20.6	201,846	198,754	94.3	18.3
45-54	188,952	186,705	94.5	19.1	155,708	146,612	94.6	14.2
55-64	128,944	126,872	85.6	14.0	106,405	99,609	87.5	11.3
65 +	113,467	118,630	36.4	5.9	86,447	89,508	42.9	6.0

TABLE J-2 continued

CENSUS YEARS

Province and Age Group	1971 Population 15 Years and Over		1971 Per Cent in Labour Force		1961 Population 15 Years and Over		1961 Per Cent in Labour Force	
	M	F	M	F	M	F	M	F
ONTARIO	2,709,805	2,784,795	80.3	44.3	2,106,048	2,122,295	80.8	32.6
15-19	362,150	351,215	49.9	40.6	223,059	213,824	40.6	33.9
20-24	334,880	339,255	89.6	66.6	190,368	196,598	89.0	51.6
25-34	528,725	516,770	95.3	50.1	447,426	435,050	95.7	33.8
35-44	481,255	461,415	96.0	50.5	432,818	433,745	96.0	36.2
45-54	421,330	429,615	94.1	50.9	341,756	328,788	94.2	38.4
55-64	306,555	317,045	84.9	39.0	238,856	237,982	84.5	28.4
65 +	274,930	369,490	26.4	8.5	231,765	276,308	31.6	7.6
MANITOBA	348,430	353,020	77.6	42.3	315,107	306,473	78.1	31.5
15-19	48,905	47,435	54.5	40.9	36,287	34,521	43.5	33.3
20-24	43,035	42,445	89.0	65.5	29,714	29,293	88.4	51.5
25-34	62,090	59,670	93.9	44.2	59,963	57,354	94.2	31.4
35-44	53,585	52,510	94.2	48.4	59,757	61,017	95.0	35.1
45-54	52,500	55,000	92.6	50.9	51,090	49,410	93.5	37.7
55-64	43,915	44,810	83.8	40.2	35,939	33,947	85.8	27.0
65 +	44,390	51,170	25.2	8.4	42,357	40,931	29.2	6.5
SASKATCHEWAN	327,575	318,235	76.9	39.2	318,314	291,953	78.1	26.4
15-19	48,920	46,845	58.8	32.9	37,461	35,403	43.5	24.7
20-24	35,205	33,645	89.8	60.8	28,973	28,023	88.9	46.4
25-34	50,690	49,635	93.8	43.1	58,599	54,957	94.4	26.9
35-44	50,675	48,410	93.6	47.9	58,575	57,258	95.4	29.6
45-54	51,135	50,700	91.6	48.6	50,809	46,621	93.9	31.8
55-64	43,380	41,820	82.6	37.9	36,519	31,499	85.9	21.7
65 +	47,565	47,240	28.6	8.3	47,378	38,192	34.2	5.1

149

TABLE J-2 continued

CENSUS YEARS

Province and Age Group	Population 15 Years and Over 1951 M	F	Per Cent in Labour Force M	F	Population 15 Years and Over 1941(a) M	F	Per Cent in Labour Force 1941(a) M	F
ONTARIO	1,680,363	1,677,865	85.6	26.5	1,452,190	1,411,222	78.3	22.3
15-19	160,190	115,495	57.4	42.1	172,133	166,983	50.8	33.1
20-24	176,929	175,431	93.1	51.6	163,579	160,410	67.1	46.6
25-34	363,980	374,302	97.3	27.6	305,515	296,695	85.5	26.6
35-44	327,548	315,951	97.5	25.5	267,392	251,309	91.0	17.9
45-54	264,717	250,890	95.5	23.9	229,448	217,263	93.7	14.7
55-64	196,789	196,003	88.1	17.0	169,281	162,079	89.6	12.1
65 +	190,210	210,153	43.1	5.6	144,842	156,483	47.7	5.7
MANITOBA	280,919	272,908	82.6	24.2	280,978	257,787	76.6	19.3
15-19	28,555	28,633	57.7	36.3	36,675	36,718	47.2	21.8
20-24	28,437	30,315	93.0	49.0	34,898	34,375	64.6	41.9
25-34	58,579	62,201	95.6	24.6	59,225	58,055	84.4	24.1
35-44	53,519	52,465	96.0	22.7	45,514	42,594	90.6	14.0
45-54	40,851	38,001	94.5	21.0	44,422	38,213	93.7	10.4
55-64	35,567	31,236	85.9	14.2	35,409	27,016	89.8	9.3
65 +	35,411	30,057	35.1	4.4	24,835	20,816	43.3	4.3
SASKATCHEWAN	304,326	272,150	82.4	18.7	341,337	286,579	79.9	14.9
15-19	34,538	33,944	53.6	25.1	48,857	47,152	48.9	15.1
20-24	31,377	31,236	93.3	42.1	44,204	40,893	69.7	34.0
25-34	61,462	61,140	96.0	18.9	68,850	63,345	87.1	17.7
35-44	55,723	51,494	96.3	16.4	53,225	46,180	92.4	8.4
45-54	42,616	36,572	94.7	14.6	54,937	41,261	95.4	7.9
55-64	39,320	29,841	86.3	9.9	44,343	28,417	93.5	8.4
65 +	39,290	27,923	40.9	3.7	26,921	19,331	54.4	4.7

TABLE J-2 continued

Province and Age Group	1971 Population 15 Years and Over		1971 Per Cent in Labour Force		1961 Population 15 Years and Over		1961 Per Cent in Labour Force	
	M	F	M	F	M	F	M	F
ALBERTA	564,685	548,690	80.5	44.4	448,820	413,800	80.7	30.8
15-19	81,970	78,920	57.9	41.9	50,296	48,708	46.0	30.3
20-24	70,575	71,685	91.1	63.7	44,403	44,751	90.8	46.8
25-34	110,630	108,035	95.4	46.4	100,414	92,157	95.5	30.0
35-44	100,850	92,295	95.4	49.6	87,593	85,030	95.9	34.4
45-54	81,750	80,820	93.2	51.6	67,212	61,335	93.8	37.0
55-64	59,420	57,655	83.6	39.2	48,052	39,591	84.1	25.4
65 +	59,485	59,260	25.9	8.0	50,850	42,228	29.8	5.2
BRITISH COLUMBIA	789,070	785,570	77.5	40.4	569,041	550,898	74.1	28.3
15-19	102,765	98,360	53.5	42.2	57,726	54,927	38.2	28.6
20-24	95,155	91,995	89.0	61.1	47,758	47,472	87.0	44.8
25-34	150,030	143,045	94.5	44.6	111,057	103,212	93.7	28.4
35-44	133,930	121,845	95.3	46.2	109,420	114,393	93.8	33.0
45-54	119,225	124,080	92.3	46.9	94,209	90,614	90.7	36.8
55-64	94,415	96,805	80.7	25.8	64,483	59,052	76.9	24.4
65 +	95,540	109,465	19.0	6.6	84,388	81,228	19.6	5.1

151

TABLE J-2 continued

Province and Age Group	1951 Population 15 Years and Over M	1951 Population 15 Years and Over F	1951 Per Cent in Labour Force M	1951 Per Cent in Labour Force F	1941(a) Population 15 Years and Over M	1941(a) Population 15 Years and Over F	1941(a) Per Cent in Labour Force M	1941(a) Per Cent in Labour Force F
ALBERTA	346,247	306,448	84.0	20.4	310,860	256,857	79.6	15.7
15-19	37,882	35,059	53.7	27.8	39,335	39,023	45.9	15.5
20-24	38,333	37,194	94.2	42.6	37,524	36,090	69.0	34.6
25-34	74,053	74,613	97.1	20.1	63,955	58,583	86.6	18.1
35-44	64,370	59,110	97.2	17.8	55,124	43,813	91.5	10.2
45-54	51,657	40,823	95.3	15.8	50,885	36,711	94.4	9.5
55-64	41,225	30,433	86.5	11.6	39,935	25,494	92.4	9.4
65 +	38,727	28,216	39.2	4.3	24,098	17,143	53.0	5.4
BRITISH COLUMBIA	441,951	418,872	78.3	23.4	346,364	296,364	74.7	18.6
15-19	35,767	34,463	49.5	34.8	33,727	32,893	38.1	21.5
20-24	35,407	40,417	91.2	48.8	34,153	35,094	63.3	42.0
25-34	86,569	95,801	95.3	25.8	68,359	65,617	84.3	23.3
35-44	85,604	83,215	95.8	24.2	57,935	48,461	88.9	15.1
45-54	66,879	57,814	92.5	21.7	57,741	46,723	90.4	12.0
55-64	57,766	50,984	78.3	13.1	55,565	38,388	84.1	9.6
65 +	69,959	56,178	29.6	3.8	38,884	29,188	41.4	4.8

Notes: (a) Excludes Yukon and Northwest Territories prior to 1971. Excludes Newfoundland prior to 1951. Population figures for 1971 randomly rounded.
(b) Excludes persons in Active Service from the gainfully occupied (Labour Force) count for 1941.

Source: Statistics Canada Information: 1971 Census Labour Force Data. (1974), Table 1. 1961 Census of Canada. Bull. 3.1-1, Table 2.

TABLE J-3 NUMERICAL AND PERCENTAGE DISTRIBUTION OF THE LABOUR FORCE 15 YEARS OF AGE AND OVER, BY MAJOR OCCUPATIONAL DIVISIONS AND BY SEX, FOR CANADA SINCE 1901, AND THE PROVINCES AT CENSUS YEARS SINCE 1911

Occupation division (as of 1951)	1971(a) M No.	%	F No.	%	1961 M No.	%	F No.	%	1951 M No.	%	F No.(d)	%(d)	1941(b) M No.	%	F No.	%
Canada(c)																
All occupations	5,474,000	100.0	2,714,000	100.0	4,694,294	100.0	1,763,862	100.0	4,114,407	100.0	1,162,232	100.0	3,352,428	100.0	831,129	100.0
Proprietary & managerial	680,000	12.4	105,000	3.9	449,191	9.6	51,720	2.9	357,893	8.7	35,003	3.0	209,246	6.2	16,305	2.0
Professional	690,000	12.6	461,000	17.0	360,478	7.7	273,793	15.5	217,896	5.3	167,762	14.4	152,161	4.5	130,071	15.7
Clerical	332,000	6.1	862,000	31.8	315,252	6.7	503,660	28.6	243,811	5.9	319,111	27.5	151,377	4.5	152,206	18.3
Agricultural	481,000	8.8	89,000	3.3	573,042	12.2	75,868	4.3	793,924	19.3	32,169	2.8	1,056,092	31.5	18,812	2.3
Fishing hunting & trapping	24,000	0.4	-	-	36,581	0.8	396	*	52,624(₫)1.3(d)		262(d)*	(d)	50,922	1.5	321	*
Logging	54,000	1.0	-	-	79,557	1.7	125	*	101,146	2.5	23	*	78,710	2.4	-	-
Mining & quarrying	57,000	1.0	-	-	64,590	1.4	21	*	65,271	1.6	18	*	70,494	2.1	16	*
Manufacturing & mechanical (e)	1,736,000	31.7	297,000	10.9	862,417	18.4	174,525	9.9	737,017	17.9	169,988	14.6	544,553	16.2	128,07	15.4
Construction	-	-	-	-	335,078	7.1	799	0.1	290,455	7.1	897	*	195,737	5.8	312	*
Transportation (f)	393,000	7.2	46,000	1.7	457,532	9.8	39,291	2.2	378,718	9.2	33,661	2.9	252,003	7.5	14,054	1.7
Commercial	335,000	6.1	220,000	8.1	262,514	5.6	177,158	10.0	194,398	4.7	120,870	10.4	151,918	4.5	71,957	8.7
Financial	-	-	-	-	49,386	1.1	3,570	0.2	30,755	0.8	1,550	0.1	22,335	0.7	766	0.1

153

TABLE J-3 continued

Occupation division (as of 1951)	1971 M No.	%	1971 F No.	%	1961 M No.	%	1961 F No.	%	1951 M No.	%	1951 F No.	%	1941(b) M No.	%	1941(b) F No.	%
Canada(c)																
Service	384,000	7.0	601,000	22.1	401,097	8.5	398,703	22.6	269,446	6.6	246,914	21.2	153,486	4.6	284,896	34.3
Personal	-	-	-	-	197,972	4.2	390,447	22.1	136,790	3.3	244,550	21.0	105,874	3.2	284,029	34.2
Labourers(g)	304,000	5.6	32,000	1.2	322,918	6.9	20,925	1.2	329,758	8.0	20,830	1.8	253,711	7.6	11,624	1.4
Not Stated					124,661	2.7	43,308	2.5	51,295	1.3	13,174	1.1	9,683	0.3	1,714	0.2

Occupation Division	1951 M No.	%	1951 F No.	%	1921 M No.	%	1921 F No.	%	1911 M No.	%	1911 F No.	%	1901 M No.	%	1901 F No.	%
Canada (c)																
All occupations	3,244,788	100.0	663,329	100.0	2,658,463	100.0	485,140	100.0	2,341,437	100.0	347,044	100.0	1,544,883	100.0	237,949	100.0
Proprietary & Managerial	209,101	6.4	10,652	1.6	218,689	8.2	9,920	2.0	121,070	5.2	5,707	1.6	74,506	4.8	2,754	1.2
Professional	120,289	3.7	117,781	17.8	78,744 (h)	3.0	927,758	19.1	56,482	2.4	45,487	12.7	47,426	3.1	35,044	14.7
Clerical	142,951	4.4	117,613	17.7	126,103	4.7	90,577	18.7	69,408	3.0	33,542	9.4	44,571	2.9	12,660	5.3
Agricultural	1,094,396	33.7	23,946	3.6	1,007,498	37.9	17,880	3.7	912,471	39.0	15,865	4.4	709,345	45.9	8,936	3.8
Fishing, hunting & trapping	46,964	1.5	493	0.1	28,868(d)	1.1	48 (d)*		34,166	1.5	264	0.1	27,160(d)	1.8	24 (d)*	

TABLE J-3 continued

Occupation Division	1931 M No.	%	1931 F No.	%	1921 M No.	%	1921 F No.	%	1911 M No.	%	1911 F No.	%	1901 M No.	%	1901 F No.	%
Logging	42,030	1.3	-	-	36,602	1.4	-	-	41,396(i)	1.8	-	-	17,055(h)	1.0	-	-
Mining & quarrying	57,320	1.8	-	-	46,365	1.7	1	*	60,923(j)	2.6	3	*	27,903	1.8	2	*
Manufacturing & mechanical(e)	267,248	11.3	84,494	12.7	272,888	10.3	86,413	17.8	273,897	11.7	93,723	26.3	213,476	13.8	70,431	29.6
Construction	183,456	5.7	63	*	147,041	5.5	76	*	128,412	5.5	46	*	83,906	5.4	27	*
Transportation(f)	229,196	7.1	15,982	2.4	157,664	5.9	14,436	3.0	147,179	6.3	5,301	1.5	77,725	5.0	1,079	0.5
Commercial	156,202	4.8	54,829	8.3	118,707	4.5	40,746	8.4	95,032	4.1	24,051	6.7	50,134	3.3	(k)	-
Financial	27,695	0.9	533	0.1	18,332	0.7	256	0.1	7,282	0.3	63	*	50,134	3.3	5,804	2.4
Service	137,235	4.2	225,067	33.9	91,784	3.5	129,960	26.8	72,037	3.1	132,766	37.2	45,555	3.0	100,006	42.0
Personal	98,222	3.0	224,316	33.8	57,084	2.2	125,296	25.8	65,884	2.8	132,342	37.1	39,414	2.6	99,837	42.0
Labourers(g)	429,353	13.2	11,579	1.8	303,688	11.4	463	0.1	321,682	13.7	226	0.1	127,121	8.2	1,182	0.5
Not Stated	1,352	*	297	*	5,485	0.2	1,626	0.3	-	-	-	-	-	-	-	-

	1971 Both Sexes	1961 M	1961 F	1951 M	1951 F	1941(b) M	1941(b) F	1931 M	1931 F	1921 M	1921 F	1911 M	1911 F
Newfoundland													
All occupations		88,702 100.0	23,608 100.0	89,384 100.0	17,027 100.0								
Proprietary and managerial		7.5	7.4	6.2	6.4								
Professional		5.5	19.9	3.3	15.7								
Clerical		5.8	18.9	4.1	17.4								
Agricultural		1.8	0.4	4.0	0.7								
Fishing, hunting and trapping		9.2	0.1	20.5	0.1								
Logging		6.5	*	10.2	0.2								
Mining and quarrying		2.5	-	2.5	-								
Manufacturing & mechanical (e)		13.4	3.6	10.5	5.4								
Construction	See regional	8.6	*	7.8	*								
Transportation	data under	13.8	2.2	11.9	2.2								
Commercial	P.E.I.	4.1	16.2	2.9	17.6								
Financial		0.3	*	0.1	*								
Service		7.6	27.7	5.4	33.0								
Personal		3.9	27.4	3.2	32.8								
Labourers(g)		10.0	0.4	9.4	9.4								
Not stated		3.5	3.2	1.1	0.7								
Prince Edward Island													
All occupations	618,000 100.0	26,068 100.0	8,080 100.0	26,001 100.0	5,099 100.0	26,001 100.0	5,099 100.0	27,613 100.0	4,316 100.0	26,788 100.0	3,995 100.0	27,853 100.0	3,913 100.0
Proprietary and managerial	8.6	7.1	2.9	6.0	3.3	4.0	2.0	4.1	1.9	5.8	1.6	2.8	0.8
Professional	12.9	3.8	19.9	2.8	20.4	2.6	21.1	2.2	19.9	1.8	20.4	2.1	14.8
Clerical	13.1	3.4	17.3	2.6	16.8	1.4	9.2	1.6	10.5	1.9(h)	10.4	1.3	4.9
Agricultural	3.2	32.8	8.0	45.0	4.2	62.6	6.1	63.8	13.0	66.6	11.5	68.5	14.8
Fishing, hunting & trapping	2.6	6.9(d)	0.3	6.9(d)	0.1(d)	6.0	0.1	5.2	-	4.4(d)	0.1(d)	4.8	0.4
Logging	1.5	0.9	-	0.9	-	0.8	-	*	-	0.3	-	0.2	-
Mining & quarrying	1.0	*	-	*	-	*	-	*	-	*	-	0.1	-
Manufacturing & mechanical (e)	23.8	8.8	7.9	6.8	8.2	4.8	1.8	4.1	6.5	3.6	9.5	5.7	19.4

	1971 Both Sexes	1961 M	1961 F	1951 M	1951 F	1941(b) M	1941(b) F	1931 M	1931 F	1921 M	1921 F	1911 M	1911 F
Prince Edward Island cont'd.													
Construction	7.3	6.77	0.02	5.51	0.05	3.94	-	3.35	-	3.13	-	3.13	0.08
Transportation(f)	7.3	8.30	2.38	7.45	2.60	4.84	1.59	3.98	1.88	2.80	1.08	3.60	0.43
Commercial	-	4.56	10.45	3.35	11.58	2.65	8.81	2.48	7.25	2.49	8.99	2.16	5.70
Financial	-	0.38	0.05	0.22	0.08	0.20	0.02	0.29	-	0.24	0.03	0.09	0.03
Service	13.9	7.81	27.15	6.31	30.49	1.77	47.70	1.56	36.49	1.19	36.24	1.08	38.44
Personal	-	2.64	26.37	1.91	30.42	1.20	47.62	1.14	36.47	0.85	35.22	1.01	38.36
Labourers(g)	4.9	5.73	1.05	5.27	1.18	4.44	0.59	7.21	2.50	5.68	-	4.56	0.05
Not stated	-	2.10	2.77	0.83	1.12	0.10	0.14	0.04	0.05	0.03	0.15	-	-
Nova Scotia													
All occupations		178,559 100.0	58,260 100.0	177,905 100.0	42,680 100.0	153,712 100.0	36,952 100.0	152,632 100.0	27,811 100.0	155,740 100.0	28,528 100.0	147,864 100.0	23,997 100.0
Proprietary and managerial		8.44	3.80	7.44	4.24	5.59	2.69	5.66	2.52	7.69	2.75	4.08	1.90
Professional		5.43	20.42	3.72	18.49	3.03	17.00	2.57	20.25	2.28	18.66	1.88	15.20
Clerical		5.22	24.25	4.44	22.02	3.25	13.50	2.63	12.26	3.09h	13.00	2.93	5.34
Agricultural		6.69	0.03	12.88	1.17		1.73	27.80	4.66	30.38	5.17	31.76	6.44
Fishing, hunting & trapping		4.25	-	5.64(d)	0.04(d)	6.94(d)	0.01	7.48	0.09	7.83(d)	0.05(d)	9.78	0.13
Logging		1.93	-	2.82	-	3.49	-	1.39	-	1.44	-	2.07(i)	-
Mining & quarrying		4.03	-	6.75	-	9.22	-	9.71	-	9.15	-	11.34(j)	-
Manufacuring & mechanical(e)		14.25	5.52	13.03	6.66	11.47	6.25	8.06	6.69	8.14	9.52	9.62	18.71
Construction		7.86	-	7.58	-	7.25	0.02	5.46	0.01	6.23	0.01	4.73	0.02
Transportation(f)		10.62	2.62	10.96	2.76	9.62	1.77	8.10	2.40	6.31	2.56	7.13	1.17
Commercial		4.79	12.04		12.58		10.44	3.21	8.66	2.78	8.92	2.78	6.33
Financial		0.65	0.15	0.40	0.08	0.39	0.03	0.46	0.06	0.35	0.03	1.83	-
Service		15.72	27.56	9.83	29.91	3.40	45.39	3.52	41.30	1.56	39.14	1.66	44.64
Personal(g)		3.41	26.77	2.56	29.60	2.27	45.33	2.24	41.21		37.80		44.58
Labourers		8.10	0.74	9.40	0.71	8.71	1.09	13.92	1.08	11.24	0.01	9.88	0.03
Not Stated		2.00	2.00	1.50	1.34	0.23	0.09	0.03	0.03	0.13	0.18	-	-
New Brunswick													
All occupations		132,549 100.0	45,806 100.0	134,728 100.0	34,034 100.0	118,794 100.0	27,358 100.0	117,008 100.0	21,927 100.0	111,874 100.0	19,647 100.0	102,669 100.0	16,237 100.0
Proprietary and managerial		8.62	4.00	7.34	3.94	4.96	2.28	5.20	1.86	6.43	2.64	3.60	1.67
Professional		5.62	19.94	3.53	18.46	2.77	17.85	2.48	19.61	2.00	19.36	1.94	16.17
Clerical		5.48	23.23	4.62	21.66	2.90	13.74	2.91	13.99	3.35(h)	15.54	2.34	6.53
Agricultural		9.16	1.28	19.37	1.19	34.25	2.36	38.09	4.50	40.47	5.09	43.51	5.55

Note: For "Proprietary and managerial", "Professional", and "Clerical" of Nova Scotia and New Brunswick — See regional data under P.E.I.

TABLE J3 continued

	1971 Both Sexes	1961 M	1961 F	1951 M	1951 F	1941(b) M	1941(b) F	1931 M	1931 F	1921 M	1921 F	1911 M	1911 F
New Brunswick con't.													
Fishing, hunting and trapping		2.77	0.06	3.42(d)	0.04(d)	3.67	0.04	3.75	0.14	2.62(d)	0.03(d)	2.76	0.04
Logging		6.81	0.03	10.83	-	9.85	-	2.43	-	3.62	-	4.22(i)	-
Mining & quarrying		0.33	-	0.69	-	1.30	-	0.78	-	0.67	-	0.79(j)	-
Manufacturing and mechanical(e)		13.99	6.77	12.05	9.41	9.77	7.00	7.27	8.26	7.21	12.46	8.80	23.64
Construction		7.29	0.02	6.25	0.03	5.05	0.01	4.40	-	4.57	-	4.06	0.03
Transportation(f)		11.64	2.40	11.55	2.54	9.49	1.59	6.49	2.13	6.12	2.28	5.85	0.96
Commercial		5.09	11.45	3.78	12.04	3.20	9.92	3.26	8.52	3.37	9.22	3.26	6.09
Financial		0.60	0.10	0.39	0.06	0.36	0.06	0.46	0.05	0.31	0.03	0.18	0.02
Service		10.40	27.10	4.99	27.43	3.27	43.90	2.81	39.65	2.14	33.09	2.19	39.24
Personal		3.17	26.64	2.35	27.28	2.10	43.83	1.99	39.57	1.42	32.04	2.00	39.14
Labourers(g)		9.40	1.04	9.61	1.52	8.96	1.05	19.62	1.24	17.03	0.09	16.50	0.05
Not Stated		2.29	2.59	1.58	1.68	0.19	0.21	0.04	0.05	0.09	0.17	-	-
Quebec													
All occupations	2,197,000 / 100.0	1,289,423 / 100.0	478,694 / 100.0	1,126,696 / 100.0	340,591 / 100.0	922,292 / 100.0	259,312 / 100.0	813,323 / 100.0	200,850 / 100.0	634,587 / 100.0	136,900 / 100.0	546,537 / 100.0	98,429 / 100.0
Proprietary and managerial	9.5	9.00	2.68	8.42	2.77	6.06	1.89	6.77	1.56	8.62	2.14	5.72	1.85
Professional	14.7	7.89	16.74	5.50	15.38	5.31	16.53	4.19	18.03	3.24	21.80	2.77	13.21
Clerical	14.8	7.61	25.00	6.38	22.38	4.64	13.94	5.22	13.93	5.17(h)	13.18	2.96	5.77
Agricultural	4.5	9.09	3.20	16.47	2.16	26.72	1.34	26.82	2.28	32.99	2.64	36.67	3.06
Fishing, hunting and trapping		0.27	0.01	0.49(d)	0.01(d)	0.87	0.02	0.77	0.02	0.61(d)	0.01(d)	0.80	0.01
Logging	0.6	2.47	0.01	3.06	-	3.25	-	1.82	-	1.62	-	2.01(i)	-
Mining & quarrying	0.5	1.01	-	1.05	-	1.06	0.01	0.73	-	0.61	-	1.00(j)	-
Manufacturing and mechanical(e)	26.7	20.11	16.24	19.55	22.47	18.20	23.08	12.63	18.66	11.78	26.37	14.22	33.16
Construction	-	8.06	0.03	7.99	0.04	7.10	0.02	7.07	0.01	6.58	0.01	5.51	1.19
Transportation(f)	5.4	9.83	2.03	8.99	2.54	7.41	1.33	7.00	1.98	5.42	2.31	6.28	5.58
Commercial	6.2	5.83	8.18	4.92	8.26	4.82	7.16	5.30	7.02	5.05	6.06	4.76	-
Financial	-	0.99	0.11	0.67	0.07	0.65	0.05	0.86	0.05	0.58	0.04	0.34	0.01
Service	13.0	7.52	21.18	5.75	20.39	4.70	32.25	4.33	33.10	3.17	24.71	3.01	36.11
Personal	-	4.32	20.72	3.35	20.23	3.11	32.16	3.03	33.04	1.95	24.01	2.72	36.00
Labourers(g)	4.1	7.31	1.36	8.88	2.19	8.80	2.12	16.40	3.34	14.19	0.01	13.95	0.03
Not Stated	-	3.00	3.20	1.90	1.34	0.41	0.26	0.04	0.03	0.37	0.73	-	-

TABLE J-3 continued

Ontario

	1971 Both Sexes	1961 M	1961 F	1951 M	1951 F	1941(b) M	1941(b) F	1931 M	1931 F	1921 M	1921 F	1911 M	1911 F
All occupations	3,079,000	1,700,567	692,448	1,458,110	444,398	1,137,584	314,487	1,094,008	249,095	917,826	193,543	829,200	151,711
	100.0	100.0	100.0	100.0	100.0	100.0	100.0	100.0	100.0	100.0	100.0	100.0	100.0
Proprietary and managerial	9.8	10.25	2.69	9.58	2.81	6.94	1.80	7.14	1.52	9.01	1.94	5.28	1.52
Professional	14.6	8.51	13.74	6.07	12.16	5.06	13.36	4.16	15.63	3.10	16.01	2.39	11.25
Clerical	16.6	7.47	32.51	7.07	32.35	5.89	23.26	5.16	21.86	5.53(l)	22.58	3.24	11.49
Agricultural	4.5												
Fishing, hunting and trapping	-	0.19	0.02	0.21(d)	0.02(d)	0.55	0.03	0.55	0.08	0.26(d)	-	0.43	0.06
Logging	-	0.70	-	1.14	-	1.25	-	0.80	-	0.82	-	1.22(i)	-
Mining & quarrying	0.8	1.52	-	1.43	-	2.08	-	1.32	-	0.89	-	1.95(j)	-
Manufacturing & mechanical(e)	25.7	21.87	10.03	23.16	15.59	22.05	17.25	15.55	14.42	14.28	20.06	15.49	29.18
Construction	5.0	7.00	0.07	7.18	0.12	6.10	0.07	6.24	0.02	6.26	0.03	5.56	0.01
Transportation(f)	7.4	8.80	2.16	8.68	3.08	7.70	1.79	7.77	2.72	6.64	3.41	6.35	1.58
Commercial	-	5.87	0.50	4.97	10.61	5.03	9.44	5.45	9.57	4.88	9.58	4.26	7.88
Financial	-	1.25	0.25	0.91	0.16	0.84	0.11	1.02	0.10	0.79	0.05	0.36	0.03
Service	10.9	8.66	21.57	7.03	17.71	5.00	29.39	4.41	30.15	3.48	23.16	3.03	33.17
Personal	-	4.45	21.12	3.50	17.52	3.41	29.30	3.03	30.05	2.03	22.25	2.76	33.07
Labourers (g)	4.6	6.60	1.36	8.17	2.18	8.10	1.49	13.29	1.38	12.65	0.19	14.42	0.09
Not stated	-	2.52	1.80	0.99	1.06	0.30	0.23	0.06	0.07	0.19	0.21	-	-

Manitoba

	1971 Both Sexes	1961 M	1961 F	1951 M	1951 F	1941(b) M	1941(b) F	1931 M	1931 F	1921 M	1921 F	1911 M	1911 F
All occupations	See regional data under Sask.	246,198	96,444	231,899	66,135	215,180	49,764	224,883	44,812	183,703	31,444	154,917	21,749
		100.0	100.0	100.0	100.0	100.0	100.0	100.0	100.0	100.0	100.0	100.0	100.0
Proprietary and managerial		8.95	2.22	8.36	2.25	6.15	1.40	6.03	1.08	8.00	1.50	5.63	0.90
Professional		6.45	14.02	4.46	13.14	3.96	15.48	3.56	17.48	3.00	19.38	2.63	13.31
Clerical		6.77	28.61	6.13	29.99	4.77	20.45	4.96	20.52	5.84(h)	24.16	4.02	14.19
Agricultural		21.32	7.70	30.28	5.09	41.96	3.01	40.36	4.14	46.12	4.03	44.32	4.14
Fishing, hunting and trapping		0.55	0.01	0.67(d)	0.02(d)	2.36	0.10	1.75	-	0.24(d)	0.01(d)	0.27	0.01
Logging		0.38	-	0.56	-	0.69	-	0.23	-	0.13	-	0.17(i)	-
Mining & quarrying		1.15	-	0.93	-	1.03	-	0.65	-	0.15	-	0.58(j)	-
Manufacturing & mechanical(e)		13.88	7.33	12.94	10.40	11.16	7.67	8.33	6.24	6.46	7.31	7.83	12.62
Construction		6.22	0.05	6.16	0.11	5.16	0.03	5.01	-	6.95	-	6.15	0.02
Transportation(f)		10.13	2.35	9.45	2.41	7.47	1.68	7.00	1.97	6.95	3.15	7.63	3.01

159

TABLE J-3 continued

	1971 Both Sexes	1961 M	1961 F	1951 M	1951 F	1941(b) M	1941(b) F	1931 M	1931 F	1921 M	1921 F	1911 M	1911 F
Manitoba con't.													
Commercial		5.04	10.19	4.71	11.77	4.49	9.39	4.85	9.04	5.25	11.33	5.43	7.89
Financial		0.94	0.23	0.69	0.12	0.59	0.08	0.81	0.08	0.91	0.08	0.41	0.01
Service		9.13	24.13	6.69	22.78	4.53	40.09	4.45	38.63	3.82	28.82	3.52	43.82
Personal		4.15	23.66	3.56	22.51	3.12	39.86	3.21	38.43	2.32	27.40	3.22	43.76
Labourers(g)		6.63	0.97	7.23	1.12	5.53	0.53	11.96	0.62	8.25	0.05	11.40	0.08
Not Stated		2.44	2.18	0.76	0.82	0.14	0.10	0.05	0.07	0.14	0.19	-	-
Saskatchewan													
All occupations	1,338,000	248,479	77,110	250,709	50,936	272,823	42,681	300,740	37,400	239,743	24,588	194,606	12,926
	100.0	100.0	100.0	100.0	100.0	100.0	100.0	100.0	100.0	100.0	100.0	100.0	100.0
Proprietary and managerial	9.6	8.13	2.72	7.26	2.58	5.13	1.75	4.84	1.31	6.03	1.35	3.74	1.29
Professional	13.4	5.63	18.19	3.64	19.87	2.80	19.65	2.42	23.18	2.09	23.64	1.66	13.44
Clerical	13.2	3.64	21.49	2.97	21.86	1.86	13.84	2.20	13.13	2.54(h)	16.79	1.71	9.31
Agricultural	17.2	43.18	15.94	56.43	11.35	67.43	7.42	66.58	9.58	70.95	9.08	67.31	12.41
Fishing, hunting and trapping		0.48	0.02	0.54(d)	0.04(d)	0.96	0.12	0.66	0.26	0.30(d)	-	0.92	0.25
Logging		0.41	0.01	0.24	-	0.34	-	0.08	-	0.04	-	0.23(i)	-
Mining & quarrying	0.8	0.80	-	0.34	-	0.30	-	0.24	-	0.14	-	0.33(j)	-
Manufacturing and mechanical (e)	25.7	7.81	-	5.88	2.31	4.57	-	3.57	1.64	2.53	2.62	2.97	6.31
Construction	-	4.49	0.02	3.05	0.02	1.97	0.01	2.30	-	2.17	-	4.11	-
Transportation (f)	5.0	8.95	2.58	7.55	2.87	4.96	1.68	4.33	1.89	3.44	2.92	3.74	0.97
Commercial	7.4	4.06	9.21	4.19	9.75	3.49	6.33	3.54	5.22	3.31	6.54	2.75	4.15
Financial	-	0.60	0.11	0.41	0.08	0.32	0.03	0.51	0.03	0.50	0.04	0.17	0.01
Service	10.9	5.28	24.54	3.51	28.13	2.73	47.20	2.54	43.59	2.34	36.92	2.14	51.76
Personal	-	2.98	24.25	2.22	27.95	2.00	47.13	1.96	43.48	1.42	35.96	1.98	51.62
Labourers(g)	4.6	4.26	0.49	3.50	0.42	2.98	0.10	6.17	0.17	3.56	0.03	3.21	0.10
Not Stated	-	2.25	2.85	0.48	0.73	0.16	0.11	0.01	0.01	0.06	0.06	-	-
Alberta													
All occupations	See regional data under Sask.	361,961	127,550	290,931	62,566	247,456	40,375	252,315	33,425	194,497	21,087	149,147	11,664
		100.0	100.0	100.0	100.0	100.0	100.0	100.0	100.0	100.0	100.0	100.0	100.0
Proprietary and managerial		9.77	2.72	8.08	2.95	5.43	2.05	5.22	1.45	6.38	1.51	4.99	1.53
Professional		7.46	15.78	4.74	16.42	3.39	19.23	2.86	21.97	2.63	22.19	2.12	15.63
Clerical		5.15	27.77	4.04	27.71	2.75	16.28	2.88	16.38	3.57(h)	20.54	2.43	12.21
Agricultural		25.16	10.25	38.36	5.31	56.04	5.91	56.41	9.03	57.63	8.10	53.01	10.65

TABLE J-3 continued

	1971 Both Sexes	1961 M	1961 F	1951 M	1951 F	1941(b) M	1941(b) F	1931 M	1931 F	1921 M	1921 F	1911 M	1911 F
Alberta con't.													
Fishing, hunting and trapping		0.23	0.02	0.34(d)	0.01(d)	1.21	0.04	0.85	0.02	0.26(d)	0.01(d)	0.59	0.03
Logging		0.63	-	0.47	-	0.38	-	0.18	-	0.17	-	0.43(i)	-
Mining & quarrying		1.47	-	2.57	-	3.05	-	3.49	-	4.35	-	3.40(j)	-
Manufacturing and mechanical (e)		11.28	3.15	9.18	4.10	6.89	3.73	5.24	2.91	4.22	5.04	4.48	8.61
Construction		6.49	0.05	6.12	0.09	3.24	0.01	3.08	-	2.87	-	5.11	-
Transportation(f)		9.89	2.57	8.46	2.52	5.83	1.56	5.20	1.88	4.93	2.44	5.70	1.43
Commercial		5.39	10.16	4.50	11.94	3.69	7.80	3.78	6.97	3.32	7.18	2.86	4.99
Financial		0.96	0.15	0.74	0.17	0.42	0.15	0.64	0.08	0.73	0.05	0.27	-
Service		8.07	24.03	6.26	27.25	3.43	42.86	3.52	39.02	3.72	32.84	3.29	44.88
Personal		3.75	23.51	2.76	26.96	2.53	42.73	2.76	38.93	2.51	31.29	3.04	44.50
Labourers (g)		5.72	0.84	5.60	0.74	4.10	0.27	6.62	0.29	5.60	-	11.32	0.04
Not Stated		2.33	2.50	0.53	0.79	0.15	0.10	0.03	-	0.12	0.09	-	-
British Columbia													
All occupations	847,000 / 100.0	421,786 / 100.0	155,862 / 100.0	345,952 / 100.0	97,908 / 100.0	258,586 / 100.0	55,101 / 100.0	262,264 / 100.0	43,684 / 100.0	193,705 / 100.0	25,408 / 100.0	188,644 / 100.0	16,418 / 100.0
Proprietary and managerial	11.2	10.08	4.18	9.80	4.08	7.06	3.18	7.15	2.46	9.82	2.92	6.39	1.59
Professional	13.1	8.08	15.05	5.86	14.47	4.84	16.50	4.08	18.29	4.05	21.23	3.01	12.82
Clerical	14.5	5.49	31.21	5.30	30.74	4.10	19.49	4.26	19.83	5.05(h)	22.02	3.24	13.33
Agricultural	3.0	5.07	1.97	7.76	1.59	15.49	2.55	16.05	3.25	17.67	2.92	12.69	2.46
Fishing, hunting and trapping	1.5	1.18	0.05	1.52(d)	0.06(d)	3.65	0.06	3.57	0.11	2.40(d)	0.02(d)	2.37	0.44
Logging	0.7	3.15	0.01	5.21	0.02	5.37	-	4.68	-	6.06	-	6.09(i)	-
Mining & quarrying		1.16	-	2.10	0.01	4.14	-	3.87	-	5.29	-	8.02(j)	0.02
Manufacturing and mechanical (e)	24.6	18.65	4.52	17.78	6.23	16.16	6.42	11.21	6.32	9.95	7.60	9.68	19.22
Construction	5.7	6.88	0.03	7.81	0.06	7.04	0.01	6.61	-	6.57	0.03	7.95	0.02
Transportation(f)	8.0	11.72	2.40	11.39	4.19	9.53	2.85	9.27	4.11	7.37	4.86	7.99	2.02
Commercial		5.99	11.82	5.19	12.47	4.69	11.18	4.97	10.23	4.52	9.88	4.05	6.36
Financial		1.37	0.40	1.16	0.33	0.98	0.27	1.21	0.19	1.07	0.16	0.32	0.01
Service	13.1	9.83	24.32	8.76	23.29	6.96	36.69	6.93	34.49	6.61	28.07	5.64	41.70

161

TABLE J-3 continued

	1971 Both Sexes	1961 M	F	1951 M	F	1941(b) M	F	1931 M	F	1921 M	F	1911 M	F
Personal	-	4.98	23.79	4.70	22.93	5.28	36.38	5.45	34.12	4.77	26.85	5.29	41.43
Labourers(g)	4.3	7.44	1.00	8.90	1.26	9.66	0.55	16.10	0.70	13.35	0.17	22.55	0.02
Not Stated	-	3.02	3.03	1.46	1.20	0.32	0.16	0.03	0.01	0.22	0.12	-	-

Note: The labour force was counted as gainfully employed prior to 1951. All occupations on base of 1951 classification. No provincial data for 1901.

(a) Provisional figures from a labour force survey for September 1971. The 1961 occupational categories adapted for the 1951 classification for the sake of comparability. Adaptation only approximate. Data from Provinces for both sexes only, 1971 annual averages.
(b) Excludes persons on Active Service on 2 June 1941.
(c) Excludes Yukon and Northwest Territories. Includes Newfoundland for 1951, 1961, 1971.
(d) Excludes Indians living on reserves, and all Indians for 1901.
(e) Includes stationary enginemen and occupations associated with electric power production.
(f) Includes communication.
(g) Labourers in all industries except extraction industries (agriculture, mining, fishing, logging).
(h) Includes proofreaders, shippers, weighmen and postmen classified elsewhere in other years:
(i) Includes pulp mill employees, stationary engineers and occupations associated with electric power production.
(j) Includes almost all mine and smelter employees except clerical workers.
(k) No separate data available.

* Value smaller than 0.05 per cent.

Source: Labour Force Survey Division, Statistics Canada, unpublished tabulations for 1971; The Labour Force Survey, September 1971, table 14; 1961 Census of Canada, Bull.3.1-1, tables 3,3,38.

162

TABLE J-3 continued   PERCENT DISTRIBUTION OF THE LABOUR FORCE 15 YEARS AND OVER, BY MAJOR OCCUPATIONAL GROUPINGS, FOR CANADA BY SEX, AND FOR THE PROVINCES, 1971

Occupation Group	CANADA		NFLD.	PEI.	NOVA SCOTIA
	M	F	M&F	M&F	M&F
All occupations	5,665,700	2,961,200	148,000	43,000	286,400
Managerial,Administrative and Related Occupations	5.5	2.0	3.5	2.8	3.4
Occupations in Natural Sciences, Engineering and Mathematics	3.8	0.6	2.0	1.4	2.2
Occupations in Social Sciences and Related Fields	0.9	1.0	0.5	0.7	0.8
Occupations in Religion	0.4	0.1	0.4	0.5	0.4
Teaching and Related Occupations	2.4	7.1	4.7	4.4	4.4
Occupations in Medicine and Health	1.5	8.2	3.9	4.2	4.0
Artistic, Literary, Recreational and Related Fields	1.0	0.7	0.5	0.7	0.7
Clerical and Related Occupations	7.7	31.8	11.4	9.8	13.3
Sales Occupations	10.0	8.4	9.1	7.9	9.6
Service Occupations	9.2	15.1	11.0	13.3	15.7
Farming and Animal Husbandry Occupations	7.2	3.6	1.1	14.2	3.0
Fishing, Hunting, Trapping and Related Occupations	0.5	(500)	4.9	5.1	2.3
Forestry and Logging Occupations	1.2	0.1	1.6	0.2	1.1
Mining and Quarrying Including Oil and Gas Field Occupations	1.0	(400)	1.4	0.2	1.2
Processing Occupations	4.9	2.0	6.4	5.6	4.5
Machining and Related Occupations	4.0	0.5	1.4	0.7	1.9

163

TABLE J-3 continued

Occupation Group	CANADA M	CANADA F	NFLD. M&F	PEI. M&F	NOVA SCOTIA M&F
Product Fabricating, Assembling and Repairing Occupations	8.5	5.1	4.3	3.0	5.2
Construction Trades Occupations	9.9	0.2	10.1	7.4	8.9
Transport Equipment Operation Occupations	5.8	0.3	6.4	4.2	5.0
Materials Handling and Related Occupations	2.9	1.4	2.8	1.6	2.5
Other Crafts and Equipment Operating Occupations	1.7	0.5	1.5	0.7	1.2
Occupations, Not Elsewhere Classified	2.6	0.7	1.3	1.6	1.0
Occupations Not Stated	7.4	10.8	9.8	9.5	7.6

Occupation Group	NEW BRUNSWICK M&F	QUEBEC M&F	ONTARIO M&F	MANITOBA M&F	SASKATCHEWAN M&F
All Occupation	223,500	2,169,100	3,354,400	413,900	371,100
Managerial,Administrative and Related Occupations	3.2	4.8	4.7	4.1	3.2
Occupations in Natural Sciences, Engineering and Mathematics	2.1	2.5	3.1	2.4	1.6
Occupations in Social Sciences and Related Fields	0.8	1.0	1.0	0.9	0.7
Occupations in Religion	0.5	0.3	0.2	0.3	0.4
Teaching and Related Occupations	4.4	4.5	3.8	3.9	4.0
Occupations in Medicine and Health	3.8	3.7	3.7	4.8	3.9
Artistic, Literary, Recreational and Related Fields	0.6	1.1	1.0	0.2	0.6
Clerical and Related Occupations	13.3	16.0	17.6	15.4	10.8

TABLE J-3 continued

	NEW BRUNSWICK M&F	QUEBEC M&F	ONTARIO M&F	MANITOBA M&F	SASKATCHEWAN M&F
Sales Occupations	9.4	9.1	9.6	9.1	8.6
Service Occupations	13.2	10.4	10.6	11.7	10.8
Farming and Animal Husbandry Occupations	3.4	3.6	4.5	11.8	27.4
Fishing, Hunting, Trapping and Related Occupations	1.2	0.1	(1200)	(300)	(300)
Forestry and Logging Occupations	2.9	0.9	0.3	0.2	0.3
Mining and Quarrying Including Oil and Gas Field Occupations	0.7	0.5	0.6	0.8	0.9
Processing Occupations	6.2	4.5	3.7	2.4	1.6
Machining and Related Occupations	1.9	2.6	3.8	3.0	1.0
Product Fabricating, Assembling and Repairing Occupations	5.2	9.0	8.3	6.8	3.7
Construction Trades Occupations	8.8	5.8	6.2	6.6	5.5
Transport Equipment Operation Occupations	4.8	4.0	3.6	3.9	3.4
Materials Handling and Related Occupations	3.0	1.8	2.5	2.1	1.9
Other Crafts and Equipment Operating Occupations	1.2	1.3	1.4	1.2	0.9
Occupations, Not Elsewhere Classified	1.0	2.3	2.3	1.8	1.34
Occupations Not Stated	8.4	12.2	7.1	7.7	7.6

TABLE J-3 continued

Occupation Group	ALBERTA M&F	B.C. M&F	YUKON & N.W.T. M&F
All occupations	688,300	910,100	19,100
Managerial,Administrative and Related Occupations	3.9	3.6	3.7
Occupations in Natural Sciences, Engineering and Mathematics	2.9	2.6	3.1
Occupations in Social Sciences and Related Fields	0.9	0.9	1.0
Occupations in Religion	0.2	0.2	0.5
Teaching and Related Occupations	4.1	3.5	4.2
Occupations in Medicine and Health	4.0	3.7	2.6
Artistic, Literary, Recreational and Related Fields	0.7	0.9	1.0
Clerical and Related Occupations	14.6	15.6	12.0
Sales Occupations	9.6	10.6	5.2
Service Occupations	11.7	13.1	14.1
Farming and Animal Husbandry Occupations	13.0	3.0	5.0
Fishing, Hunting, Trapping and Related Occupations	(200)	0.5	2.1
Forestry and Logging Occupations	0.3	2.1	1.0
Mining and Quarrying Including Oil and Gas Field Operations	1.1	0.6	4.2
Processing Occupations	2.2	4.9	1.6
Machining and Related Occupations	1.7	2.1	1.0
Product Fabricating, Assembling and Repairing Occupations	4.5	5.8	5.8
Construction Trades Occupations	7.5	7.6	8.4
Transport Equipment Operation Occupation	3.8	4.4	5.8

TABLE J-3 continued

Occupation Group	ALBERTA M&F	B.C. M&F	YUKON & N.W.T. M&F
Materials Handling and Related Occupations	2.2	3.6	2.1
Other Crafts and Equipment Operating Occupations	1.0	1.1	2.1
Occupations, Not elsewhere Classified	1.7	1.0	1.6
Occupations Not Stated	8.2	8.6	15.7

Comment: The 1971 census started a new series of occupational division of the labour force. Excludes persons looking for work, who last worked prior to January 1, 1970 or who never worked. Data rounded to the nearest 100. Included persons 15 years of age and over who, during the week preceding the census, worked for pay or profit, did unpaid family work, looked for work, were on temporary layoff or had jobs from which they were temporarily absent.

Source: Statistics Canada Daily, Dec. 27, 1973, pg. 2,3.

TABLE J-4 PER CENT DISTRIBUTION OF THE CANADIAN LABOUR FORCE, BY OCCUPATIONAL GROUP, LEVEL OF EDUCATION AND SEX, 1966, AND BY SEX, EDUCATION AND OCCUPATIONAL GROUP, 1972

Level of Education(a)	All Occupations	White Collar(b)	Blue Collar(c)	Service and Recreation	Transportation and Communication	Primary Occupations(d)
All Levels in 000s (e)	8,085	3,821	2,327	958	413	565
Elementary T	23.5	8.1	37.1	32.9	35.4	47.8
M	26.8	14.9(f)	50.5(f)	46.3(f)	49.8(f)	66.9(f)
F	17.4	8.2(f)	56.9(f)	45.8(f)	*	59.0(f)
Secondary T	53.8	52.9	54.9	57.3	58.1	45.5
M	51.4	56.1(f)	47.2(f)	50.6(f)	47.8(f)	31.5(f)
F	58.4	73.3(f)	42.2(f)	52.4(f)	85.5(f)	39.2(f)
Post-secondary T	22.7	39.1	8.0	9.7	6.8	6.4
M	21.8	29.0(f)	2.3(f)	3.1(f)	*	1.6(f)
F	24.5	18.0(f)	*	*	*	*

* Based on estimate of less than 10,000
Note: Based on supplementary information from the Labour Force Survey, January 1966 and April 1972. Since data are from a single month at a time, considerable fluctuation in categories may be expected.

(a) Refers to either some or completed education.
(b) Includes persons in managerial, professional and technical, clerical and sales occupations.
(c) Includes craftsmen, production process and related workers, and labourers not included elsewhere.
(d) Includes farmers and farm workers, logger and related workers, fishermen, trappers and hunters.
(e) Sample reinflated to estimate population in labour force for 1966 and in labour force and employed in 1972.
(f) For 1966, the estimated number for all occupations was 7,079,000, and for the occupation groups as follows (in 000s): white collar, 2,981; blue collar, 2,231; service, 814; transportation, 410; primary, 643.

Sources: The Labour Force, February 1973, tables S-3, S-6; Lagace, Educational Attainment in Canada, tables 4, F2.

TABLE J-5 OCCUPATIONAL DISTRIBUTION OF THE IMMIGRANT AND NATIVE-
BORN LABOUR FORCE, FOR CANADA, 1967.

Occupation	Post War Immigrants	Native-Born
Total	1,003,000(a)	5,977,000(a)
Managerial	8.0	10.0
Professional	15.0	12.7
Clerical	11.7	15.0
Sales	4.7	7.1
Service	12.9	11.4
Transportation and Communication	2.3	6.4
Primary	3.3	8.8
Craftsmen	36.8	24.8
Other	5.2	3.8

Note: Based on a DBS labour force survey, February 1967.
      (a) Reinflated sample estimate.

Source: N.H.W. Davis and M.J.Gupta, Labour Force Characteristics,
        table D12.

TABLE J-6 AVERAGE INCOME OF PERSONS REPORTING INCOME BY OCCUPATION AND SEX, FOR SELECTED AGE GROUPS, FOR CANADA, 1971.

Occupation and Sex	All Ages	Under 25	30-34	40-44	50-54
Professionals					
M	$27,115	$4,505	$21,383	$32,123	$32,422
F	8,009	3,889	7,425	10,095	7,906
Salesmen					
M	9,097	4,290	7,662	10,575	10,210
F	5,023	3,771	4,893	5,155	5,799
Employees					
M	8,001	4,891	8,999	10,049	9,834
F	4,831	3,908	5,200	5,120	5,339
Business Proprietors					
M	7,795	4,565	7,452	8,698	8,188
F	5,064	3,660	4,746	5,476	4,973
Investors and Property Owners					
M	9,249	6,397	10,335	12,866	11,752
F	5,980	5,762	5,757	7,044	6,649
Farmers and Fishermen					
M	6,074	4,005	6,081	6,738	6,486
F	4,394	3,430	4,280	5,446	4,831
Pensioners					
M	4,809	2,033	1,700	4,346	5,459
F	3,578	3,069	2,593	3,115	3,647
Unclassified					
M	6,351	2,996	7,943	7,709	8,448
F	5,151	2,366	4,740	5,944	5,501

Notes: Based on a 6 per cent sample of all returns for tax purposes of T1 Short and T1 General for 1971. Occupational classification is based on the taxpayer's method of earning income rather than on the type of work performed. Averages based on taxable returns.
Professionals: self-employed persons with fees as principal source of income.
Salesmen: only those reporting commission income from self-employment.
Employees: anybody working for an employer, disregarding the kind of work performed.
Property owners: those receiving the bulk of their income from the rental of real estate.
Unclassified: those whose principal source of income is alimony, or certain miscellaneous types of income, e.g., hunters, trappers, and guides.

Source: Department of National Revenue, Taxation Statistics, 1973, (Ottawa: Information Canada, 1973), table 12.

TABLE J-7 ESTIMATED MEDIAN AND AVERAGE INCOMES FOR SELECTED OCCUPATIONAL GROUPS AS DEFINED BY INCOME TAX RETURNS, CANADA, 1969.

Occupational Groups (a)	Taxable Returns (b) No.	Median Income	All Returns (c) No.	Average Income
All Returns	7,363,963	$5,157	8,882,006	$5,232
Employees				
Employees of Businesses	4,584,104	5,282	5,347,328	5,300
Employees of Institutions	471,288	4,116	555,086	4,104
Teachers and Professors	302,498	6,784	324,131	7,176
Federal Employees	249,336	6,643	277,885	6,598
Provincial Employees	310,849	5,949	350,827	5,889
Municipal Employees	277,741	6,308	310,251	5,867
Unclassified	116,222	3,540	153,109	3,368
Self-employed				
Medical Doctors and Surgeons	17,940	32,338(d)	18,174	31,946
Dentists	5,372	19,687	5,500	21,290
Lawyers and Notaries	9,088	21,044	9,325	25,254
Accountants	5,092	14,558	5,212	17,655
Consulting Engineering and Architects	2,442	16,935	2,633	20,783
Entertainers and Artists	6,409	4,081	8,454	4,814
Other Professionals	12,725	5,406	14,697	7,844
Salesmen	21,210	5,769	26,704	6,314
Business Proprietors	273,776	5,161	361,678	5,305
Investors	234,766	3,612	296,170	5,314
Property Owners	60,494	3,933	91,154	4,620
Farmers	124,482	4,058	283,859	2,845
Fishermen	9,115	4,026	14,751	3,695
Pensioners	256,569	2,820	360,533	2,889
Unclassified	12,445	3,234	64,605	978

Note: Estimated from a 7 per cent sample of T1 short and T1 General Income Tax Returns for 1969.

(a) Occupational group is determined by the taxpayer's method of earning income. "Other professionals" includes nurses, osteopaths, chiropractors, surveyors, veterinarians, tax consultants, investment counsellors. Employees of individuals or farmers and other employees who cannot be included elsewhere are shown as "unclassified". Employees of Crown Corporations are shown as employees of businesses.
(b) Taxable returns are those where the earnings after deductions remain subject to tax. In general, this group contains full-time employees and those whose investment and professional income exceeds the minimum nontaxable income.
(c) All returns include those under (b) and those whose income after deductions is not taxable. In general, this group may contain those not fully employed in the customary way.
(d) Average income, as median income could not be calculated due to the open top category of 25,000 and over.

Source: Dept. of National Revenue, Taxation Statistics, 1971, table 13.

BIBLIOGRAPHY

Allingham, J.D., The Demographic Background to Change in the Number
and Composition of Female Wage Earners in Canada, 1951-1961.
Special Labour Force Studies, Series B., No. 1. Ottawa: Queen's
Printer, 1967. (26 pp.)

Women Who Work: Part I: The Relative Importance of Age, Education
and Marital Status for Participation in the Labour Force. Special
Labour Force Studies, Series B, No.5. Ottawa: Queen's Printer
1967. (26 pp.)

Allingham, J.D., and Spencer, B.G., Women Who Work: Part II:
Married Women in the Labour Force: the Influence of Age, Education
Childbearing Status and Residence. Special Labour Force Studies,
Series B, No. 2. Ottawa: Queen's Printer, 1968. (21 pp.)

Bertram, G., The Contribution of Education to Economic Growth.
Staff Study No. 12. Ottawa: Economic Council of Canada, 1966. (146 pp.)

Chernick, S.E., Interregional Disparities in Income. Staff Study
No. 14. Ottawa: Economic Council of Canada, 1966. (91 pp.)

Davis, N.H.W., and Gupta, M.J., Labour Force Characteristics of
Post-War Immigrants and Native-Born Canadians, 1956-1967. Special
Labour Force Studies, No.6. Ottawa: Queen's Printer, 1968. (45 pp.)

Denton, F.T., The Growth of Manpower in Canada. 1961 Census Monograph
Ottawa: Queen's Printer, 1970. (83 pp.)

Denton, F.T., and Ostry, S., Historical Estimates of the Canadian
Labour Force. 1961 Census Monograph. Ottawa: Queen's Printer
1967. (49 pp.)

_____, Working-Life Tables for Canadian Males. 1961 Census
Monograph. Ottawa: Queen's Printer, 1969. (56 pp.)

Meltz, N.M. Changes in the Composition of the Canadian Labour Force,
1931-1961. Occasional Paper No. 2. Ottawa: Department of Labour
1965. (136 pp.)

Ostry, S., The Occupational Composition of the Canadian Labour
Force. 1961 Census Monograph. Ottawa: Queen's Printer, 1967.
(90 pp.)

_____, Provincial Differences in Labour Force Participation.
1961 Census Monograph. Ottawa: Queen's Printer, 1968. (37 pp.)

_____, Unemployment in Canada. 1961 Census Monograph. Ottawa:
Queen's Printer, 1968. (83 pp.)

_____, The Female Worker in Canada. 1961 Census Monograph.
Ottawa: Queen's Printer 1968. (63 pp.)

172

_____, Geographical Composition of the Canadian Labour Force. 1961 Census Monograph. Ottawa: Queen's Printer, 1968. (41 pp.)

_____, Labour Force Participation and Childbearing Status. Demography and Educational Planning. Edited by B. MacLeod. Toronto: Ontario Institute for Studies in Education, 1970, pp. 143-156.

Podoluk, J.R., Incomes of Canadians. 1961 Census Monograph. Ottawa: Queen's Printer, 1968. (356 pp.)

Royal Commission on Bilingualism and Biculturalism, The Work World. Book III, parts 1 and 2. Ottawa: Queen's Printer, 1969. (440 pp.)

Scoville, J.G., The Job Content of the Canadian Economy, 1941, 1951, 1961. Special Labour Force Studies, No. 3. Ottawa: Queen's Printer, 1967. (28 pp.)

Wilkinson, B., Studies in the Economics of Education. Department of Labour, Occasional Paper No. 4. Ottawa: Queen's Printer, 1966. (148 pp.)

4 Comparative Perspectives

No profile of a country would be complete were there not a set of parallel data from other countries against which to draw comparisons. The choice of countries for comparison should rest on specific assumptions of comparability and specific assumptions as to which of the social indicators summarize social conditions most acceptably. It can be argued that comparisons should be made with countries in geographical proximity, with common historical and political tradition or, at least, similar in social and economic development.

Social conditions are reflected both in the behaviour of individuals as monitored by government statistics, and in the social infrastructure, that is, in the arrangements for schooling, employment and income distribution. No doubt, the number of comparisons possible is as inexhaustible as one's imagination. As short-cut indicators, however, a few behaviour indices and a few sketches of social infrastructure should place Canadians and Canadian society in a perspective with the United States and, to a much lesser degree, with a few other countries.

Looking at some of the simple indices of behaviour, one cannot but notice the very recent drop in Canada's birthrate, which, perhaps only temporarily (e.g., in 1970), was slightly lower than that of the United States, contrary to a long-standing difference in the opposite direction (see table C-1). The "youngness" of Canada's population is apparent in its low crude death rate (7.3). However, it is the difference between the death rate and the birthrate that determines the country's natural growth, and Canada's has been about twice as large as that of the United Kingdom, for instance. In the past, a high natural rate of growth was considered a sign of demographic vigour; now we have to think of it as careless reproduction in the face of our ecological crisis.

Countries with a history of development similar to that of Canada -- for example, Australia or New Zealand -- show lower rates of infant mortality than Canada. This can be explained by the unevenness of Canada's public health coverage as it pertains to its remote populations and native peoples. When the fertility and marriage rates of Canada and the United States are compared, both rates appear higher for the latter, even though in the past Canada has generally had a higher fertility but lower marriage rate. Where there is a substantial difference between these two countries is in their divorce rates, the American rate being much higher, as it has been in the past as well. It is not only due to different legislation that such is the case, nor to a heavier Catholic composition of Canada's population. More likely than not, the high divorce rate for the United States is a reflection of a low age at first marriage, which requires occasional rematching of partners: their interests are not defined for them by a close-knit community and their diverging personal growth is abetted by a development-oriented society. Demographically, divorce functions as does male mortality at higher ages, producing a low sex ratio for the unmarried; divorced men tend to remarry to younger women and divorced women add to the female widowed population.

In a way, where there are many people in similar circumstances, coping mechanisms are institutionalized more easily than where there are just a few individuals interspersed in the population. Divorce, then, may result in diversified life

Chart 8.   Crude Birth Rates for Four Countries, 1921-1968

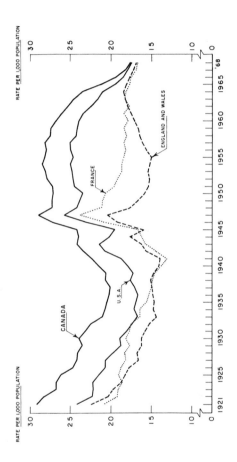

Source: Dominion Bureau of Statistics.   Vital Statistics 1968.   Ottawa: Queen's Printer, 1970, Chart A, page 18.

175

styles of all those without spouses (usually without husbands).
The different age at marriage, the higher resistance to death
and longevity of women, together with the effects of divorce, all
add to the unmarried population at higher ages; such a population
is then large enough to make social provisions for living alone.

One of the demographic features which did separate the
developed from the underdeveloped countries was the practice of
early marriage of women: the proportion marrying early was
inverse to the level of economic development. In North America,
however, a high fertility of very young married women has been
until now a matter of record, even though the proportion marrying
young was fairly low.

Recently, however, those married between fifteen and nineteen
years of age in Canada have shown a dramatic decline in fertility
(see table C-2) as compared with earlier years and with teenage
women in the United States. This is somewhat puzzling in view of
the traditionally higher fertility for Canadian women in all age
categories. One explanation may be that the proportions of women
in the United States who marry in their late teens are composed
of two major racial groups and the Blacks have retained their
fertility, forcing the national rates upward. The same argument
may apply to the increasing rate of illegitimate births,
traditionally higher in the United States than here. Illegitimacy
is, of course, not only an expression of tolerance of births, but also
of tolerance of diverse life styles and of other peoples errors.
What this portends for Canada and the United States (that is, for
the low-fertility segments of their young population) is the
dissociation of marriage and childbearing with the slow population
growth and greater personal growth of women that this dissociation
implies. The cost of the latter may be, at least temporarily,
an increased illegitimacy rate.

One traditional, even though not universal, practice of
limiting population size is self-destruction. Of the many causes
of death, those attributed to cirrhosis of the liver (1),
automobile accidents (2) and suicide are a fair indication of
man's willingness to forfeit his opportunity to stay alive.
Canada has fewer deaths due to cirrhosis of the liver than the
United States,but both have a higher rate than Ireland, which
has been a source of immigrants to both countries for a long
time (see table C-3). Deaths due to automobile accidents and
suicide are evenly matched for both Canada and the United States
but all three causes of death combined represent a slightly
higher proportion of all deaths in Canada. The highest index
of "self-destruction" is shown for France, where the high suicide
rate combined with a high death rate due to cirrhosis account for
over 7 per cent of all deaths.

Mental illness is not as much an attribute of modern living
as its visibility is an attribute of efficient mental-health
diagnosis and treatment capabilities of each society. When
Canada and the United States are compared on incidence of mental
illness (see table C-4), Canadians appear to be hospitalized
more often than Americans. Caution is necessary in interpreting
the data, however, as they may represent differential access to
mental-health facilities and a differential health coverage of
the two countries. In Canada, where the general health services
cover the majority of the population and the personal costs to

---

(1) Technically, cirrhosis of the liver is not identical with
    alcoholism death, only a fair indicator.
(2) Not all deaths caused by motor vehicles, of course.

Chart 9. Standardized Death Rates for Cardiovascular Diseases for Selected
Countries, by Sex, 1964

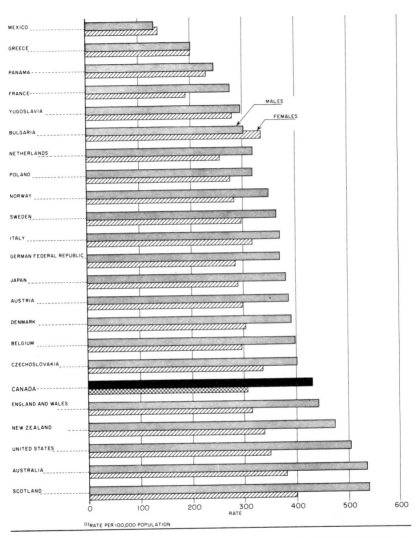

Source: Statistics Canada. Cardiovascular-renal Mortality 1950-1968, Ottawa:
Information Canada, 1973, Chart 15, page 45.

patients in direct payments are negligible, the reporting of
incidence of mental illness would be more intensive than in the
United States. There, the middle strata have to finance their
own health plans and thus either undergo private treatment, which
may go unreported, or abstain from utilizing the public treatment
facilities.(3) Thus, only those segments of the population which
are under government tutelage, by receiving transfer payments,
for instance, are covered by public-health measures and reported.

The disproportionate number of divorced, separated or widowed
males whose mental illness incidence rate for the United States is
double the rate for Canada appears to be recruited from the
category of the disadvantaged. Altogether, men appear to be more
susceptible to mental disorders than women, more so in the United
States. There is a possibility that women are more likely underreported, as their performance at home need not be monitored as
closely as one's performance at work. Data from private mental
hospitals in the United States, however, show heavier admissions
for women, especially for those in middle-age categories and with
disorders of a neurotic nature.(4) Men, on the other hand, are
more prone to disorders stemming from alcoholism and drug dependency
and also from psychoses, all harsh mental illnesses: this is true
more for Americans than for Canadians.

Canadians have a self-image as law-abiding citizens. This
self-image is fairly well supported by data in comparison with the
United States, even though increasing at about the same pace in
both countries. On the whole, the countries become more alike as
one moves toward soft crimes, that is, crimes against property;
nonetheless, both countries show a disturbing rate of growth in
all crime, a pace which outstrips the population growth by about
tenfold (see table C-5).

The dissimilarities between the two countries become more
pronounced in dealing with offenders. Four features seem to
separate the data on both countries: thefts result in arrests
more often in the United States than in Canada; American offenders
are not as exclusively men as offenders in Canada nor are they as
exclusively adult; juveniles in the United States are arrested
about twice as often as juveniles are charged in Canada; and,
finally, car thefts appear to be less frequent in Canada than in
the United States (see table C-6). Some of the differences may be
due, of course, to uneven practices of reporting, crime detection,
and prosecution. The national differences may also suggest that
the urban racial minorities in the United States, more likely
than the rest of the population, find themselves in conflict with
the law(5); it may be that respect for the law is not well
anchored in the American central city, nor has it ever been.

The few indices of individual behaviour suggest that, on
balance, and as compared with Americans, Canadians appear more
prudent, are better taken care of by their government

---

(3) The upper strata are numerically not significant apart from
    being fairly free of mental illness.
(4) The reported figures for the United States refer to all
    admissions to state and county mental hospitals. Of these,
    about 50 to 60 per cent are first admissions. Private hospitals
    and outpatient clinics admit and treat additional patients.
    In terms of first admissions, the figures probably would not
    add to the figures reported in table C-4, thus overinflating
    the American incidence figures.
(5) The breakdown of the United States data by race would confirm
    this interpretation.

institutions in matters of health or public safety; but also, Canadians seem less inclined to violence, disregard of personal safety, and pronounced mental anguish than Americans. Whether their caution in all matters is also reflected in the national economy is a matter of conjecture but the economic vigour of their southern neighbour is obviously not being matched.

The efficiency of a national economy may be a matter of natural resources, supply of skills, as well as of the level of administrative organization of the labour force. Thus, the occupational distribution of the labour force is a good indicator of overall performance of national economies. Occupational distribution for Canada and for the United States is dissimilar only as regards the proportions of the labour force in extractive industries and traditional occupations, where the American labour force has been pared in favour of occupations at clerical and, more importantly, at administrative levels (see table C-7). However, as compared to other immigrant countries -- for example, Australia or New Zealand -- Canada is clearly more like the United States in the makeup of its labour force.

Whether the consistently higher rate of unemployment in Canada as compared to that of the United States is a function of the traditional profile of its labour force or whether it is a result of permissive immigration policies is a matter of conjecture. The Canadian labour force appears undereducated as compared with the United States, especially with respect to postsecondary education and training (see table C-8). As least until now, post-secondary education was closely connected with obtaining jobs on administrative levels, which in turn characterizes advanced economies. Curiously enough, the male lead in education in the United States is greater than the corresponding male lead in Canada. This may mean that the modernization of the Canadian economy, being imported from the outside(6), proceeds at a faster rate than would have been the case under "natural" conditions.

The proportion of population at school, in particular those in universities and colleges, still shows the Americans at an advantage, even though the gap has been narrowing over time (see table C-9). It should be borne in mind that the respective age cohorts in the two countries are likely to retain their educational distance throughout their forty or so years of participation in the labour force, with the obvious implications for the two economies. In view of this, short-term savings, which either government may wish to effectuate by means of grants to educational institutions, may prove somewhat shortsighted.

Education and the type of jobs people hold are reflected in the income people derive from the economy as a whole and from individual wages and salaries. The superficial parallel between the standard of living for Canadians and Americans is not substantiated by actual income figures, the median income for Canadians being quite a bit lower (see table C-10). (7)

---

(6) Imported skills and technological innovations bring modern features to the importing society which the exporting society may not have.
(7) United States figures include income for individuals and families, which make the absolute figures higher for the United States. However, the internal distributions within income ranges show that United States income figures include more earners in the higher categories than do the Canadian figures.

What is particularly revealing is the clustering of income recipients in income ranges and in income deciles; in both instances the Americans appear well represented at the top, whereas the Canadian income distribution tends toward the middle incomes. This is so not entirely because the top professional occupations in the United States yield more money than they do in Canada, but because there are proportionately more people in those occupations in the United States; such a distribution is, thus far, a result of education and training.

The overall income picture of the two countries is reflected as well in the official poverty figures. Canadians as a proportion of population, are more likely to be below the poverty line than Americans (see table C-11). It is in the United States that massive actions and "war" on poverty have been undertaken, as it appears that the smaller the proportion of population below the poverty line the less likely such a condition is taken for granted. The Canadian approach to proverty takes a subdued administrative route of commission reports in the tradition of a parliamentary democracy. Which of the approaches will prove successful in the end is difficult to foretell; as regards the visible poverty, slums are certainly not a Canadian phenomenon.

On balance, the indicators of social infrastructure show Canada lagging behind the United States. However, the latter appears tolerant of a greater measure of behaviour errors, which in turn may make life less pleasant, at least in some urban areas. Quality of life must, in the final analysis, be judged as a balance of benefits of wealth and of cost of wealth's corollaries. Whether crime rates, for instance, always have to increase with societal wealth is difficult to judge, as the North American civilization is unprecedented. On the other hand, whether an exercise in societal constraints should be initiated to limit the behaviour errors of a few at the cost of the personal freedoms of all and at the cost of economic development, is a decision which would be equally unprecedented and would run counter to the history which made this continent so attractive to so many.

TABLE C-1 POPULATION AND PRINCIPAL VITAL STATISTICS FOR CANADA AND SELECTED COUNTRIES, 1970.

Country	Population (or Estimate)	Birth Rate(a)	Death Rate(a)	Infant Mortality Rate(b)	Fertility Rate(c)	Marriage Rate(a)	Divorce Rate(d)	Life Expectancy M	Life Expectancy F
Canada, 1970	21,568,311(e)	17.4	7.3	18.8	58.7	8.8	136	68.8(f)	75.2(f)
Australia, 1970	12,296,000(g)	20.5	9.0	17.9	71.2(h)	9.2	100	67.9(i)	74.2(i)
New Zealand, 1970	2,777,000(g)	22.1	8.8	16.7	80.4(j)	9.2	110(j)	68.4(i)	73.7(i)
South Africa 1967	19,180,000(g)	22.8	8.7	24.2	-	9.7	-	49(k)	
United Kingdom 1970	54,022,000(g)	16.2	11.8	18.6	62.0(j)	8.1(j)	110	68.5(l)	74.7(l)
United States 1970	203,184,772	18.2	9.4	19.8	61.6(j)	10.7	350	66.6(h)	74.0(h)

(a) Per 1,000 population.
(b) Per 1,000 live births.
(c) Per 1,000 women 10-49 years of age.
(d) Per 100,000 population.
(e) 1971 Census.
(f) For 1966.
(g) Estimate for 1969.
(h) For 1968.
(i) For 1960-62.
(j) Estimate from a survey covering a 12 month preceding period.
(k) For 1965-1970.
(l) For 1967-1969.

Sources: United Nations, Demographic Year Book, 1970 (New York: United Nations, 1971), table 3.18;
Vital Statistics, 1970 (Preliminary Report), tables 1,3; Vital Statistics, 1969, tables
L1,S1.

TABLE C-2 CHILDBEARING BEHAVIOUR OF MARRIED AND UNMARRIED WOMEN, AGED 15-19 CANADA AND THE UNITED STATES, FOR SELECTED YEARS SINCE 1941 (RATES PER 1,000)

Year	Canada(a)		United States (b)	
	Married	Unmarried	Married	Unmarried
1969	350.4	14.7(c)	496.5(d)	19.8(d)
1966	465.8	12.2(c)	455.6	17.5
1961	541.2	12.7	538.1	16.6
1951	498.5	9.8	461.7	13.1
1941	453.1	5.8	401.7	7.4

(a) Excludes Newfoundland, Northwest Territories and Yukon prior to 1950.
(b) Estimates only. A number of states do not register births by marital status of mothers.
(c) Estimate from recalculation of fertility rates for all women.
(d) For 1968.

Sources: Vital Statistics of the United States, 1968, vol. 1. Natality (Rockville, Md.: U.S. Dept. of Health, Education and Welfare, 1970), tables 1.7, 1.26; Vital Statistics 1969, table B6; J.Henripin, Tendances et Facteurs, table 11.7.

TABLE C-3 DEATHS ATTRIBUTED TO CIRRHOSIS OF THE LIVER, MOTOR
VEHICLE ACCIDENTS, AND SUICIDE, FOR CANADA AND SELECTED
COUNTRIES, FOR RECENT YEARS. (RATES PER   100,000 POPULATION)

Countries	Cirrhosis	Motor Vehicle	Suicide	All Three Combined	Per Cent of All Deaths
Canada,1969	7.8	27.0	10.9	45.7	6.2
Australia, 1968(a)	5.8	28.7	12.7	47.2	5.2
England and Wales, 1968 (a)	3.0	13.1	9.4	25.5	2.1
Ireland, 1968	3.1	14.2	2.5	19.8	1.7
France, 1968	34.9	28.6	15.3	78.8	7.2
New Zealand, 1968	2.9	13.0	7.0	22.9	2.6
South Africa, 1966 (Whites only)	5.9	38.6	14.0	58.5	6.8
United States, 1968	15.0	26.8	10.9	52.7	5.6

(a) Data by registration, not necessarily by occurrence.

Source: Vital Statistics, 1969, tables 11 A,B.

TABLE C-4 INCIDENCE OF MENTAL ILLNESS BY AGE, SEX, MARITAL STATUS AND MAJOR DIAGNOSTIC CLASS, FOR CANADA AND THE UNITED STATES, FOR RECENT YEARS (RATES PER 100,000 POPULATION).

Diagnostic Class Age, Marital Status	Canada, 1970. Males	Females	United States, 1969. Males	Females	U.S. Ages
All classes					
Age 15 yrs. +(a)	346	319	311	195	14 yrs. +
15-19	306	307	114	100	14-17
20-39	373	368	321	182	18-35
40-64	351	296	378	248	35-64
65+	278	240	213	127	65+
Single(b)	434	354	387	207	Never Married(b)
Married	284	300	156	131	Married
Divorced, widowed	608	332	1,481	258	Divorced
Alcohol and drug disorders(c) Age 15+	109	22	143	24	18+
Psychoses Age 15+	97	107	122	128	18+
Neuroses Age 15+	127	80	47	38	18+

Note: Incidence of mental illness estimated by first admissions to all facilities in Canada. U.S. figures are based on a sample representing admissions to state and county mental hospitals, omitting private hospitals and outpatient services. Even though the U.S. data include all admissions, these figures compensate for the first admissions to facilities not surveyed. Diagnostic class is based on the "International Classification of Diseases", 8th Revision (1965) for Canada and the Diagnostic and Statistical Manual of Mental Disorders, 3rd ed. (1968) for the United States. The classes are comparable.

(a) The two countries do not use the same age categories. However, since rates only are reported, the age groups are roughly comparable.
(b) Comparable uses.
(c) Not included in psychoses and neuroses.

Sources: Mental Health Statistics, 1970 (Ottawa: Information Canada, 1972), vol. 1, table 1; National Institute of Mental Health, Socio-Economic Characteristics of Admissions to Inpatient Service of State and County Mental Hospitals, 1969, DHEW Publication No. (HSM) 72-9048 (Supertintendent of Documents, U.S. Government Printing Office, Washington, D.C.: 1971), tables 1,3.

TABLE C-5 CRIME AND CRIME RATES, BY TYPE, FOR CANADA AND THE UNITED STATES, SINCE 1961.

| | Canada | | | | | U.S. | | | | |
Type of Crime	1961 No.	Rate	1971 No.	Rate	Per Cent Change	1960 No.	Rate	1970 No.	Rate	Per Cent Change
Murder(a)	249	1.4	426	2.0	71.1	9,000	5.0	15,810	7.8	75.7
Rape(b)	573	3.1	1,249	5.8	117.9	16,860	9.9	37,270	18.3	121.1
Assault(c)	a.27,818(c) b. 8,856(c)	149.7 48.6	85,626	397.0	207.8	125,000	84.7	329,940	162.4	117.1
Robbery	3,828	21.0	11,551	53.6	201.7	107,390	59.9	348,380	171.5	224.4
Burglary(d)	71,670	393.0	192,748	893.7	168.9	897,400	500.5	2,169,300	1,067.7	141.7
Larceny(e)	59,370(f)	319.5	177,491	822.9	198.9	506,200	282.3	1,746,100	859.4	244.9
Car theft	38,482(f)	207.1	68,107	315.8	76.9	325,700	181.6	921,400	453.5	182.9

Note: Crime refers to actual offences committed, and known to police, per 100,000 population.

(a) Excludes attempted murder; includes nonnegligent manslaughter for the U.S.; excludes manslaughter for Canada; includes capital and noncapital murder.
(b) Includes attempted rape; excludes statutory offences.
(c) Canadian data since 1962. Assault has been defined more broadly than until 1961, thus the major discrepancy in the 1961 column. The 1961 roughly corresponded to aggravated assault (U.S.definition).
(d) Breaking and entering.
(e) Refers to value of stolen goods, $50 or more.
(f) 1962 data. 1961 not subdivided.

Sources: Crime in the United States -- Uniform Crime Reports, 1970 (Washington, D.C.: Department of Justice, 1971) table 2; Preliminary Statistics -- Crime, Police, Personnel and Traffic, Canada 1971, table 3; Crime Statistics (Police) 1962, table 1D; Crime Statistics (Police) 1961, table 2.

TABLE C-6 PERSONS CHARGED (ARRESTED) UNDER SELECTED CRIME CATEGORIES, BY SEX AND AGE STATUS, CANADA AND THE UNITED STATES, FOR RECENT YEARS.

	CANADA 1969				UNITED STATES, 1970			
Crime Category	All Charges	Rate per(a) 100,000 Population	Per Cent Male	Per Cent Juvenile	All Charges	Rate per(a) 100,000 Population	Per Cent Male	Per Cent Juvenile
Murder(b)	505	2.4	86.7	5.3	12,836	8.5	84.6	10.5
Rape(c)	760	3.6	99.7	4.2	15,411	10.2	100.0	20.8
Assault(d)	24,797	117.7	93.9	5.2	125,971	83.1	87.4	16.5
Robbery	3,724	17.7	94.7	18.4	87,687	57.8	93.9	33.4
Burglary(e)	33,283	158.0	97.3	44.7	285,418	188.3	95.3	51.9
Larceny(f) ($50,+)	14,275	67.8	90.7	25.9	616,099	406.4	72.1	50.6
Car theft	13,779	65.4	97.7	2.0	127,341	84.0	94.9	56.1

Note: "Charges" laid in Canada are somewhat similar in procedure to "arrests" in the United States. Age status refers to adults (18 years of age or over) and juveniles.

(a) In Canada, for the estimated population as of 1, June, 1969, 21,061,000. In the U.S., data reported by 5,270 agencies representing 151,604,000 population. Thus the rates are comparable but the absolute numbers underestimate the U.S. figures.
(b) Includes attempted murder and manslaughter for Canada; excludes attempts to kill for the U.S. data.
(c) Excludes statutory offences; includes attempted rape for the U.S. data.
(d) Aggravated assault only for the U.S. data; for Canada, all assault data.
(e) Breaking and/or entering.
(f) Theft of goods valued $50. or more.

Source: Crime in the United States -- Uniform Crime Reports 1970 (Washington, D.C.: Department of Justice, 1971), table 30; Crime Statistics (Police) 1969, table 1B.

TABLE C-7 PER CENT DISTRIBUTION OF THE LABOUR FORCE BY OCCUPATIONAL GROUPS, FOR CANADA AND SELECTED COUNTRIES, FOR RECENT YEARS.

	Canada (1971)	U.S. (1970)	Ireland (1966)	U.K. (1966)	Australia (1966)	N.Zealand (1966)
Occupational Group	100.0	100.0	100.0	100.0	100.0	100.0
Professional, technical and related	13.3	13.2	7.8	9.6	9.3	10.2
Administrative,executive and managerial	9.2	9.8	1.3	3.1	6.3	5.9
Clerical	14.2	16.6	8.1	13.7	14.7	13.7
Sales	6.4	5.9	9.8	9.6	7.7	8.2
Farmers, fishermen,hunters loggers and related	7.1	3.7	3.2	3.5	9.7	13.7
Miners, quarrymen and related	0.7⎫		0.4	1.5	0.7	0.4
Transport and communication	5.1⎭	17.4	5.2	6.0	6.1	5.9
Craftsmen, production-process workers, labourers and not elsewhere classified	26.4	17.2	27.5	39.3	35.3	34.7
Service, sport and recreation workers	11.3	11.9	7.8	12.0	7.4	6.3
Not classifiable by occupation	-	-	0.2	0.7	1.6	0.5
Members of the armed forces	0.2(a)	3.7	0.7	1.0	1.2	1.1
Seeking work for the first time	1.1	0.6	-	-	-	-
Unemployed	5.2	3.5(b)	-	-	-	-

Note: This table does not distinguish between the self-employed and those
working for an employer.
(a) 1968; (b)March, 1969.
Source: Yearbook of Labour Statistics, 1971 (Geneva: International Labour
Organization, 1972), table 2B. The American Almanac for 1970
(New York: Grosset and Dunlap, 1970), table 310.1251.

TABLE C-8 PER CENT DISTRIBUTION OF EDUCATIONAL ATTAINMENT AND LABOUR FORCE PARTICIPATION FOR THE POPULATION OF CANADA AND THE UNITED STATES, FOR RECENT YEARS

Educational Attainment	CANADA, 1971 (a) Population 14 yrs. and over (%)	Labour Force Particip- ation Rate	Unemployment Rate 14 and over %	Population 14 and over %	UNITED STATES, 1970 Civilian Labour Force % (b)	Labour Force Participation Rate(c)	Unemployment Rate (c)
Grade 8 or less							
Male	32.1	70.3	8.5	25.9	19.9		
Female	30.1	21.8	3.9		13.7		
Secondary(d)							
Male	50.1	72.2	6.7	53.7	52.6		
Female	54.2	38.3	5.3		62.4		
Postsecondary(e)							
Male	17.8	87.0	5.2	20.3	27.1		
Female	15.3	56.9	5.1		23.9		
Total (No.)							
Male	7,601	76.7	6.3	147,472	48,891	80.6	4.4
Female	7,743	36.1	5.0		30,064	43.4	5.9

(a) As of May, 1971 survey.
(b) Population 18 years and over.
(c) Population 16 years and over.
(d) For Canada, grades 9-13; for the U.S., grades 9-12.
(e) University or other postsecondary.

Sources: Statistics Canada, The Labour Force, December 1971 (Ottawa: Information Canada, 1972), table S1; U.S. Bureau of the Census, Statistical Abstracts of the United States, 1971 (Washington, D.C., 1971), table 165; U.S. Department of Labor, Handbook of Labor Statistics (Washington, D.C.), tables 3,12.

TABLE C-9 SCHOOL ENROLLMENT AS PROPORTION IN CORRESPONDING AGE GROUPS, FOR CANADA AND THE UNITED STATES, FOR SELECTED ACADEMIC YEARS SINCE 1956-57.

Age Group Enrollment	1971-72(a)		1960-61		1956-57	
	Canada	U.S.	Canada	U.S.	Canada	U.S.
14 - 17 Secondary(b)	102	95	67	86	56	83
18 - 21 University (c)	22(37)	54	13	26	10	23
18 - 24 University(c)	13(21)	32	8	15	6	14

(a) Population bases estimated from 1966 single age-group distribution and an upward adjustment for immigration, based on age-group totals for 1971.
(b) In Canada, grade 9 and higher until graduation, which may be grade 11, 12 or 13. In the United States, grades 9 - 12.
(c) Refers to full-time enrollment in Canada. Includes teachers' colleges for 1971-72; the numbers in parentheses include all students in post-secondary institutions. For the United States, degree credit enrollment in institutions of higher learning.

Sources: Statistics Canada, Advance Statistics of Education, 1972-73 (Ottawa: Information Canada, August 1972), table 7,9; U.S. Bureau of the Census, Statistical Abstracts of the United States, 1972, 93rd ed. (Washington, D.C., 1972), tables 33,34,161; Z.Zsigmond and C.Wenas, Enrollment in Educational Institutions by Province, 1951-52 --1980-81, Staff Study No. 25 (Ottawa: Economic Council of Canada, 1970), tables 3-7.

TABLE C-10 DISTRIBUTION OF INCOME OF INDIVIDUALS AND FAMILY UNITS, BY INCOME GROUP AND INCOME RANK FOR CANADA AND THE UNITED STATES, IN 1969.

Income Group (in $)	Canada Per Cent of Total Income 100.0	United States Per Cent of Total Income 100.0
Under $1,000	2	(b)
1,000-1,999	5	(b)
2,000-2,999	5	2
3,000-3,999	7	2
4,000-4,999	8	2
5,000-5,999	9	3
6,000-7,499	15	7
7,500-9,999	20	13
10,000-14,999	17	29
15,000 and over	13	42

Income Rank by deciles	Per Cent of Total Income			
	Canada		United States	
	Mean Income(a) (in $)	(b)	Lowest Income(a) (in $)	(b)
Lowest decile	(b)	(b)	1	
2nd decile	2	930	3	2,400
3rd decile	3	1,310	5	3,400
4th decile	5	2,120	6	5,810
5th decile	7	3,240	8	7,300
6th decile	9	4,270	9	8,690
7th decile	12	5,450	11	10,400
8th decile	14	6,780	12	12,200
9th decile	18	9,400	16	14,460
Highest decile	30	14,330	29	18,410

Note: For Canada, income refers to individuals; for the U.S. for families and individuals combined. Both are based on a sample of population, the Canadian sample being 17,606, representing 11 million income recipients.

(a) By using only individual income as compared to family units income, there is a downward bias for the Canadian figures. Even then, however, the U.S. income advantage is not to be denied.
(b) Not available, or less than 0.5 per cent.

Sources: Statistics Canada, Income Distribution by Size in Canada, 1969 (Ottawa: Information Canada, 1972), tables 45,46; U.S. Bureau of the Census, Statistical Abstracts of the United States. 1971, 92nd ed. (Washington, D.C., 1971), table 504.

TABLE C-11 PROPORTION OF HOUSEHOLDS WITH INCOME BELOW POVERTY LEVEL, FOR CANADA AND THE UNITED STATES, FOR RECENT YEARS.

Household Status	Canada, 1967		United States, 1969	
	No. (000s)	Per Cent	No. (000s)	Per Cent
All Units	1,417	23.8	9,801	14.9
Families of 2 or more	832	18.2	4,950	9.8
Unattached individuals	585	38.9	4,851	33.6

Note: For Canada, based on a sample of 17,000.

	Canada	U.S.
Poverty levels by annual income: Unattached individuals	1,740	1,834
2-person family	2,900	2,364
3-person family	3,480	2,905
4-person family	4,060	3,721
5-or-more person family	4,640	4,386

Sources: StatisticsCanada, Household Facilities by Income and Other Characteristics, 1968 (Ottawa: Information Canada, 1972), pp. 15-17; U.S.Bureau of the Census, Statistical Abstracts,1971 (Washington, D.C., 1971), tables 512,513,514,517.

BIBLIOGRAPHY

For sources of a general nature, consult the Suggested Readings, appendix A.

Dominion Bureau of Statistics/Statistics Canada, Nuptiality 1950-1964. Ottawa: Queen's Printer, 1967.

Henripin, J., and Keyfitz, N., "Les Tendences Démographiques au Canada et aux États-Unis", The Canadian Review of Sociology and Anthropology 2 (1965): 77-91.

Keyfitz, N., and Flieger, W., World Population: An Analysis of Vital Data. Chicago: University of Chicago Press, 1968. (671 pp.)

Shryock, H.S., Siegel, J.J., et al, The Methods and Materials of Demography. Vols. I and II. Washington: U.S.Government Printing Office, 1971. (888 pp.)

United States Department of Health, Education and Welfare.

Changes in Mortality Trends in England and Wales, 1931-61. By H.Campbell. National Center for Health Statistics Series 3, No. 3. Washington, D.C., 1965. (49 pp.)

_____, International Comparisons of Perinatal and Infant Mortality: The United States and Six West European Countries. National Center for Health Statistics Series 3, No. 6. Washington, D.C., 1967. (97 pp.)

_____, Trends in Illegitimacy: United States, 1940-1965. By A.J.Clague and S.J.Ventura. National Center for Health Statistics Series 21, No. 16. Washington, D.C., 1968. (90 pp.)

_____, Leading Components of Upturn in Mortality for Men, United States, 1952-1967. By A.J.Klebba. National Center for Health Statistics, Series 20, No. 11. Rockville, Md., 1971. (46 pp.)

_____, Marriages: Trends and Characteristics. By A.M. Hetzel and M. Capetta. National Center for Health Statistics Series 21, No. 21. Rockville, Md., 1971. (35 pp.)

Appendix A   Suggested Readings

The titles listed below are of a more general nature than those listed after each section. The list of readings is based on two criteria: recency of publication and preponderance of sociological analysis.

Adams, I., Cameron, W., Hill,B., and Penz,P., The Real Poverty Report. Edmonton: Hurtig, 1971. (225 pp.)

Archibald, K., Sex and the Public Service. Report to the Public Service Commission of Canada. Ottawa: Queen's Printer, 1970. (218 pp.)

Armstrong, D.E., Education and Economic Achievement. Documents of the Royal Commission on Bilingualism and Biculturalism, no. 7. Ottawa: Information Canada, 1970. (101 pp.)

Blishen, B., Jones, F.E., Naegele, K.D., Porter J., eds., Canadian Society: Sociological Perspectives. 3rd ed. (Abridged) Toronto: Macmillan, 1971. (575 pp.)

Boissevain, J., The Italians of Montreal: Social Adjustment in a Plural Society. Studies of the Royal Commission on Bilingualism and Biculturalism, no. 7. Ottawa: Information Canada, 1970. (87 pp.)

Boydell, C.L., Grindstaff, C.F., Whitehead, P.C., eds., Critical Issues in Canadian Society. Toronto: Holt Rinehart and Winston, 1971. (597 pp.)

Canadian Committee on Corrections, Toward Unity: Criminal Justice and Corrections. Ottawa: Queen's Printer, 1969. (505 pp.)

Curtis, J.E., and Scott, W.G., eds., Social Stratification: Canada. Scarborough, Ontario: Prentice-Hall, 1973. (275 pp.)

Denniss, M., and Fish, S., Programs in Search of a Policy: Low Income Housing in Canada. Toronto: Hakker, 1972. (392 pp.)

Elliot, J.L., ed., Native Peoples. Minority Canadians. Vol I. Scarborough, Ontario: Prentice-Hall, 1971. (169 pp.)

_____, Immigrant Groups. Minority Canadians. Vol. II. Scarborough, Ontario: Prentice-Hall, 1971. (215 pp.)

Gallagher, J.E., and Lambert, R.D. Social Process and Institution: the Canadian Case. Toronto: Holt, Rinehart and Winston, 1971. (531 pp.)

Geoffroy, R., and Sainte-Marie, P., Attitude of Union Workers to Women in Industry. Studies of the Royal Commission on the Status of Women in Canada, no. 9. Ottawa: Information Canada, 1971. (137 pp.)

Harp, J., and Hofley, J.R., eds., Poverty in Canada. Scarborough Ontario: Prentice-Hall, 1971. (357 pp.)

Hawkins, F., Canada and Immigration: Public Policy and Public Concern. Montreal and London: McGill-Quenn's University Press, 1972. (444 pp.)

Ishwaran, K., ed., The Canadian Family. Toronto: Holt, Rinehart and Winston, 1971. (557 pp.)

Lambert, R.D., Sex Role Imagery in Children: Social Origins of Mind. Studies of the Royal Commission on the Status of Women in Canada, no. 6. Ottawa: Information Canada, 1971. (156 pp.)

Lorimer, J., and Phillips, M., Working People: Life in a Downtown City Neighbourhood. Toronto: Lewis and Samuel, 1971. (273 pp.)

Mann, W.E., ed., Social and Cultural Change in Canada. Toronto: Copp Clark, 1970. (Vol. I, 315 pp.; Vol. II, 342 pp.)

_____, Canada: A Sociological Profile. 2nd ed. Toronto: Copp Clark, 1971. (558 pp.)

_____, Poverty and Social Policy in Canada. Toronto: Copp Clark, 1970. (429 pp.)

_____, Social Deviance in Canada. Toronto: Copp Clark, 1971. (412 pp.)

Marsden, L.E., Population Probe: Canada. Toronto: Copp Clark 1972. (179 pp.)

Michelson, W., Man and His Urban Environment: A Sociological Approach. Don Mills, Ontario: Addison-Wesley, 1970. (242 pp.)

Ossenberg, R.J., ed., Canadian Society: Pluralism, Change and Conflict. Scarborough, Ontario: Prentice-Hall, 1971. (214 pp.)

Royal Commission on Bilingualism and Biculturalism, Education Report. Book II. Ottawa: Queen's Printer, 1968. (347 pp.)

Royal Commission on the Status of Women in Canada, Report on the Status of Women in Canada. Ottawa: Information Canada, 1970. (488 pp.)

Systems Research Group, Canada 2000: Family, Household and Housing Projections. Toronto: Systems Research Group, 1970. (91 pp.)

_____, Canada 2000: Population Projections. Toronto: Systems Research Group, 1970. (120 pp.)

Watts, R.L., Multicultural Societies and Federalism. Studies of the Royal Commission on Bilingualism and Biculturalism, no. 8. Ottawa: Information Canada, 1970. (187 pp.)

Appendix B Glossary of Demographic Terms

Age-specific birth rate. The number of live, registered births per 1,000 females in a specific age group (i.e. 25-29 years) at mid-year.

Age-sex-specific death rate. The number of registered deaths in a specific age and sex group per 1,000 persons in that group at mid-year.

Child-woman ratio. A ratio of the number of children 5 years of age and under in a population to the total number of women in reproductive ages (ie., 15 to 49 years) in that population.

Crude birthrate. The total number of registered births during a one-year period per 1,000 population at mid-year.

Crude death rate. The total number of registered deaths during a one-year period per 1,000 population at mid-year.

Crude marriage rate. The total number of registered marriages within a specified one-year period per 1,000 population at mid-year.

Dependency ratio. The ratio of the total number of persons under 15 and over 65 years of age to the total population between ages 15 to 64.

General divorce rate. The number of registered divorces during a one-year period per 1,000 married couples at mid-year.

General fertility rate. The number of registered live births in a one-year period per 1,000 females of childbearing age (defined by the United Nations as 15 to 49 years).

General marriage rate. The number of registered marriages during a one-year period per 1,000 unmarried persons between ages 15 to 49 years at mid-year.

Gross migration. The sum of arrivals (in-migrants) and departures (out-migrants) in a specific geographical area during a specified time period.

Illegitimacy rate. The number of illegitimate births during a one-year period per 1,000 live births during the same period.

Infant mortality rate. A ratio of the total number of infants under one year of age who die in a given year to the total number of live births in the same year.

Labour-force participation rate. The percentage of the population 15 years of age and older in the labour force (defined to include all persons having a job or actively looking for work).

Life expectancy. The average number of years of life remaining to males or females at a specific age under a given set of mortality conditions.

Natural increase. The difference between the number of births and number of deaths during a specified time period.

Net migration. The difference between the number of arrivals (in-migrants) and departures (out-migrants) in a specific geographical area during a specified time period.

Occupational composition. The types of occupations and the number of workers in each within a defined population.

Population density. A ratio of the number of people to the area of land that they occupy (ie., the average number of people per square mile, acres, etc.)

Population equation. A method of summarizing the amount of growth experienced by a specified geographical area during a given time period that results from the interaction of the demographic processes of fertility, mortality and migration. The equation is written as:

$$P_t = P_o + (B-D) + (M_i - M_o)$$

where

P_t denotes the population size at the end of the specified time period;

P_o denotes the population size at the beginning of the time period;

B denotes the number of births during the interval between P_o and P_t;

D denotes the number of deaths during the interval between P_o and P_t;

M_i denotes the amount of in-migration during the interval between P_o and P_t;

M_o denotes the amount of out-migration during the interval between P_o and P_t;

Population projection. An estimate of the future population size of a specific geographical area on the basis of a set of assumptions regarding the future fertility, mortality and migration behaviour of the population within that area.

Ratio. A single term indicating the relative size of one number to another. As examples, see sex ratio, child-women ratio, etc.

Sex ratio. The number of males per 100 females in a defined population.

Standard Rate. A rate which has been adjusted to permit the comparison of several populations with respect to one variable (ie. fertility, mo tality, etc.) while holding constant the effect of one or several other variables (ie., age, population size, etc.).

Total Fertility Rate. Number of live births per 1,000 women were all women to survive until the end of their childbearing period and experience age-specific fertility prevailing at the time of computation.

Unemployment Rate . The percentage of the total labour force which is without a current job.

Appendix C   How to Read the Tables

A statistical table is a means of communicating information in an intelligible and efficient manner. Effective table reading involves correctly interpreting the information presented. Since there are probably as many ways to approach reading tables as there are ways of constructing them, it is difficult to provide a set of specific rules which should be followed to ensure correct table interpretation. However, you may find the following general comments of assistance.

There is always a temptation when confronted with a statistical table to leap before looking; that is, to begin examing the numbers contained in the table before examining its overall framework. In the authors' estimation, this is a bad policy because the numbers in a table become meaningful only to the extent that you know and understand the context within which they are relevant. Information about the kinds of things to which the numbers refer can only be obtained through a careful examination of the framework of a table; its title, structure and accompanying footnotes. The first and most basic suggestion, therefore, is to briefly overview all aspects of the table. Then, carefully scrutinize its framework before examining the figures in detail. Find out what the table is about before you try to interpret the numbers in it.

A great deal of information about a table is found in the title. The title tells you about the subject matter the table deals with, the categories the subject matter has been broken down into and the relation of these categories to one another. In addition, it indicates the specific population to which the numbers in the table refer. The title should be carefully read, several times if necessary. When you are finished, you should be able to identify all those characteristics of the table which are given in its title.

Next, look at any footnotes accompanying the table. Footnotes provide supplementary information which helps you to understand more clearly the nature of the table and its content. For example, they may be employed to define major concepts in the table which, for one reason or another, are not generally understood. Concepts like "regions of metropolitan development", "migrant", "primary occupations" and "license" are examples of this. Or, they may be employed to explain the nature of the numerical units (ie., rounded to the nearest hundred thousand, etc.) in which the information is presented. Or, they may be used to explain the reason for missing or incomplete data in the table or to indicate the type of data-collection technique (ie., survey, census) employed to obtain the data. In all these instances, footnotes help you to properly interpret the table. For this reason, you should read them carefully.

The structure of a table refers to the way in which the various categories are organized. After a careful reading of the title and footnotes of a table, its structure should be examined. This will help you to determine how the data is ordered and classified. Following this, examine the figures and try to grasp their significance.

To illustate what has been said above, let's examine a concrete example: Table J-4, Per Cent Distribution of the Canadian Labour Force, by Occupational Group, Level of Education and Sex, 1966, and by Sex, Education and Occupational Group, 1972. The title indicates that the table deals with certain characteristics of the Canadian labour force at the two time periods 1966 and 1972. The employment data are cross-classified by the variables of type of occupation, level of education and sex. Further, we are told that the original raw numbers have been transformed and are presented in terms of percentages.

The accompanying footnotes tell us several things. First, the general note indicates that the figures presented in the table are based on survey data and therefore represent estimates of the labour-force population falling within each of the cells of the table. Second, footnotes a,b,c,and d provide us with a more precise understanding of which occupations and which educational attainment levels are grouped together. Finally, and most important, footnote f indicates the estimated number of persons employed in 1966, by occupational groups.

Examing the structure of the table, we find that the column categories consist of types of occupations, while the row categories represent levels of education and sex. This type of organization permits us to examine the estimated percentage of the male and female labour-force population at each level of educational attainment, both within and between the occupational categories.

An interpretation of this table might be as follows. The table tells us about the educational attainment of males and females in the Canadian labour force in 1972 generally and in specific occupations in 1966. For example, an examination of the figures in the "all occupations" column indicates that 82.9 per cent of females in the labour force have some secondary-school education or higher, while only 13.2 per cent of the males fall into this category. It would appear, therefore, that in 1972 females in the labour force had, in general, a higher level of educational attainment than their male counterparts. You should try to think of an explanation for this fact. For 1966, the figures in the table indicate, not unexpectedly, that white collar occupations are occupied, regardless of sex, by those with higher levels of education. Twenty-nine per cent of the males and 18.5 per cent of the females have at least some university education, while only 14.9 per cent of the males and 8.2 per cent of the females have no education above the elementary-school level. In constrast, only a very small percentage of the males and females in other occupations have some or completed university education. The majority in service, recreation, transportation and communications occupations have some or completed secondary-school education, while the majority in blue-collar and "primary" occupations have some or completed elementary-school education. This indicates that in Canadian society (at least in 1966) educational attainment and type of occupation are correlated, the more skilled occupations being filled by those with higher levels of educational attainment.

It is not within the scope of this section to discuss all the intricacies of tabular organization. However, some additional aspects of tables encountered throughout the text should be mentioned.

The tables in the text vary in terms of their complexity and comprehensiveness. To illustrate, compare tables P-1 and P-12. Table P-1 simultaneously presents information about three major demographic features of Canadian society, by province, since 1851. In contrast, table P-12 deals with a single variable, religious denomination. Variations in the size of principal religious denominations of the Canadian people are traced through time since 1871. At first encounter, you may be tempted to avoid multivariate tables - like table P-1 - which appear to be extremely complex. The authors' best advice here is not to be frightened by complexity. In actual fact, the more complex tables are no more difficult to read than simple, one variable tables, provided you follow the guidelines for table reading outlined above and analyze the information in the table in a systematic manner. With practise, you will probably find multivariate tables more enjoyable since they present, at once, a great deal more information than univariate tables.

Generally speaking, two major types of tables are found throughout this text. One type includes those tables which depict differences in the numerical composition of relevant social and demographic characteristics of Canadian society through time. This type of table is frequently referred to as a trend or time-series table. Table P-6, which traces the changes in the size of the population living in metropolitan areas in Canada since 1901, illustrates this type. Additional examples are tables H-1, D-1, J-1 and F-3. The other major type of table found in the text focuses on showing differences between a number of categories at a specific period in time. The labour force table, examined in detail above, is an example of this type which, for lack of a better term, can be called a static table. Further examples are provided by tables E-8, J-6, J-7, and H-8. You should recognize that the two types have different purposes and, therefore, should be approached in a slightly different manner. When confronted with a trend table, concentrate your attention on the time dimension. Examine the changes in the size of the categories over the time periods specified. In attempting to analyze a static table, the emphasis should be on isolating and interpreting differences between the specified categories.

Another aspect about the tables you should bear in mind is that the figures in them are of two major types; specifically, basic and derived. Basic data are simple raw numbers based on counting. Tables E-5, E-11 and P-7 illustrate the use of this type of data. A major advantage of presenting information in terms of basic figures is that the detail and completeness of the information is preserved. The exact number of cases falling within each category is known. However, presenting information in this way has its disadvantages, one of them being that basic figures are often large and awkward to handle, thereby increasing the difficulty of table analysis. Furthermore, for comparative purposes, the use of raw number is often not meaningful. Examine table P-10, for example. To compare the variation in the ethnic and racial backgrounds of Canadians over census years since 1851 in terms of raw numbers is not nearly as meaningful or concise as to examine these variations in terms of percentages. This is because percentages, in this instance, specify the relative changes in the ethnic composition of the total Canadian population. In so doing, they make meaningful comparisons across the specified census years possible. Percentages are one of a group of summary measures frequently referred to as derived figures. The other types of derived figures most often encountered in the tables are ratios and rates. An example of the use of ratios is found in table P-4, while table D-1 standardizes mortality information in terms of rates. As with percentages, ratios and rates are derived from basic-count data through simple calculating procedures.

One final comment may be made. A major purpose of this text is to present a statistical picture of the major changes in the demographic and social structure of Canadian society that have occurred up to the present time. Each of the tables seeks to illustrate one or more facets of this overall picture. You would do well to keep this fact clearly in mind. In the authors' opinion, this will not only help you in terms of analyzing the information presented in each table but will also provide you with a framework in which to organize and interrelate the seemingly isolated facts gleaned from each of the tables.

In summary, we return to our original advice. Regardless of the type of table or its content being analyzed, find out what it is about before you try to interpret it. Read the words before you examine the numbers.

Date P